WATER ISSUES
IN SOUTHEAST ASIA

WATER ISSUES
IN SOUTHEAST ASIA

PRESENT TRENDS
AND
FUTURE DIRECTIONS

EDITED BY
LEE POH ONN

ISEAS

INSTITUTE OF SOUTHEAST ASIAN STUDIES
Singapore

First published in Singapore in 2013 by
Institute of Southeast Asian Studies
30 Heng Mui Keng Terrace
Pasir Panjang
Singapore 119614
E-mail: publish@iseas.edu.sg
Website: <http://bookshop.iseas.edu.sg>

The responsibility for facts and opinions in this publication rests exclusively with the editor and contributors and their interpretations do not necessarily reflect the views or the policy of the publisher or its supporters.

ISEAS Library Cataloguing-in-Publication Data

Water issues in Southeast Asia : present trends and future directions / edited by Lee Poh Onn.
    1.   Water resources development—Southeast Asia—Congresses.
    2.   Water utilities—Southeast Asia—Congresses.
    3.   Water supply—Southeast Asia—Congresses.
    I.   Lee, Poh Onn.
    II. Forum on Water Issues in Southeast Asia : Present Trends and Future Directions (2005 : Singapore).
HD1698 A9W31   2013

ISBN 978-981-230-982-2 (soft cover)
ISBN 978-981-230-983-9 (E-book PDF)

Typeset by International Typesetters Pte Ltd
Printed in Singapore by Oxford Graphic Printers Pte Ltd

Contents

List of Tables, Figures, Boxes and Photos vii

Acknowledgements xi

About the Contributors xiii

CHAPTER 1 Introduction 1
Lee Poh Onn and Ng Boon Yian

CHAPTER 2 China and the Potential for Conflict over 27
Water among Eurasian States
Michael Richardson

CHAPTER 3 River Basin Agreements as Facilitators of 56
Development
Chris Perry

CHAPTER 4 Privatization of Water Services via Public- 76
Private Partnership and Implications for
Southeast Asia
Eric Teo Chu Cheow

CHAPTER 5 Indonesia's Water Management Reform 100
Budhi Santoso

CHAPTER 6 Water Resource Management Issues in 119
Malaysia
Salmah Zakaria

CHAPTER 7 Privatization Issues in Water Supply in 136
Malaysia
Syed Danial Syed Ariffin

CHAPTER 8   Troubled Waters: Rehabilitating the Pasig   174
               River, the Philippines
               Donovan Storey

CHAPTER 9   The Privatization of Water Services in Metro   212
               Manila: Lessons from a Mixed Outcome
               Lorraine Carlos Salazar

CHAPTER 10   Singapore's Experience in Water Resource   243
               Management
               Wong Kai Yeng

CHAPTER 11   Thailand's Water Sector: Overview and   255
               Implications
               Sukontha Aekaraj

CHAPTER 12   Water Resources and Issues Concerning   286
               Sustainable Watershed Management
               Practices in Vietnam
               Le Dinh Thanh

Index   317

List of Tables, Figures, Boxes and Photos

TABLES

Table 1.1	Water Availability and Access to Sanitation	3
Table 1.2	Past, Present, and Future Water Trends	6
Table 3.1	Elements of Sustainable Water Management — Examples	72
Table 7.1	Implementation of Major Privatized Project in Malaysia in 2004 and 2005	141
Table 7.2	Share of Private-Public Responsibility for Water Supply in Malaysia	143
Table 7.3	Percentage of Non-Revenue Water: Selected States	145
Table 7.4	Reported Cases of Pollution in Selangor	146
Table 7.5	Capital Costs of Privatised Projects	150
Table 7.6	Summary of Debts	156
Table 7.7	Development of Rasa WTP	157
Table 7.8	Percentage of Account Billed, Jan–Dec 2004	161
Table 7.9	Demand and Supply of Water (mld), 1995–2005	163
Table 7.10	Water Quality in Gombak and Klang Rivers, Malaysia	169
Table 9.1	Pre-Privatized MWSS Operational Highlights, 1997	219

Table 9.2   Service Targets (in per cent coverage)   223
Table 9.3   Bidders Tariff for the Concessions   226
Table 10.1   Some of the Ministries and Statutory Boards
              Involved in the Clean-up   247
Table 12.1   Ten Biggest River Basins of Vietnam   292
Table 12.2   Water Quality in Vietnam's Rivers   302

FIGURES

Figure 5.1   Water Balance in Jakarta and West Java, 2000   103
Figure 5.2   Condition of Irrigation Infrastructure, 2001   106
Figure 5.3   Delegation of Authority and Responsibility   111
Figure 7.1   Sectoral Distribution of Privatized Projects,   140
               1983–2003
Figure 7.2   Ageing of Outstanding Receivables at   154
               30 April 2004
Figure 7.3   Amount Owing to the Water Treatment   154
               Operators
Figure 7.4   Summary of Indebtedness   156
Figure 7.5   NRW Level from 1992 to 2003   157
Figure 7.6   Overall Operating Deficit   158
Figure 7.7(a) Overall Operating Deficit: Emoluments and   159
               Allowances Expenses
Figure 7.7(b) Increases in Various Operating Cost   159
               Elements: Repair and Maintenance
Figure 7.7(c) Capital Expenditure   160
Figure 7.8   Ageing of Active Consumers   161
Figure 7.9   Ageing of Terminated Consumers   162
Figure 7.10   Ageing of Disconnected Consumers   163
Figure 7.11   Water Supply Planning   164
Figure 10.1   Extent of Clean-up   246
Figure 12.1   Mekong River Basin   287
Figure 12.2   The Major River Basins in Inland Vietnam   291
Figure 12.3(a) River Run-off per Region (bcm)   292
Figure 12.3(b) Exploitable Groundwater (bcm)   293
Figure 12.4   Maximum Inundation Depth of 2000 Flood   299
               in Mekong Delta
Figure 12.5   Water Resources Management in Vietnam   306

BOXES

Box 3.1	The Dublin Principles	58
Box 3.2	Definition of Integrated Water Resources Management	59
Box 3.3	Themes for Discussion at Third World Water Forum	60

PHOTOS

Photo 8.1	The Pasig River	184
Photo 8.2	Solid Waste	184
Photo 8.3	Meulle del Rio Linear Park	191
Photo 8.4	West Rembo Linear Park	191
Photo 8.5	Polluted *estero*, Guadalupe	195
Photo 8.6	Stagnant *estero*, Makati	195

Acknowledgements

I would like to thank the Konrad Adeneur Foundation for funding the forum which has subsequently resulted in the production of this book. Thanks are also due to the Hyflux Group of Companies for making a financial contribution towards the running of the forum.

The first version of these chapters were presented at the "Forum on Water Issues in Southeast Asia: Present Trends and Future Directions" from 16 to 17 August 2005.

The authors have subsequently revised and updated their papers based on feedback from the forum participants, and newer developments in their respective country and/or case studies and incorporated such changes in the present publication. A great thank you is done to the various authors for painstakingly working on their respective chapters and for adding new and important dimensions to their initial presentations.

The studies here illustrate the multi-dimensional and political-economic aspects involved in water and water management issues in a very clear and forceful manner. My greatest debt is owed to the ISEAS Publications Unit for making this volume publishable. Any remaining errors are due to the editor and authors alone.

Lee Poh Onn
Fellow
ISEAS

About the Contributors

Sukontha AEKARAJ is Director, Foreign Relations and International Cooperation, Department of Water Resources, Ministry of Natural Resources and the Environment, Bangkok, Thailand.

Syed DANIAL Syed Ariffin is Chief Operating Officer of both Puncak Niaga Holdings Berhad (PNHB) and Puncak Niaga (M) Sdn Bhd (PNSB). YBhg Dato's Syed is also Director of Syarikat Bekalan Air Selangor Sdn Bhd (SYABAS).

LEE Poh Onn is Fellow at the Regional Economic Studies Unit, Institute of Southeast Asian Studies (ISEAS), Singapore.

NG Boon Yian is Deputy Director, ASEAN Political-Security Community Branch, Ministry of Foreign Affairs, Singapore. She was formerly Research Associate at the Institute of Southeast Asian Studies (ISEAS), Singapore.

Chris PERRY is an independent consultant. Formerly, he was Deputy Director General of the International Water Management Institute (IWMI).

Michael RICHARDSON has been a Visiting Senior Research Fellow at the Institute of Southeast Asian Studies (ISEAS) since September 2003. He focuses on a wide range of challenges to growth and stability in Asia, and is currently completing a book for ISEAS on climate change and Southeast Asia.

Lorraine Carlos SALAZAR was a Visiting Research Fellow at the Institute of Southeast Asian Studies (ISEAS) at the time of writing. She is currently Senior Research Analyst at McKinsey & Company's Singapore Office.

Budhi SANTOSO is Senior Water Expert, National Development Planning Agency (BAPPENAS), Indonesia.

Donovan STOREY is coordinator of the Development Planning programme at the School of Geography, Planning and Environmental Management, University of Queensland. His research focuses on exclusion from participation and decision making and how this affects urban planning and sustainable development in the cities of the global South.

Eric TEO Chu Cheow was a business consultant and strategist, and Managing Director of Savior Faire Corporate Consultants, a political and economic risks consultancy, based in Singapore. This chapter was completed prior to Dr Teoh's passing away on 22 August 2007 though some minor editorial changes have been made posthumously.

Le Dinh THANH is Dean of the Faculty, and Vice Rector of the University, Coastal Engineering, Hanoi Water Resources University, Vietnam.

WONG Kai Yeng is Group Director, Urban Redevelopment Authority (URA) International, Singapore. Formerly he was Director (Policy & Planning), Public Utilities Board (PUB), Singapore.

Salmah ZAKARIA is Economics Affairs Officer, Water Security Section, Environment and Development Division, United Nations Economic and Social Commission for Asia and the Pacific (ESCAP). Formerly, Dr Salmah was Secretary, Malaysian Water Partnership (MyWP); Director, National Hydraulic Research Institute of Malaysia (NAHRIM), Ministry of Natural Resources and Environment, Malaysia.

I

INTRODUCTION

Lee Poh Onn and Ng Boon Yian

The availability of freshwater resources will be one of the most pressing environmental challenges in the years ahead. International dialogues in water have gone through several stages.[1] From 1970 to the early 1980s (first stage), human health issues were the catalyst which ignited the international discussion of water. Then it was the Mar del Plata Action Plan in 1979 which called countries to develop national plans and programmes regarding the provision of water supplies and sanitation at a community level.

From the 1980s to the early 1990s (second stage), there was a growing recognition of water as an element of sustainable development. The Dublin Principles in 1992 referred to the economic value of water, and the importance of "integrated water resource management".

From 1992 onwards (third stage), water issues have jumped in importance to become a priority issue. Water was recognized to be in a short supply; and in the Millennium Development Goals, the goal was set to include reducing or halving the proportion of population without sustainable access to safe drinking water by 2015. The Johannesburg Plan of Implementation in 2002 also reaffirmed the water supply goals of the Millennium Development

Goals and also set a sanitation goal. In 2003, the United Nationals World Water Development Report also recognized that there was a water crisis globally, identified the causes, and provided tools to assess progress towards building a better future. In 2006, the United Nations World Water Development Report 2 recognized water as a shared responsibility recognizing the diverse functions of water as a resource, and also the stewardship roles that could be played by governments, communities, and individuals.

Narrowing the focus, Southeast Asia's annual per capita freshwater resources increased at an average rate of 38 per cent from 1996 to 1999 but has started to decreased at an average rate of 17 per cent beginning from 2000 to 2004, partly as a result of increases in the region's population and also development activities.[2] From the State of Water Resources Management Report, it has been reported that most countries in Southeast Asia anticipate that water demand would increase by about 33 per cent by 2025.[3] However, the region as a whole is not expected to suffer from any severe water shortage up to 2025.[4]

Access to sustainable sources of water and sanitation between 1990 and 2006 have also improved for all Southeast Asian countries, as indicated in Table 1.1 (where data is available), with the exception of Indonesia and Myanmar:

In terms of water resources, Indonesia produced the largest volume of freshwater resources in the Southeast Asia amounting to about 41 per cent of the region's total resources, followed by Myanmar (20 per cent), Malaysia (14 per cent). Brunei and Singapore, on the other hand, produced the smallest volume (0.08 per cent and 0.01 per cent respectively).[5]

Water management issues in Southeast Asia involve many dimensions and aspects. First, there is the issue of managing water supply and demand in the present and also that of anticipating future needs. Then there is also the issue of allocation requirements among the various stakeholders in an area and that of irrigating agricultural areas adequately. The issue of water pollution is also

TABLE 1.1
Water Availability and Access to Sanitation
(Percentages)

	(A) Urban 1990	(A) Rural 1990	(A) Urban 2008	(A) Rural 2008	(B) Urban 1990	(B) Rural 1990	(B) Urban 2008	(B) Rural 2008
Brunei Darussalam	n.a.	n.a.	n.a.	n.a.	n.a.	n.a.	n.a.	n.a.
Cambodia	47 (1995)	14 (1995)	81	56	43 (1995)	2 (1995)	67	18
Indonesia	92	63	89	71	73	42	67	36
Lao PDR	73 (1995)	34 (1995)	72	51	48 (1995)	6 (1995)	86	38
Malaysia	100	96	100	99	95	93	96	95
Myanmar	86	47	75	69	47	15	86	79
Philippines	92	75	93	87	71	46	80	69
Singapore	100		100	98	100		100	
Thailand	98	94	99	98	92	72	95	96
Viet Nam	87	43	94	92	62	21	94	67

(A) Population Using Improved Water Sources (percentage); (B) Population Using Improved Sanitation Facilities (percentage)
Source: Key Indicators for Asia and the Pacific 2010 (41st edition), Manila: Asian Development Bank, August 2010.

severe in some Southeast Asian countries. In this respect, governance, reorganization, and capacity-building issues come to the forefront. There is also the potential for conflict across boundaries when a river system transverses several countries.

This is especially so for the riparian countries along the Mekong River, where water availability and sharing issues are quite complex. Five countries in Southeast Asia derive water from this river, namely Cambodia, Lao PDR, Myanmar, Thailand and Vietnam. However, China has come under increasing scrutiny of these water-dependent neighbours in Southeast Asia, especially in recent years when it has been building a number of new dams which have affected these downstream countries.

In the years to come, in view of increasing pressures on water exerted by rising populations in this area, and demands placed by agriculture, this issue of "water sharing" would need to be carefully managed, addressing the concerns of these countries as well as that of China. Agricultural demands in these countries comprise 70 per cent to 90 per cent of total demand.

Water statistics and water usage patterns differ across countries in Southeast Asia. For most countries in the region, the availability of groundwater supplies range from between 10 per cent to 20 per cent of total water supplies with the rest coming from surface supplies.[6] In terms of exceptions, in Brunei Darussalam, over 99 per cent of its water supplies have been sourced from surface water. In the Philippines, one-fifth of its total water supplies came from groundwater sources.[7]

In Cambodia, over 94 per cent of its freshwater is used for agricultural purposes. In Singapore, the industrial and domestic sectors accounted for about 50 per cent each of its total water supplies.[8]

In terms of accessibility, on average, only about 77 per cent of residents in Southeast Asia can get clean safe water for their everyday needs, with Cambodia and Lao PDR having the lowest accessibility rates of 34 per cent and 43 per cent respectively.[9]

WATER IN SOUTHEAST ASIA

Presently, water consumption in most countries generally does not exceed sources of supply. However, ASEAN countries do experience the familiar scenario of "localised, sometimes severe, water stress coupled with the traditional water sharing systems to cope with growing demand, with new users, and with competition between sectors and between individual users".[10] Table 1.2 presents a breakdown of sectoral demands as well as available sources of water within each Southeast Asian country. In 2007, the region had about 5,674.5 billion cubic metres of internal renewable freshwater resources.

The relevance of the following case studies and chapters on water management in countries or across countries and boundaries would serve to highlight some of the pertinent issues involved in water management and perhaps shed some light on and offer answers to the complexities involved.

The chapters in this book have been revised between 2006 to 2010 by the respective authors and hence are updated papers based on presentations at a two-day forum on water issues in Southeast Asia held at the Institute of Southeast Studies (ISEAS) in late 2005.

In that forum itself, many important insights were presented. The issue of potential water scarcity by 2050 was highlighted by the then minister for the environment and water resources, Singapore, who opened the forum and was the keynote speaker. Dr Yaacob also touched on touched on issues such as: The need for sustainable water development; the need for sound management of water supply infrastructure; the need to mobilize the general public's engagement and support for water conservation; the need to manage water demand; and also harnessing the newer water technologies such as membrane filtration. Importantly, Dr Yaacob stressed the need to cooperate between governments, industries, communities and the individual.

TABLE 1.2
Past, Present, and Future Water Trends

Country	Renewable Freshwater Resources – 2007 (billion m³)	Total Available Internal Water Resources (mcm)	Current Industry Demands	Current Agriculture Demands	Current Domestic demands	Total 2005/ Estimated Demand in 2025
Brunei Darussalam	8.5	3,425	35	Na	48	83/151
Cambodia	120.6	133,600	30	455	136	767/1,742
Indonesia	2838.0	1,852,576	2,759	78,272	5,125	90,656/123,440
Lao PDR	190.4	308,000	570	4,674	456	5,700/na
Malaysia	580.0	630,000	1,909	7,300	2,413	1,622/14,504
Myanmar	880.6	901,000	80	28,000	153	28,243/na
Philippines	479.0	145,990	2,233	25,533	2,189	29,955/138,571
Singapore	0.9	600	197	0	250	447/664
Thailand	210.0	216,123	1,311	48,172	3,188	67,997/na
Vietnam	366.5	335,000	3,074	62,200	1,042	73,599/100,257

mcm = million cubic metre na = not available

Source: State of Water Resources Management in ASEAN. Jakarta: ASEAN Secretariat, October 2005, p. 5; Fourth ASEAN State of the Environment Report 2009, Jakarta: ASEAN Secretariat, October 2009.

Water has been dubbed the "oil of the twenty-first century" as its scarcity is increasingly felt globally. Over the last fifty years, the world's population had risen by more than two-and-a-half times to about 6.4 billion. At the same time, however, the demand for fresh water went up by four times. Dr Yaacob referred to the United Nations Environment Programme Report 2003 which predicted that, at this rate, up to seven billion people in sixty countries may possibly face water scarcity by the year 2050. Without access to clean water, not only would public health suffer because of poor hygiene and sanitation, agricultural and industrial activities could also get disrupted.[11]

Dr Yaacob also spoke about Singapore's sound management of its water infrastructure. Singapore protects its water catchments by implementing a comprehensive catchment management policy, backed by strong anti-pollution enforcement measures and reinforced with public education and engagement. Water leakages are also kept low by programmes to replace old pipes and connections. The appropriate pricing of water in Singapore has also played an important role in reinforcing the value of water and minimizing wastage. Last, but not least, the development of new technologies in recent years has helped Singapore to develop a sustainable source of domestic water supply. Singapore's success with NEWater and desalination cannot be over-emphasized enough. Such issues are further elaborated in the Singapore chapter in this book by Wong Kai Yeng (Chapter 10).

The then Director of ISEAS, Ambassador K. Kesavapany, stated that it was important to bring together a broad range of country and technical expertise on the water issue in order to advance the exchange of ideas and yield useful lessons for policy-makers, business people, practitioners, NGOs and academia interested in the area. A longer-term research programme on water issues, which would explore topics such as water conflicts and its regional security implications, water pollution, sustainable water development, privatization, watershed management, water scarcity management and strategies undertaken by the respective water authorities in ASEAN was also necessary, and in part would be fulfilled by research at ISEAS.

Dr Colin Duerkop of the Konrad Adenaur Stiftung observed that water was one of the most important issues facing Southeast Asia, with wide-ranging implications for the region's ecosystem, public health, regional security and general well-being. Such aspects are discussed in varying intensities in the following chapters in this book.

Indeed these remarks made during the forum back then echo similar sentiments now. Economic development had generated greater demand for water from different sectors such as agriculture, industry and domestic users. The situation is likely to exacerbate and prove more challenging in the future.

Such trends pose several important questions that policy-makers would have to address. These include: How likely are regional conflicts as countries compete for the increasingly scarce water resources? What are the mechanisms to forestall such conflicts? At the national level, what are the best practices that countries can use to manage their own water resources so as to ensure sustainable development? How can governments ensure that water sources are protected through legislation and also clear direction from the authorities? How can overlaps in water management by the various bodies be addressed? As privatization is increasingly considered as an option, how should it be designed to promote efficiency as well as equity? What role does technology have to play in overcoming water shortages?

OUTLINE OF THE BOOK

The present book deals with a variety of topics covering selected countries across Southeast Asia. Chapter 2 deals with the potential of upstream-downstream conflicts between China and the various Indochinese states. Chapter 3 offers a solution for cross-border conflicts in the form of river basin agreements between countries and the preconditions for success, while Chapter 4 discusses public-private partnership issues in Southeast Asia. Chapter 5 then discusses reforms in the context of Indonesia. Chapters 6 and 7 focus on Malaysia; the former examines water resource management issues in the context of Malaysia as a whole while the latter looks at the privatization exercise of a single water utility.

Chapters 8 and 9 then bring the focus to the Philippines. Chapter 8 looks at the politics of river pollution in the Philippines, while Chapter 9 examines the water privatization exercise of two entities, of which one was a success and the other a failure. Chapter 10 then looks at Singapore's experience of managing its scarce water supplies, and the use of new technologies to augment its traditional sources of water. Chapter 11 examines Thailand's water supplies while Chapter 12 examines Vietnam's supplies from a water management perspective.

REGIONAL IMPLICATIONS

As water flows do not stop at sovereign borders, shared water resources among nation-states could potentially lead to conflicts as use by one party might diminish the benefits to others. This is a relevant concern for the Southeast Asian region as the Mekong River — one of the world's largest rivers — runs through six countries: China, Myanmar, Laos, Thailand, Vietnam and Cambodia.

The China Factor

When assessing the potential for water conflict in the region, it is impossible to overlook the impact of China. Such issues are discussed by Michael Richardson in Chapter 2 of this book. Like its appetite for energy, the vast country's thirst for water has been rising dramatically. Global warming and melting glaciers in and around the Qinghai Tibet Plateau is threatening Asia's future water supplies. And since 1949, water consumption for human use, agriculture and industry in China has risen nearly six-fold, from around 100 billion cubic metres to the current level of around 560 billion cubic metres.

Rapid economic growth, urbanization and industrialization over the past twenty-five years has intensified shortages and pollution in many areas of China. As a relatively resource-scarce country, the future prospects for China's water supply do not look bright. Chinese experts have already warned that by 2030, when the population reaches 1.6 billion, per capita water resources would drop to 1,760 cubic metres a year, perilously close to the 1,700 cubic metres level that is the internationally recognized benchmark for chronic shortage.

Aware of the country's water problems, the Chinese leadership has been carrying out some controversial schemes to harness water, which has caused spillover effects into its neighbouring countries. In this regard, much attention has been focused on China's dam-building activities on the upper reaches of the Mekong River, known locally as Lancang Jiang, which flows mainly through the southern province of Yunnan.

China has the upper hand in harnessing the Mekong waters for power, irrigation and flood control because it is an upstream country. It has completed the first two dams in a series of seven hydropower plants, and already it has been criticized by some officials and environmental activists in Southeast Asia for controlling water at the expense of the downstream countries. Dam building in the upstream has been reported to affect issues such as water levels, sedimentation and biodiversity, and undermining the livelihood of many who have depended on the Mekong River for farming, fishing and navigation.

While it has at times remained debatable whether China's developments has led to lower water levels, the bigger concern has been over the lack of institutional safeguards to check against

Chinese actions in this international river basin. China is not party to the Mekong Agreement nor is it a member of the Mekong River Commission (MRC), which helps to coordinate the management and conservation of the Mekong Basin. Yet even if China joined these institutions, they are too weak to have any real impact on developments in the river. For instance, even if China signed the Mekong Agreement, the lower riparian states would still have no right to demand impact studies or mitigation measures as China's projects will be intra-basin, requiring only prior notification but not the agreement of all MRC members.

China is, however, more likely to use "softer" means such as diplomacy, trade and investment to protect its strategic water interests. China had also so far shown itself to be sensitive to its neighbours' concerns by offering compensation for its actions. At the same time, however, its own internal environmental problems, including water, are growing, and whether that would cause the country to be more aggressive in harnessing water in the region remains to be seen.

River Basin Agreements as Facilitators

While there could be many policy approaches for sustainable water resource management, Christopher Perry in Chapter 3 proposed a broad framework that he argued would be effective for resolving conflicts if the proposed steps were systematically followed. He cited the joint management of the Indus River basin by India and Pakistan, despite their political antagonism, as an example of the framework's robustness. Its component parts include:

- *Assessment* of available resources;
- *Bargaining* through the political process over development and allocation;
- *Codification* of the agreed allocations into laws;

- *Delegation* of implementation to appropriate institutions and agencies;
- *Engineering* to create the necessary infrastructure to deliver the agreed services.

CHALLENGES OF NATIONAL WATER MANAGEMENT

Aside from the China issue, the growing water scarcity in the region means that national water management strategies will become more critical to achieving sustainable development of the various countries' water resources. At a national level, most countries in Southeast Asia are already facing issues such as rising water consumption, pollution and a weak institutional capacity in managing water resources. The case studies in this book deal with such issues with varying intensities as the challenges are dissimilar across countries.

Rising Water Demand

Water consumption has been rising in Vietnam, Malaysia, Thailand and Indonesia due to rapid economic development.

In Malaysia, the overall water demand has been growing at an annual rate of 4 per cent and is projected to reach 20 billion cubic metres by 2020, up from 14.8 billion cubic metres in 2000, as highlighted by Salmah Zakariah in Chapter 6. Some parts of Malaysia are already experiencing water crises situations. For instance, Negri Sembilan has had to ration water supply to customers in 2005 where over 420,000 residents were affected by the rationing.[12]

In Indonesia, water demand has also been growing rapidly. Industrial and municipal water use in the country is expected to double in the next two decades, and it is widely anticipated that the various Indonesian government agencies will be unable to meet the growing demands caused by a rising population in the coming years. This is discussed by Budhi Santhoso from a regulatory perspective in Chapter 5.

As noted earlier, in many of the Southeast Asian countries, agriculture is the biggest user of water. In years to come, with additional population pressures and demands placed on agriculture, this could pose significant strains on water resources. Vietnam, for example, is seeing a rise in water consumption because of irrigation demand. In 2000, the total irrigation demand was 76.6 billion cubic metres. By 2010, this could increase to about 88.8 billion cubic metres, as highlighted by Le Dinh Thanh who examined Vietnam's water management strategy from sustainable watershed management perspective in Chapter 12.

Even as water demand is growing, developing countries in Southeast Asia have yet to devise efficient ways of managing water resources. In Vietnam, for example, although the country receives abundant rainfall of about 1,944 millimetres (mm) per year, about 1,003 mm is lost through evaporation.

Variations in rainfall over both time and space still lead to bouts of floods and droughts in other countries such as Malaysia and Thailand as they have been also unable to manage the water flows effectively. Such disasters take a severe toll on their economies. For instance, the costs imposed by floods in Malaysia had been estimated to be in the vicinity of RM1 billion per year (Chapter 6). The poor state of water delivery infrastructure in countries like the Philippines also means that most Filipinos, especially the poor ones, continue to face difficulties in accessing clean water supplies.

Pollution

Pollution is severe problem facing Southeast Asian countries like Indonesia and the Philippines. According to Budhi Santoso in Chapter 5, the main problem faced by the country is a deterioration of its water quality in its river basins. The number of river basins in a critical condition has almost doubled every 10 years, from 22 in 1984, 39 in 1992 to 59 in 1998. Most people still treat the rivers around them as a "backyard" where junk could be tossed. In this respect, it is crucial to change the public's attitude toward rivers so that they would learn the value of keeping them clean in order to foster a sustainable water solution. This is still a challenge which has yet to achieve significant results.

Waterways in the Philippines are also highly polluted, as the case study on the Pasig River undertaken by Donovan Storey reveals in Chapter 8. About 180 of the country's 421 main rivers and other water bodies have been so heavily polluted that they might soon be declared biologically dead. In fact, fifty of these major rivers are already considered biologically dead.

In Malaysia, there has also been a slow but steady deterioration in the water quality of sampled rivers. This pollution comes from various sources including untreated sewerage and waste disposals from factories, squatter areas, hawkers and sediments from construction sites, among others. Vietnam too is not immune from the issue, and pollution is especially evident in lakes and rivers situated near industrial, urban and tourist activities. Part of the problem is the people's mindset towards the water bodies around them.

Weak Institutions

Beyond changing mindsets, strong institutional capacity is also needed to enforce solutions to water problems. That is, however, still lacking in many Southeast Asian countries. In Malaysia, for example, agencies that regulate, manage, and provide services for the various water sectors sometimes have the technical expertise but no legislative or enforcement powers, and *vice versa*. There has also been a lack of policy coordination as water resources development is sectorally based whereby the development of domestic, industrial and irrigation water supplies are undertaken unilaterally by the respective agencies, as Salmah Zakaria has shown in Chapter 6. Many government bodies suffer from inadequate funding and labour shortages as well. More fundamentally, federal agencies are hobbled by the absence of legal jurisdiction over the management of natural resources including water, as they fall under state jurisdiction according to the Malaysian Constitution. Water only becomes a federal matter if a dispute arises in the case of a river basin which crosses a state's boundary. Given such a bureaucratic maze, it is hard to push through reforms effectively. To do so, a high-profile political champion for the issue is needed but such a figure is still lacking in Malaysian politics. The severe water problems in Indonesia has also escaped the radar screen of the leadership because of the lack of such a prominent champion.

Vietnam faces the same institutional problem. The overlapping of responsibilities among the various ministries is one reason why enforcement measures have been poorly carried out, as found in some of the studies ensuing. For example, the Ministry of Industry, the Ministry of Construction, and the Ministry of Natural Resources and the Environment may be responsible for water in one area but the lack of coordination among these ministries have made an integrated approach towards river basin management difficult, as discussed by Le Dinh Thanh in Chapter 12.

In other countries like Thailand and the Philippines, decentralization has inadvertently weakened their institutional capacity to manage water resources. For instance, in Thailand, the 1997 decentralization movement meant that Local Government Units (LGUs) had been given the authority to manage local water. However, according to the study by Sukontha Aekaraj (Chapter 11), the LGUs were not ready to take on this responsibility as they were limited in managerial capabilities such as personnel and in their budgets. A similar situation arose in the Philippines where the 1991 Local Government Code had decentralized many functions from the central authority to LGUs. However, decentralization in terms of environmental policy has been incomplete, leaving jurisdictions and responsibilities somewhat blurred between the centre and local governments. Such fuzziness is further exacerbated by tensions among the state, national bureaucracy and local authorities in the anarchic politics of the Philippines, as Donovan Storey highlights in Chapter 8.

Despite these problems, some institutional improvements have been made in countries such as Malaysia and Thailand. In the former, a National Water Resources Council (NWRC) was set up after the 1997 water crisis in order to pursue effective water management and services. In Thailand, a Department of Water Resources was also set up in 2003 in a bid to amalgamate many water-related agencies. While such moves are heartening, much remains to be done in these countries to further integrate water management across their territories and improve the capacity of local governments to deliver services.

Overcoming Water Constraints — The Case of Singapore

As a small island-state, Singapore, with inadequate water resources of its own, faces unique challenges in securing adequate water supplies to meet its needs as well as managing water demand to a sustainable level. So far, it had successfully managed to do so, even though there is still room for improvement in areas such as promoting greater consciousness of the importance of water among the public, as Wong Kai Yeng discusses in Chapter 10.

In terms of water supply management, Singapore's overall approach in ensuring sufficient water to meet its needs is based on three inter-related strategies, which include diversification of sources, leveraging on research and development (R&D) and technology, as well as management of the water loop. Indeed, technology has allowed Singapore to develop its so-called "Four Taps" or four diversified, independent sources of water supply.

Other than local water sources and imported water, the two other relatively new sources are NEWater and desalinated water. Both are examples of Singapore's use of technology to increase water for its use.

Singapore has won accolades for its water management strategies and technologies. Singapore water companies and also its Public Utilities Board (PUB) have been making sure but steady inroads into the global water market industry. The inaugural Singapore International Water Week, which was held in June 2008, is a testament of the country's endeavours to tap and develop its water industry to meet its own domestic as well as international demands in the years to come. The country has not only developed economically viable ways to recycle water but also spawned a whole industry of private water players which are now expanding overseas in markets in China, the Middle East, and India.[13]

NEWater is basically high-quality recycled water that is derived from a three-step process of microfiltration, reverse osmosis and UV radiation. Most of it is for direct non-potable use in industries and commercial sector, although a small portion is also injected back into the city-state's reservoirs for indirect potable use. As at end-2010, four NEWater plants supplying a total of 52 million gallons per day (mgd) are in operation. Meanwhile, desalinated water had also been fed into Singapore's water supply with the opening of the new desalination plant in September 2005. Both these new sources will supply over 50 per cent of Singapore's total water demand by the year 2012, according to Wong Kai Yeng.

Singapore has also been working to enlarge its water catchment areas, especially since technological breakthroughs in membrane technology has made it possible to convert previously untapped regions in Singapore into water catchment areas. One such example is the Marina Basin, which was completed in 2009. Construction has been completed to dam up the mouth of the Marina Channel with a barrage, thus creating Singapore's first "reservoir in the city". Together with other ongoing schemes, the project would increase Singapore's water catchment areas from half to two-thirds of the country. In addition, the barrage would also help to control flooding and offer a variety of new waterfront lifestyle opportunities for Singaporeans right in the heart of the city.

Singapore has continued to engage the so-called 3P (people, public and private) sectors and make sure everyone plays their part by not polluting water catchment areas. PUB has already embarked on community-driven public education programmes such as the Water Efficient Homes Programme and Water Efficient Buildings Programme to encourage house owners and building owners to adopt water conservation measures. The results so far have been encouraging. Per capita domestic consumption level has decreased from 162 litres per day in 2004 to 154 litres per day in 2010. The aim is to lower this further to 147 litres per day by 2020.

EXPERIMENTS WITH PRIVATIZATION

As countries try to find the most efficient way of delivering water to the people, privatization is an option that is increasingly undertaken in the region, as seen in Malaysia and the Philippines. Thailand too is moving towards it with a committee already established to design a regulatory framework for the process. However, this option is not without controversy. For instance, Eric Teo in Chapter 4 cautioned that full-fledged privatization of the water sector may not be acceptable for several reasons, including the growing tide of public opinion against "unbridled capitalism" and the peculiar character of water as a "social good" which has social redistribution implications.

In the chapter, Teo argued for the public-private partnership (PPP) as a privatization model for the water sector in Southeast Asia. In this concept, the assets of the water sector would still belong to the state, which also sets the overall development strategy and regulatory framework. The private sector, in turn, would build and operate the facilities, so as to deliver water services more efficiently and effectively. Such a partnership should clearly establish the quality of service, pricing formula, future tariff increases and the duration of the concession or contract.

Beyond these socio-economic aspects, there should also be sound public relations management of a PPP in the water sector in order to assuage three forces that might be unleashed: Nationalistic feelings, fears of unemployment, and concerns about rising utilities prices. The public relations exercise should highlight that savings could be achieved by greater private sector involvement, as wastage is cut down to the minimum, and that the labour force and the plants are used more efficiently. At the same time, however, consumers should also be made to understand that reasonable price increases are to be expected, in line with inflation. If not, the private service providers would bleed financially and their ultimate failure may not benefit the consumers in the long run.

Lorraine Carlos Salazar in Chapter 9 argued that "government failure" does not automatically justify private sector involvement in the water sector as making a state monopoly a private monopoly could worsen the situation, if the monopolist took advantage of its privileged position. Two privatization exercises in Metro Manila in the Philippines have come up with very different outcomes, as discussed in the chapter. Privatization should be accompanied by the introduction of an effective regulatory system as well which was not always the case in the privatization exercises examined.

Forms of private sector participation could come in many ways because of the nature of the water supply chain, which could be vertically unbundled. This would allow for the entry of various service providers at different stages, such as raw water supply, water treatment, water distribution, waste-water collection and waste-water treatment. The different forms of private sector participation in the water sector include service contracts, management contracts, leases, BOO/BOT (build-operate-own/build-operate-transfer) contracts, concessions and divestiture.

Malaysian Privatization of Water

The forum also explored two detailed case studies of privatization in Southeast Asia in Malaysia and the Philippines. The outcomes of these cases appear to be mixed so far.

For Malaysia, Syed Danial Syed Ariffin pointed to several reasons which have prompted the rise of privatization in the water sector, using the case of Puncak Niaga, the largest water supply concessionaire in Malaysia. Reasons include: The escalating cost of water supply expenditure; increasing rate of non-revenue water; deterioration of raw water quality; insufficient funds to improve assets and finance further capital expenditure, as well as the need to ensure sufficient water supplies for the future. In line with the National Privatization Policy unveiled in 1983, more Malaysian states have been moving towards privatization to lessen the burden of the high development cost of water supply programmes. These states include Johor, Penang and Kelantan, which has privatized the construction, operation and maintenance of source works, treatment plants and distribution systems as well as billing and revenue collection. Selangor has also recently privatized its water treatment plants and other distributional aspects of water supply.

The results have been largely positive so far. Penang and Johor have registered the highest figures of revenue over expenditure of 57 per cent and 46 per cent respectively. These contrast sharply with the state water supply departments of Sabah and Pahang, which registered a deficit of 71 per cent and 18 per cent respectively.

Even so, Syed Danial's discussion showed that the process of privatizing a previously malfunctioning state operator is fraught with challenges, including the inheriting of massive debts and the difficulties in revamping operations and changing the mindset of former state employees. As the water sector is a highly capital-intensive one, being able to secure huge financing is another challenge. So far, the private operators have benefited from a low-interest rate environment and the growth of new financial instruments like Islamic bonds. Looking ahead, there is a need for more financial expertise in the sector to help it obtain the funds needed. At the macro-level, other issues such as the need to rationalize the regulatory environment, reduce raw water pollution, cut non-revenue water and increase R&D, also need to be tackled to ensure the sustainability of water resource development in Malaysia.

Philippine Privatization

The Philippines also took steps toward privatizing its water sector in 1994 when the disastrous job done by state agency, Metropolitan Waterworks and Sewerage System (MWSS), threatened to throw the country into a "water crisis". Former President Fidel Ramos then decided that the solution was to involve the private sector in the operation and management of the MWSS, with the help of the International Finance Corporation (IFC) as the financial and technical adviser. After a competitive bidding process, two twenty-five-year concessions were awarded to two joint ventures. The post-privatization outcomes were mixed. As the process coincided with the 1997 Asian financial crisis, both companies were hit by the peso devaluation, which almost doubled the debt burden they inherited overnight.

Still, Manila Water managed to improve the provision of water services, along with enhancing the company's fiscal discipline and cost-effectiveness. This was in contrast to the failed case of Maynilad Water, which pulled out of its water contract by March 2003, blaming its losses on the heavy debt burden assumed by the company in 1997. Despite the problems and challenges, the privatization of the Manila water system was necessary and had beneficial results. Even people who were critical of the failure of Maynilad acknowledged the general improvement in infrastructure and level of service in the metropolitan area, in contrast to the former situation under the MWSS where water was supplied in low quantities and of poor quality at a very high price.

In 2007, a new and all-Filipino partnership of DM Consunji Holdings Incorporated and Metro Pacific Investments Corporation (DMCI-MPIC) took over the management of Maynilad Water Services. The process of recovery is still ongoing and the new partnership can draw on lessons from the past few years to avoid a repetition of history.[14]

POLICY LESSONS

Some key policy lessons were drawn about managing water resources in the region from the forum and also the subsequent chapters discussing the above issues in more detail.

The need for an account of the environmental costs of water resource development to reflect the "true" costs of environmental degradation in terms of complex ecological losses such as biodiversity is recognized.

At the regional level, there is a need to build institutional capacity in more concrete terms. This was especially so when it came to managing the Mekong River. In order to clarify and strengthen the institutional structures and processes for ensuring environmental security in the Mekong Basin, the unsatisfactory division of labour, which currently exist between the Mekong River Commission and the Asian Development Bank (ADB), should be resolved. While the MRC was the most relevant institution as it had a mandate specifically related to integrated river basin planning, its effectiveness was seriously hampered by its lack of influence.

The ADB, on the other hand, has exercised the greatest sway over riparian governments because it provided the funds for water development projects. However, the ADB is seen as essentially a financial institution with little environmental interest. Therefore, there was an urgent need to find some way of strengthening and formalizing the MRC's specific concerns with sustainable river basin management in tandem with the ADB-led economic development plans in the region. To strengthen the MRC, its credibility had to be bolstered by strong leadership and links to international institutions like the United Nations, as well as the deployment of more influential officials to the commission.

Overall, it was understood that there was a need to raise the environmental awareness of the people in Southeast Asia through education and campaigns. Such an attitudinal shift by the public is crucial for ensuring continued supply of clean water. It is also important for governments in the region to engage the masses in managing water resources because conservation efforts without public cooperation were not likely to be successful. Indeed, for major projects that involved human impact such as resettlement, it is critical that the authorities establish the "relevance" of such works to the affected people by, for instance, highlighting that it would enhance their welfare in tangible ways. Water policies tend to be more sustainable when they increase the people's sense of security and ownership over "their" environments. Even so, strong state institutions and political support are still needed to enforce solutions to water problems. For instance, in some Southeast Asian countries like Vietnam, water laws against pollution still need to be strictly monitored and enforced. The case of Singapore has also demonstrated that technology can be successfully harnessed to increase water supply in the forms of NEWater and desalinated water.

Finally, the privatization case studies yielded other policy lessons as well. Firstly, in order to successfully implement a privatization project, there is a need to ensure the articulation of clear objectives, firm political will, focused execution of the government's action plan and unwavering support from the private sector. Secondly, there should be a clear and transparent regulatory framework, which would help lower the political risks for private-sector concessionaires. Thirdly, concessionaires need a strong balance sheet and cash flow to address the risks from regulatory uncertainty as well as liquidity problems resulting from uncontrollable factors such as a financial crisis.

Possible water conflicts, competition for water by the different sectors in each country, water accessibility, privatization, public private partnerships, institutional challenges, and future trends in water supplies will be some of the issues covered in the chapters following. The private-public partnership discussion will also highlight how governments and corporations can work together to ease water shortages. River basin agreements form another means for cooperation. The urban management of water is also relevant as countries become more urbanized in the years to come. With rates of urbanization expected to increase, the management of pollution in waterways and rivers are important. So is the need to management water in a water-scarce context, as in the case of Singapore and increasingly in other Southeast Asian countries as demands increase exponentially over existing supplies. In this instance, new technologies to harness and produce water will also play a central role in the years to come.

Notes

1. Yatsuka Kataoka, "Water Resource Management in Asia: Integration and Interaction for a Better Future", in *Sustainable Asia 2005 and Beyond: In the Pursuit of Innovative Policies* (Japan: Institute for Global Environmental Strategies (IGES), 2005).
2. *Third ASEAN State of the Environment Report 2006: Towards an Environmentally Sustainable ASEAN Community* (Jakarta: ASEAN Secretariat, November 2006), p. 39.
3. *State of Water Resources Management in ASEAN* (Jakarta: ASEAN Secretariat, October 2005), p. 4.
4. *Third ASEAN State of the Environment Report 2006*, op. cit., p. 42.

5. Ibid., p. 40.
6. See, for example, *State of Water Resources Management in ASEAN*, op. cit., p. 3.
7. *Third ASEAN State of the Environment Report 2006*, op, cit. p. 41.
8. Ibid., p. 41.
9. Ibid.
10. *State of Water Resources Management in ASEAN*, op. cit. p. 9.
11. See *United Nations World Water Development Report: Water for People, Water for Life* (United States: UNESCO-WWAP, 2003) and also *United Nations World Water Development Report 2: Water, A Shared Responsibility* (United States: UNESCO-WWAP, 2006).
12. "Negri Trying to Ease Water Woes", *The Star*, 11 July 2005.
13. See Tan Yong Soon, Lee Tung Jean, and Karen Tan, *Clean, Green, and Blue: Singapore's Journey Towards Environmental and Water Sustainability* (Singapore: Institute of Southeast Asian Studies, 2009) and Teng Chye Khoo, "Singapore Water: Yesterday, Today and Tomorrow", in *Water Management in 2020 and Beyond*, edited by Asit K. Biswas, Cecilia Tortajada and Rafael Izquierdo (Berlin: Springer-Verlag Berlin Heidelberg, 2009).
14. *Maynilad on the Mend: Rebidding Process Infuses New Life to a Struggling Concessionaire* (Manila: Asian Development Bank, May 2008).

References

Kataoka, Yatsuka. "Water Resource Management in Asia: Integration and Interaction for a Better Future". In *Sustainable Asia 2005 and Beyond: In the Pursuit of Innovative Policies*. Japan: Institute for Global Environmental Strategies (IGES), 2005.

Maynilad on the Mend: Rebidding Process Infuses New Life to a Struggling Concessionaire. Manila: Asian Development Bank, May 2008

"Negri trying to Ease Water Woes". *The Star*, 11 July 2005.

State of Water Resources Management in ASEAN. Jakarta: ASEAN Secretariat, October 2005.

Tan Yong Soon, Lee Tung Jean, and Karen Tan. *Clean, Green, and Blue: Singapore's Journey Towards Environmental and Water Sustainability*. Singapore: Institute of Southeast Asian Studies, 2009.

Teng Chye Khoo. "Singapore Water: Yesterday, Today and Tomorrow". In *Water Management in 2020 and Beyond*, edited by Asit K. Biswas, Cecilia Tortajada and Rafael Izquierdo. Berlin: Springer-Verlag Berlin Heidelberg, 2009.

Third ASEAN State of the Environment Report 2006: Towards an Environmentally Sustainable ASEAN Community. Jakarta: ASEAN Secretariat, November 2006.

United Nations World Water Development Report: Water for People, Water for Life. United States: UNESCO-WWAP, 2003.

United Nations World Water Development Report 2: Water, A Shared Responsibility. United States: UNESCO-WWAP, 2006.

2

CHINA AND THE POTENTIAL FOR CONFLICT OVER WATER AMONG EURASIAN STATES

Michael Richardson

Managing freshwater in rivers that cross borders or form boundaries between nations is a global issue with particular relevance for Asia. It places China in the focus of a new spotlight — one that will bring the world's most populous nation under the increasingly critical scrutiny of its water-dependent neighbours in Southeast Asia, South Asia, Central Asia and Russia. China itself has a growing thirst for water. It has 20 per cent of the planet's population but only 7 per cent of its total freshwater resources. Yet China is Eurasia's dominant headwater power. Most of its great rivers and many of those that enable nearby nations to flourish start from the snow-fed highlands on the "roof of the world", the Qinghai-Tibetan Plateau, which is centred in western China. Chinese control over the critical upstream sections of these transborder rivers is a factor that must be added to the country's rise as an economic, political, military and cultural force in regional affairs. It is an aspect of growing Chinese influence on nearby states that is seldom recognized and therefore underestimated.

Geography has dictated that many of the big rivers sustaining people, agriculture and industry in Southeast Asia, South Asia, Central Asia and Russia east of the Ural Mountains start in Chinese territory. Southeast Asia's largest rivers come from deep inside China. Among them are the Salween, Mekong and Red rivers. Other transboundary rivers that emerge from China include the Songhua, Ili and Irtysh rivers flowing into Russia and/or Kazakhstan. Long stretches of the headwaters of the Brahmaputra River pass through China before they reach India's Ganges River and Bangladesh. What China does to this vital supply of freshwater (by building dams, diverting flows for its own use or polluting the upstream sections of the rivers) affects its downstream neighbours. This was graphically illustrated in late 2005 when a toxic chemical spill into China's Songhua River was carried into Russia's adjoining Amur River, drawing Russian protests and raising fears about long-term pollution of a vital drinking and fishing source. China's diversion of water from the Ili River in arid northwestern China is contributing to the drying up of Kazakhstan's Lake Balkhash, the second largest body of water in Central Asia. Meanwhile, China's diversion of water from the Irtysh River for agriculture is causing concern in both Kazakhstan and Russia because the river runs from northwestern China into both countries.

China's dam building on its stretches of these long transboundary rivers flowing into other parts of Asia and Russia is the main focus of this chapter. Of all China's regional neighbours, Southeast Asia is most affected by this activity. Facing growing public pressure at home to provide more clean water and electric power to its 1.3 billion people, China is intensifying use of its freshwater resources by harnessing previously free-flowing rivers or building additional dams on rivers to control flooding; store water for human consumption, farming and industry; and to generate electricity. The latter is the single most important purpose of modern Chinese dams. Hydropower generators on rivers in

China presently provide about 100 million kilowatts of electricity, about 23 per cent of total capacity. The government has said it plans to triple hydropower supply by 2020. The programme includes a series of huge dams on Chinese sections of the Mekong and Salween rivers that downstream countries in Southeast Asia fear will affect the amount and quality of water they receive. But they, too, are building dams to exploit water on the sections of transborder rivers they control. And, like China, they often show little consideration for the interests of their neighbours further downstream.

TRANSBOUNDARY MAZE

There are over 260 freshwater rivers or lakes shared by more than one country. Hundreds of underground acquifers are similarly shared. The catchment basins of these water resources contain over half the world's land territory and population. The territory of 145 nations falls within these international basins, thirty-three of them almost entirely within. In Asia, for example, six nations share the Mekong River while three each share the Salween and Brahmaputra rivers.[1]

Shared rivers and lakes offer many opportunities for food and energy production, transport, trade and fisheries. However, they need sound environmental management. There are some international guidelines or principles on sharing transboundary water resources; but there is no binding treaty. Water is unevenly distributed between countries. At a time of looming shortages, there is potential for water-related disputes between states and a temptation for those in an upstream position to take the lion's share of the water or use it in ways that may damage the interests of downstream communities. If global warming intensifies this century as many scientists predict, water politics will become more prominent and the potential for conflict between states over shared rivers and aquifers will rise.

Transboundary basin organizations have had varying degrees of success around the globe. Among them are bodies for the Rhine River and Lake Geneva in Europe, the Great Lakes and St Lawrence seaway in North America, the Nile and Senegal rivers in Africa, and the Mekong and the Indus rivers in Asia. But many transboundary basin institutions do not have sufficient authority, capacity or resources to manage the water under their control in a sustainable way. And a lot of major transborder water sources have no inter-state water institutions at all. Indeed, some scientists, statesmen and United Nations agencies say that the risk of wars being fought over water is increasing.[2]

However, a U.S. study suggests that in recent history at least, the interdependence of countries on shared water resources was far more often a pathway to cooperation than to competition or conflict. The reseachers at Oregon State University compiled a dataset of every reported interaction between two or more nations that was driven by water in the last half century. They found that the rate of cooperation overwhelmed the incidence of acute conflict. In the past fifty years, only thirty-seven disputes involved violence and thirty of those occurred between Israel and one of its neighbours, in disagreements rooted in politics.[3]

It is also worth noting that some of the most vociferous antagonists have negotiated and maintained water agreements despite their enmity. The Indus River Commission survived two major wars between India and Pakistan. The Mekong Committee, established by Cambodia, Laos, Thailand and Vietnam in 1957, exchanged information on the river basin throughout the Vietnam War when Thailand was a U.S. ally against communist regimes in Indochina. The Mekong Committee was the forerunner of today's Mekong River Commission.[4]

Will this relatively benign situation of cooperative, though limited, transborder water management continue in an era of intensifying global warming, pollution and water shortage?

MELTING GLACIERS

The competition for dwindling reserves of water is being exacerbated as the Earth's atmosphere gets hotter. Chinese scientists have added their voices to warnings that global warming, by melting glaciers in and around the Qinghai-Tibet Plateau, is threatening Asia's future water supplies. After analysing records from China's more than 600 weather stations over the last forty years, they concluded recently that Chinese glaciers on the plateau were shrinking by 7 per cent a year and that the environmental consequences are likely to be dire. High plateau tundra will turn to desert, droughts in China will intensify, and the sandstorms that periodically lash western and northern China will intensify.[5]

Dust and sandstorms are already a growing problem, particularly in north China, due to water shortage, deforestation and poor farming practices and land management. For example, a giant sandstorm swept across one eighth of China's territory on 16 and 17 April 2006, dumping an estimated 330,000 metric tonnes of dust on Beijing and reaching as far as Korea and Japan. The Chinese capital, Beijing in northern China, has suffered drought for the last seven consecutive years. The average annual rainfall between 1999 and 2005 was only 70 per cent of the average since records began.[6]

Another development being watched closely by Chinese atmospheric and weather scientists is the depletion of the protective ozone layer over the Tibetan Plateau. Although not yet opening up into gaping holes like those over the North and South Poles, the Chinese observations suggest that the ozone level has diminished sharply since the problem was first noticed in December 2003. Ozone is one of the gases that form the Earth's atmosphere and is the major shield against Ultraviolet B (UVB) radiation from the sun. In normal concentration, ozone absorbs approximately 90 per cent of solar UVB. Excessive exposure to UVB can cause skin cancer in humans and is a major contributor to glacial melting.[7]

About 70 per cent of the world's freshwater is frozen in glaciers. The largest concentration of these slow-moving rivers of ice is in the Qinghai-Tibet Plateau — which encompasses the Tibet Autonomous Region, as well as Qinghai and Sichuan provinces in southwest China. This area is commonly known as the Tibetan Plateau or Chang Tang in Chinese. Aptly called the "roof of the world", it is the highest and biggest plateau in the world. At an average altitude of around 4,000 metres above sea level, the plateau covers an area of about 2.5 million square kilometres, roughly a quarter of China's land surface and well over three times the size of France or the U.S. state of Texas.

Glaciers form when snow from mountains accumulates in valleys and is then compressed at freezing temperatures. The Tibetan Plateau — which includes the Himalayan, Karakorum, Pamir and Kunlun mountains — has the largest concentration of glaciers outside the polar caps. These glaciers cover an area of nearly 105,000 square kilometres, almost half of which is in China and somewhat less in India and Pakistan. Of all the mountain chains in the area, the Himalayas have the biggest glacier cover, amounting to nearly 35,000 square kilometres.

China's official *Xinhua News Agency* reported in mid-2005 that Chinese scientists had found glaciers on the Tibet side of the world's tallest mountain, Mt Everest in the Himalayan chain, were shrinking faster than ever. They observed that the melting point of one Everest's glacier had risen around 50 metres in just two years, more than twice as fast as normal, while a huge, high-altitude ice cliff seen in 2002 had apparently disappeared.[8]

Why is this alarming? The United Nations' top scientific authority on global warming, the UN Panel on Climate Change, says that global warming — caused by the burning of coal, oil and other fossil fuels and the emission into the atmosphere of heat-trapping gases like carbon dioxide and methane — could drive the average temperatures up by between 1.4 and 5.8 degrees Celsius over the next 100 years. This would cause glaciers to retreat further and make oceans rise, swamping low-lying areas around the world. But the melting of glaciers on the Tibetan Plateau is a special problem for China and other parts of Asia because the vast, high-altitude plateau is the headwaters of rivers flowing to countries that are home to half of humanity.

The Himalayan and other glaciers feed eight of Asia's great rivers. They include the Yangtze and Yellow rivers that start in northeastern Tibet and flow across China. The Mekong, Southeast Asia's biggest river, originates in eastern Tibet. Myanmar's two main rivers, the Irrawaddy and the Salween, also come from the Tibetan Plateau as do the giant rivers of northern India and Pakistan — the Ganges, Indus and Brahmaputra. However, the Irrawaddy, unlike the Salween, while drawing water from tributaries that start from the the southeastern end of the Himalayas, flows wholly from within Myanmar and does not rise deep within China. Stretching for thousands of kilometres, and in the case of Yangtze for nearly 6,400 kilometres, these are among the world's longest rivers. They have enormous catchment areas in the mountains and hills that feed water via tributaries to the mainstream, providing stocks to sustain hundreds of millions of people.

Glaciers regulate the water supply to China, South Asia and Southeast Asia, where drought and water shortages are already a serious problem in many areas. The glaciers prevent winter flooding when the snow fall is heaviest but release water for drinking, farming and industry when it is most needed in spring and summer. About two-thirds of China's water is used for agricultural irrigation. It is critical for maintaining food production and rural livelihoods, thus preventing an already vast migration of country dwellers to cities and towns in search of work and a better life from becoming an uncontrollable flood.

The Chinese scientists' warning that glacial melting on the Tibetan Plateau threatens the balance of global water resources is only the latest alarm bell to ring. In March 2005, the China, India and Nepal offices of the Switzerland-based World Wide Fund for Nature (WWF) issued a joint report saying that the retreat of glaciers in the Himalayan region is accelerating as global warming increases, and that they are now receding at an average rate of between 10 and 15 metres a year. The report said that in the past forty years or more, glaciers on the Tibetan Plateau had shrunk by over 6,600 square kilometres, with the biggest retreat occurring since the mid-1980s. The melting of the glaciers could in the short term increase flooding, landslides and soil erosion in China, South Asia and Southeast Asia before creating water shortages for hundreds of millions of people across the region.[9]

> The rapid melting of Himalayan glaciers will first increase the volume of water in rivers, causing widespread flooding," said Jennifer Morgan, Director of the WWF's Global Climate Change Programme. "But in a few decades, this situation will change and the water level in rivers will decline, meaning massive economic and environmental problems for people in western China, Nepal and northern India.[10]

Other specialists have warned of the rising danger of GLOFs — glacial lake outburst floods. This has been happening with increasing frequency in recent decades as water builds up in hundreds of glacial lakes on the Tibetan Plateau. There are over 1,000 lakes larger than one square kilometre on the plateau.[11] When the walls of these lakes give way — perhaps due to structural weakness or an earthquake — huge amounts of water carrying rocks and soil are released, devastating downstream communities and causing severe damage to hydropower stations, bridges, roads and other infrastructure. The WWF report concluded the GLOFs were a danger to China, India and Nepal. But it said that the biggest threat to countries dependent on Tibetan Plateau glaciers was from long-term loss of freshwater as they melted, and that it was imperative to start vulnerability assessments now before devising adaption plans.

CHINESE WATER CRISIS

China is the world's third largest country by land area, after Russia and Canada. But relative to the size of its 1.3 billion population, China is not well endowed with natural resources, including freshwater, fertile land and forest cover to protect watersheds. The World Bank estimated in 2004 that China's internal freshwater resources per person amounted to just over 2,200 cubic metres a year, about one third of the world average and less than half the East Asia and Pacific average.[12]

With vast swathes of desert, arid or dry land, China has long had a water problem. Resources are unevenly distributed. Supplies are scarce in the north and west throughout the year. The areas south of the Yangtze River, which account for just under 37 per cent of the country's land territory, have almost 81 per cent of its total water supplies. Areas north of the Yangtze, which make up just over 63 per cent of China, have barely 19 per cent of the water. Since China's Communist Party took power in 1949, water consumption for human use, agriculture and industry on the mainland has risen nearly six-fold, from around 100 billion cubic metres to a current level of around 560 billion cubic metres. Rapid economic growth, urbanization and industrialization over the past twenty-five years have intensified shortages and pollution in many areas.

Some Chinese scientists doubt that water supply can be boosted much more by expensive storage, diversion, piping and pumping projects. In June 2002, Chinese experts warned that by 2030, when the population reaches 1.6 billion, per capita water resources will drop to 1,760 cubic metres a year — perilously close to the level of 1,700 cubic metres that is the internationally recognized benchmark for chronic shortage. The head of the Soil Conservation Institute of the Chinese Academy of Sciences said at the time that national water consumption would peak by 2030 and that if no effective measures were taken, the country was likely to suffer a serious water crisis in future.[13]

The Chinese leadership and some arms of the government are vey aware of the country's water problem and appear anxious to tackle it. They published the first guidelines on water efficient technology in May 2005 to raise public awareness of the need to save water, partly by making users pay more for an underpriced resource. The guidelines, which were jointly issued by five ministerial departments, say that China will strive for zero growth in water use for agriculture between 2005 and 2010. It will try to limit industrial users to a slight rise over the same period.[14]

But Chinese authorities are taking other measures as well. They include damming rivers in the western regions of China that flow into Southeast Asia and Central Asia. This has prompted complaints from nearby countries about unilateral Chinese action affecting downstream river flow, and the quality and availability of water. Some officials and environmental activists say that major regional disputes are brewing over this issue and that the full impact of the Chinese dam building is yet to be felt. They warn that China's ravenous appetite for hydroelectric power at home and its thrust southward into Southeast Asia to trade and extend its sphere of influence is having an adverse impact on the Mekong River Basin, changing its character in damaging and irreversible ways.

SOUTHEAST ASIA

The Mekong runs for some 4,880 kilometres through or between six countries — China, Myanmar, Laos, Thailand, Cambodia and Vietnam. It is the world's twelfth longest river. More than one-third of the Mekong runs through China although only about 18 per cent of the river's water comes from there. But the Chinese contribution is increasingly important in Southeast Asia's Mekong Basin dry season, from November to May, when the river relies for a significant part of its flow on the melting of glaciers high on the Tibetan Plateau.

China calls the Mekong the Lancang. It has the upper hand in harnessing the waters of the river for power, irrigation and flood control because it is the upstream country. Chinese engineers and workers are in midst of building a third hydroelectric power dam on the river at Xiaowan. With a dam wall nearly 300 metres high, Xiaowan will be the second largest in China after the mammoth Three Gorges Dam on the Yangtze River. When filled in 2013, its reservoir will stretch almost 170 kilometres. Two Chinese hydropower plants are already in operation on the Mekong and five more are planned by around 2020.[15] They will provide electricity not just to Yunnan, one of China's poorest and least developed provinces, but also send it via transmission lines to densely populated industrialized zones on the east coast that need power.

The Mekong River Commission (MRC) was established by the governments of Cambodia, Laos, Thailand and Vietnam in 1995 — at the end of a long period of conflict in the region. The MRC helps to coordinate the management and conservation of the Mekong Basin in Southeast Asia. It does some useful information sharing and practical work, even with its present limited membership and mandate. But the MRC cannot hope to ensure that the rich resources of the Mekong are developed in the most rational and sustainable way unless the two other riparian states, China and Myanmar, join the organization and cooperate fully in its activities. Even then, there would need to be agreement among all six members on binding rules for water allocation and uses to achieve sustainable management.

The siting, size and type of dams built on one section of the main river or the tributaries that flow into it will obviously affect other parts of the network. Ideally, Mekong dams should be part of a scientific masterplan, approved by all six states. However, no country, whether upsteam or downstream, appears willing to surrender national sovereignty to anywhere near this extent.[16] China and Myanmar attend the annual meetings of the MRC as dialogue partners. But they have refused requests to join the inter-governmental body or be bound by its guidelines. Still, China has informed the downsteam Mekong countries of the hydropower and other development plans for its section of the river. And since 2003, China and Myanmar have been providing information on water flow and river level height to the downstream states to aid in flood forecasting. The MRC is studying ways of expanding this kind of cooperation.[17]

However, the Mekong Basin is a huge resource with an ecosystem that needs to be carefully nurtured. Scientists estimate that about 1,700 species of fish, some of them migratory, live the waters of the Mekong, which supports one of the biggest inland fisheries in the world. The fish provide a key source of protein for local people. Unlike nearly all other major rivers, the Mekong has few big cities on its banks and not much industry to contribute to pollution. But this will change over the next thirty years. The population living near the river and its many tributaries is expected to increase to over 100 million, from around 70 million today. Urbanization and industrialization will intensify. And the pressure on the basin's natural resources — chiefly forests, fisheries and agriculture — will grow.[18]

Already, there are concerns that rampant logging, much of it illegal, soil erosion and over-fishing are threatening the health of the Mekong Basin. Meanwhile, the governments in the Greater Mekong Sub-region (GMS) are encouraging transportation, trade, investment and other economic activity in the area as part of a scheme to cut poverty and raise living standards. The GMS programme, launched in 1992 by six countries with assistance from the Asian Development Bank, encompasses a broader zone than just the Mekong Basin but will clearly have a heavy impact on the river and its tributaries. The GMS includes China's Yunnan province as well as Cambodia, Laos, Myanmar, Thailand and Vietnam.

Backed by China and Japan among others, the GMS programme aims to attract as much as US$15 billion in investment and loans over the next five to ten years to improve road, rail, telecommunications and power links in the sub-region. It includes a blueprint to form an inter-connected six-nation energy network based on hydropower.[19] In the race to harness the benefits of the Mekong, all six riparian countries are pressing ahead with dam building or water diversion schemes on their sections of the river or its tributaries, often without adequate consultations or environmental impact studies, despite the concerns of downstream communities that fear they will be adversely affected.

As part of a national plan to ease dependence on polluting coal and oil for energy, China plans to build as many as thirteen dams on its section of the Salween River before it flows into Myanmar, roughly parallel to the Mekong. In the past few years, controversy has swirled around the proposal to construct this cascade of hydroelectric dams on the Nu River — one of the last free-flowing rivers in China. Decisions made by Chinese government authorities on the final shape of the project will affect downstream countries, Myanmar and Thailand. Yet they are shrouded in official secrecy. In China itself, the issue is emerging as a test of national priorities. To what extent are party and government officials, both central and local, prepared to listen to dissenting voices? And how will they balance the need for energy and economic growth against conservation and sustainable development?

Beginning high on the Tibetan Plateau, the Nu, which means "angry", passes through a remote mountain region of southwest China before entering Myanmar, where it is known as the Thanlwin (in Burmese) or the Salween (in English). The river forms Myanmar's border with Thailand for 120 kilometres, then flows through Myanmar's territory before spilling into the Andaman Sea. More than two-thirds of the 2,800-kilometre-long river are in China where a group of state-owned companies announced in mid-2003 that they planned to build thirteen dams on the Chinese section of the Nu to generate electricity. Such a project would be the largest cascade dam system in the world. It would generate 22,000 megawatts, the equivalent of about two dozen big nuclear power stations. This is 4,000 more megawatts of electricity a year than the mammoth Three Gorges Dam on the Yangtze River will generate when it is finished in 2009.[20]

In April 2004, Chinese Premier Wen Jiabao — who has repeatedly expressed concern about the social and environmental consequences of uncontrolled growth — suspended the Nu River cascade project, telling officials it needed more careful scrutiny. Environmental activists and some Chinese scientists had opposed any dams along the river, arguing that they would displace at least 50,000 villagers, threaten fisheries and wildlife, and disrupt the flow of the Nu into Myanmar and along the Thai border.[21] The United Nations also entered the dispute. In 2005, its cultural protection agency, UNESCO, issued a statement expressing its "gravest concerns" about the potential damage to a wilderness area in China's Yunnan province through which the Nu flows. China had designated the area a national park and in July 2003 UNESCO listed it as world heritage site, noting that the region "may be the most biologically diverse temperate ecosystem in the world".

Latest reports suggest, however, that Chinese authorities have decided to proceed with the Nu hydropower project, initially building only four of the originally slated thirteen dams, ostensibly to limit any local disruption and damage to the environment.[22] Under China's Environmental Impact Assessement Law, which took effect in September 2003, comprehensive reviews are supposed to be made in the planning stages of major public and private development projects. This process is also supposed to involve public participation, including hearings where objections can be raised and considered. However, China's Ministry of Water Resources, noting that government reports about international rivers are considered confidential, has declared that a section of the environmental impact assessment on the Nu River project is a state secret and forbade release of the report.[23]

The governments of Myanmar and Thailand have been little more forthcoming about their plans for hydropower development on the river. They signed a memorandum of understanding in December 2005 to build at least five dams on the Salween, with participation of foreign firms including Chinese state-owned companies. The five dams would generate 11,800 megawatts of electricity. But the MOU they signed was not published until a British journalist posted it on a website in March.[24]

China's dam building and planning tend to be the activities most publicized by critics. In that sense, they are the most visible. But Myanmar, Laos, Cambodia and Vietnam, also have their own projects or plans to build hydropower dams that will affect water flow and quality in the Mekong and Salween river basins. For example, Vietnam started construction in June 2003 of a second big dam on the Sesan River, which runs through its territory and northeastern Cambodia into the Mekong. It is one of the Mekong's main tributaries. However Hanoi, in breach of its obligations as a member of the Mekong River Commission, failed to complete formal consultations with Phnom Penh on the dam. Vietnam's move to start building the second hydropower plant surprised and irritated Cambodian officials who were still discussing with their Vietnamese counterparts how to conduct a joint study on the environmental impact of the new dam. The Vietnamese government has approved planning for at least four more hydropower dams on its section of the Sesan.[25]

Yet Vietnam complains that China's dams on the Mekong, by cutting the flow of river water, are contributing to the intrusion of saltwater into the Mekong Delta in southern Vietnam where the river flows into the South China Sea. The delta produces about half Vietnam's agricultural output.

The Chinese government asserts that the Mekong dams will benefit downstream countries, by storing water in the rainy season to reduce flooding and releasing it when needed in the dry season. But in the past few years, China has been accused by some officials and environmental activists in Southeast Asia of controlling water at the expense of downstream states. They say that when water is released from the Chinese dams, water levels in the Mekong rise and fall as much as one metre in an hour. The surges disturb fish habitats, erode river banks and scour sediment and nutrients from the river as they flow southward. The critics also allege that the Chinese dams are holding back a large portion of the fertile silt that used to feed the river and surrounding areas.[26]

Some of those who live on the river in Southeast Asia seem covinced that Chinese demand for water and electric power is sucking the lower Mekong dry and undermining the livlihoods of many who depend on it for farming, fishing and navigation.[27] Are the Chinese dams really to blame for the recent low water levels in the river? A study by the Mekong River Comission, the MRC, published in 2004 says they are not, at least not so far. Instead, the study concludes that the cause of the problem was a drier than usual wet season in 2003. The MRC analysis is based on river height and rainfall data spanning several decades. If low flows in Southeast Asia's stretch of the Mekong were caused by retention of water in dams in Yunnan, the dry conditions would be more pronounced at upstream sites near China, since tributaries of the Mekong feed water into the river further downstream. In fact, the data shows it has been drier at Pakse in southern Laos than at Chiang Saen in Thailand, which is much closer to China.

The two dams already operating on China's section of the Mekong are relatively small. One was completed nearly a decade ago. Moreover, they are hydropower dams, not dams used for irrigation water supply. As a result, they release the water they retain, although usually with a different flow pattern to the natural river. In general, hydropower dam operators try to store excess water in the wet season and release more water than usual in the dry season because natural dry season flows are often insufficient to provide the electricity generating capacity that is needed. So the two Chinese dams could be expected to increase dry season flows rather than decrease them. Still, by making water levels downstream more variable and reducing sediment concentrations, the dams do have an impact on fish and other aquatic life in the Mekong. This is being studied by the MRC.[28]

CENTRAL ASIA

United Nations agencies have issued several warnings in the past couple of years that Kazakhstan's Lake Balkhash, the second largest body of water in the region could dry up, creating another major environmental crisis. Central Asia's Aral Sea has lost three-quarters of its volume since 1960, when Soviet-era planners began diverting its feeder rivers to irrigate cotton fields. Over-use of the water in the Lake Balkhash Basin by Kazakhstan itself is contributing to the new crisis. As the lake becomes shallower and more saline, it is also being increasingly polluted by local industrial waste and sewage.[29]

But competing demands from China for water from the Ili River, one of the three main rivers that feed Lake Balkhash, are certainly contributing to the problem. The Ili rises in the Xinjiang Uighur Autonomous Region — an arid area of northwestern China that is chronically short of water. The Ili flows for 624 kilometres through Chinese territory into southeastern Kazakhstan. There it flows for another 815 kilometres, passing the city of Almaty, before reaching Lake Balkhash.

Xinjiang is a valuable source of oil and natural gas for energy-short China. It has been designated as a high priority development area by Beijing, which has encouraged the settlement of Han Chinese as part of a programme to pacify restive elements of the indigenous Turkic Uigur Muslim population in Xinjiang. Cotton growing on about 40 per cent of Xinjiang's arable land consumes some of the Ili's water. But some UN officials and environmental activists say that the gradual degradation of ecosystems in and around Lake Balkhash is being hastened by China's construction of hydroelectric dams on the river.[30]

In June, the UN Environment Programme, UNEP, published a new atlas to mark World Environment Day. The atlas contains satellite images of many key natural and man-made features around the globe. It compares contemporary images with those taken up to several decades ago. The drying up of Lake Balkhash is graphically illustrated from space. The lake's basin supports more than three million people and UNEP notes that Balkhash is crucial for supply of water to farmers, urban areas and industry. It also supports an important fishery and plays a significant role in maintaining the natural climatic balance in the region.[31]

But UNEP warns that excessive water withdrawal is shrinking the lake and it may disappear altogether unless the trend is reversed. The atlas shows the drying out around the lake's edges and the rapid disappearance of two smaller, neighbouring lakes to the southeast. The Kazakh media in late 2003 reported that Balkhash had already shrunk by more than 2,000 square kilometres. Its original surface area was over 16,000 square kilometres, forty times the size of Lake Geneva. Lake Balkhash is particularly susceptible to shrinkage and water quality decline because it is relatively shallow, with an average depth of only about six metres. And although the western half is freshwater, the eastern half is saline.

UN officials say that Kazakhstan needs to secure Beijing's agreement on the amount of water Xinjiang can draw from the Ili River as a first step in a programme to prevent further damage to Lake Balkhash. In 2001, China and Kazakhstan signed an agreement to facilitate cooperation on transboundary water management. While they agreed to share information on the Ili River, Kazahk water specialists say that the joint inter-governmental commission has met every year without agreeing how to share the Ili's water. They say that what is really needed is transboundary cooperation on water allocation.[32]

Meanwhile, Chinese construction of dams, hydropower stations and canal to divert water from the Irtysh River is causing concern in both Kazakstan and Russia. Like the Ili, the Irtysh starts in China's rapidly developing Xinjiang region. It is shared not just by China and Kazakhstan but by Russia as well. From the Altai mountains in northwestern Xinjiang, the Irtysh runs for 525 kilometres through China, 1,835 kilometres through northeastern Kazakhstan and 2,010 kilometres through western Siberia in Russia until it meets the Ob River. With a total length of some 5,500 kilometres, the Irtysh-Ob is Russia's longest river and Asia's second after China's Yangtze.

Since the mid-1990s, Russian and Kazakh non-governmental organizations have voiced concerns about China's plan to build the 300-kilometre long and 22-metre wide irrigation canal. Known as the Black Irtysh-Karamai Canal, it will carry water from the upper Irtysh to an oil-rich region close to the Urumqi in Xinjiang. The Chinese reportedly plan to divert 450 million cubic metres of water per year from Irtysh, eventually raising the volume to 1.5 billion cubic metres from a total annual flow of 9 billion cubic metres.[33]

The Chinese ambassador to Kazakhstan sought to reassure critics in late 2004 when he said that China currently used only 10 per cent to 20 per cent of the Irtysh's water. He added that new infrastructure was being built in Xinjiang but that China would not use more than 40 per cent of the river's flow.[34] However, regional officials and environmental activists in both Russia and Kazakhstan worry that water withdrawals on this scale from China's section of the Irtysh will cause shortages downstream, with potentially serious consequences from several big Kazakh hydropower dams, river shipping between Russia and Kazakhstan, and farm irrigation and city water supplies to several million people in both countries. The Irtysh provides drinking water to the capital of Kazakhstan, Astana, as well as three other Kazakh cities.

However, Moscow appears reluctant to make the Irtysh an issue in its bilateral relations with China and without Russia's support, Kazakh government representations to Beijing on the issue do not carry weight. For the moment at least, Russia is giving priority to developing its strategic partnership with China as a counter-balance to U.S. and Western dominance and to increase trade, energy and arms sales to the fastest-growing market in Asia.

RUSSIA

There have been a growing number of serious toxic spills into China's rivers in recent years, mainly from industries spawned by the rapid expansion of the economy.[35] Most of these spills have been contained within China. But one in late 2005 caused alarm in Russian when it crossed the border via one of several major rivers that connect the two countries and affected water used for drinking and fishing in the Russian far east. It showed that China's pollution of the environment and its enormous demand for natural resources and energy to fuel the turbo-charged economy are injecting a new and potentially disruptive element into Beijing's relations with neighbouring states — water politics.

The water pollution crisis started on 13 November when a state-owned chemical plant in Jilin city in northeastern China exploded, leaking an estimated 100 metric tonnes of poisonous benzene compounds into the adjacent Songhua River which flows northwards into Russia's Amur River. Water supplies in downstream Harbin, a city of four million, were cut off for four days as a result. Other Chinese towns and cities along the river also had to temporarily suspend drawing water from the river as the benzene slick, which at one point stretch for 100 kilometres, passed by. Many business activities were disrupted. The accident renewed questions about the costs of China's breakneck economic boom and the culture of official secrecy that allowed some Chinese officials to withhold information from the public about the danger of the spill. Several senior officials, including the head of China's environmental protection agency, resigned as a result of the cover-up.[36]

By the end of December, the 100-kilometre chemical slick reached the Russian border city of Khabarovsk, where local officials ordered the population of nearly 600,000 people to stop using river water until the danger had passed. Both benzene and nitrobenzene can cause blood disorders in people exposed to high doses. Benzene also causes cancer. The Chinese government formally apologized to Russia after the two countries said they had agreed to set up a hotline so that Beijing could keep Moscow informed about the spill. But Russian environmentalists criticized China's response, saying it should have consulted its neighbour more quickly and extensively after the accident. Beijing only officially notified Moscow of the problem on 22 November, nine days after the accident, despite the fact that they are supposed to be "strategic partners".[37]

Russia's chief state epidemiologist, Gennady Onishchenko, said that more than one million people in the Russian Far East could be affected by the residues of benzene in the water of the Amur. Some Russians fear the slick may poison fish and cause other long-term damage. "Such a heavily-populated territory as China by definition cannot give us clean water", said Mr Onishchenko, who is also Russia's consumer rights watchdog. Some officials in the Khabarovsk region said that they would demand financial compensation from China. But the national leadership in both countries evidently decided not to allow the pollution spill to become an issue in bilateral relations or risk upsetting their growing political, energy, trade and military ties.[38]

In May 2006, China's State Environmental Protection Agency (SEPA) asserted that the the Songhua River was safe again and that a joint inspection by Chinese and Russian officials had found that benzene-related pollutants did not exceed the national standards of China and Russia. SEPA added that the two sides were discussing how to enhance environmental protection along the rivers bordering the two countries.[39] China had earlier announced it was spending the equivalent of US$1.2 million to prevent the discharge of industrial pollution and urban sewage into the Songhua and other major Chinese rivers.

However, Russian scientists continued to report substantially higher than normal levels of water pollution in the Amur River following the blast in November 2005 the Chinese chemical factory upsteam in northeast China. They found chlorophenol concentrations almost thirty times above allowable levels in the spring of 2006 as the ice sheet that covered the river in the winter months thaws, leading to a second wave of contamination. Chlorophenols are derived from benzene and have a strong medicinal taste and smell. They can affect the human liver and the immune system, as well as increase the risk of cancer, according to the U.S. Department of Health.[40]

CONCLUSION

While China was clearly at fault in the case of the Songhua River toxic spill, the evidence suggests that it is only partly responsible for the water problem in the Lake Balkhash and Mekong basins — and possibly only the minor part, at least so far. The other countries within these basins are often significant, if not major, contributors to the problem of declining water quality and flows. In the case of Irtysh River, China can argue that it is only doing in Xinjiang what the former Soviet Union did earlier in Kazakhstan — building dams and irrigation systems to bring progress to an underdeveloped region.

However, upstream river states have special responsibilities in managing transborder flows on international rivers. As noted earlier, geography has accorded China the position of dominant headwater state in Eurasia. This is a significant dimension of China's growing regional power and influence. If China's domestic water shortage becomes more acute, what is to prevent it from tapping some of the water in the big reservoirs of Yunnan's Mekong River dams, or the planned Nu River dams, for irrigation and farming as it is doing with the Irtysh in the parched northwest of China?

The Salween is one of the last big rivers in southwestern China that has not yet been dammed. Another is the Red River, which flows into Vietnam to become the largest river in the northern part of that country. A third untapped river — the mightiest of all and the one with the greatest hydropower potential — is what most people outside China call the Brahamaputra. Fed by glaciers on the Chinese side of the Himalayas in Tibet, the river skirts China's southern border for just over 2,000 kilometres before dipping into India and Bangladesh for the last 900 kilometres of its journey to the Bay of Bengal where it joins the Ganges to form a huge, fertile delta. In China, the river is called the Yarlung Zangbo (sometimes spelled Tsangpo). In India is known as the Brahmaputra; in Bangladesh, the Jamuna.

Over the last 500 kilometres of its course through China, the river plunges several thousand metres through some of the world's steepest and most spectacular gorges. Some proponents of hydropower in China believe the Brahmaputra alone has the potential to generate as much as 100,000 megawatts of electricity.[41] There have been reports from both China and India in recent years that the next great Chinese dam project when the Three Gorges project is finished in 2009, will be on the Yarlung Zangbo in Tibet. One such report in 2000 said that Chinese leaders were drawing up plans to use nuclear explosions to build hydroelectric dams on the river and that Tibetan water would also be diverted from the scheme via canals to the Xinjiang region and Gansu province.[42]

No such scheme, whether using nuclear or conventional engineering, has been confirmed by Beijing, although a relatively small hydropower plant is due to start generating electricity on Tibet's Lhasa River, a tributary of the Yarlung Zangbo, late in 2006.[43] Any large-scale Chinese project to dam its section of the Brahmaputra or divert big amounts of water to more densely populated arid regions of China would be likely to encounter fierce opposition from both India and Bangladesh. They would fear downstream shortages during the dry season as China held back water to keep its reservoir levels high, and flooding from sudden releases during the wet season to prevent the dams from overflowing.

China's growing regional influence as well as its highland position help to explain why neighbouring countries, which may suffer from Chinese actions as an upstream state, mute their complaints and are inclined instead to accept Beijing's offers of compensation in other ways. As the Asian mainland's leading economic and military power, China is in a strong position to influence and, if necessary, intimidate its neighbours — all of them, with the exception of India and Russia, far smaller than itself.

To head off protests, Beijing has held talks with affected neighbours about its plans to make fuller use of the shared rivers that start from its territory. China says it is ready to hold friendly consultations on cross-border river issues with relevant countries on the use of water resources and protection of environment.[44] When the Kazakh Foreign Minister Kasymzhomart Tokayev visited Beijing in April 2006, he was assured by Premier Wen Jiabao that China would work constructively to settle problems concerning the Irtysh and Ili transborder rivers "taking into account the long-term interests of the two states and the importance of keeping the ecological balance and using water rationally for the benefit of the peoples of the two countries".

In reality, however, China seeks to protect its strategic interests, including water, through astute diplomacy, trade, civil and military aid, concessional loans, investment and other state-supported commercial deals. This approach seems designed to placate and indirectly compensate for any downstream damage caused by Chinese activity, not to halt or seriously constrain the sources of concern. Beijing's influence is being extended by using the new leverage it gets as a senior player in key multilateral organizations in the region, including the ADB, the GMS and the Shanghai Cooperation Organization (SCO) which links China, Russia and Central Asian states.

For example, China pledged in 2005 to keep exporting increasing amounts of electricity to its neighbours sharing the Mekong River, even though parts of China itself are suffering acute power shortages.

Most of the Chinese energy goes to Myanmar and Vietnam. Yunnan province is a leading exporter.[45] China has offered preferential trade access to Thailand and other Mekong Basin nations. It has promised to help develop the hydropower potential of Laos and Myanmar. Cambodia, Laos and Myanmar want, and receive, substantial military as well as economic aid from China.

China has offered to help build a giant power station near the coal-producing town of Yekibastuz in north Kazakhstan on Irtysh River. The coal-fired plant would be designed to produce 7,200 megawatts of electricity, most of which would be exported via high-voltage power lines to China.[46] For Kazakhstan, which was previously dependent on sales to Russia, China is the closest major market for oil and natural gas. It is being linked to China by energy pipelines and pulled more closely into Beijing's diplomatic orbit by common membership of the SCO, just as the Southeast Asian Mekong River states are being tied increasingly to China through the GMS programme. Such ties are likely to grow stronger, not weaker, in future.

For all these reasons, serious conflicts between China and its neighbours over water issues seem unlikely unless Chinese upstream policies start to cause serious problems in downstream countries. But even as China seeks to ameliorate its impact, water politics may well prove costly for the environment in these countries. Some critics say that what is really needed are binding and verifiable international agreements on riverwater allocation. Of course, this would constrain national sovereignty and decision-making over use of a vital resource. As Eurasia's dominant headwater power, China is unlikely to sign such accords when demand within the country for freshwater has never been greater and will increase even more in future.

China has a strong case for harnessing its rivers. It is short of energy and needs to reduce reliance on burning coal which pollutes the atmosphere and releases gases that most scientists now believe are melting glaciers and warming the world to dangerous levels.

China's hydropower potential is huge. Yet officials say only 20 per cent has been tapped. But keeping its people and neighbouring countries in the dark about its plans will fan fears about adverse consequences, making it seem that there is much to hide.

Notes

1. The World Conservation Union (IUCN) and other International Organizations Urge G8 World Leaders to Allocate Funds to Promote Cooperation over Transboundary Waters, 28 May 2003 <www.un.org/esa/sustdev/sdissues/water/rivers_lakes_news39.pdf>.
2. *Reuters*, "Scientists say Risk of Water Wars is Rising", by Patrick McLoughlin, 24 August 2004; *Associated Press*, "Africa Could Face Water Wars if Continent's Rivers aren't Managed Better", by Anthony Mitchell, 10 September 2003; *Reuters*, "Water Must not Become New Conflict Commodity, says International Forum", by Elaine Lies, 21 March 2003.
3. Transboundary Freshwater Dispute Database <www.nasce.org/ocid/>.
4. Worldwatch Institute Global Security Brief No. 5, "Water Can Be a Pathway to Peace, not War", by Aaron T. Wolf, Annika Kramer, Alexander Carius, and Geoffrey D. Dabelko, June 2005.
5. *Reuters*, "China's 'Roof of the World' Glaciers Melting Fast", 3 May 2006.
6. *People's Daily Online*, "Drought, Floods Strike China, Affecting Tens of Millions", 13 May 2006.
7. *Xinhua News Agency*, "First ozone hole confirmed over Qinhai-Tibet Plateau", 3 May 2006.
8. *Reuters*, "China warns of Danger of Melting Everest Glaciers", 18 May 2005.
9. WWF, "An Overview of Glaciers, Glacier Retreat, and Subsequent Impacts in Nepal, India and China", March 2005.
10. WWF, "Climate Change News, Water Crisis Looms as Himalayan Glaciers Retreat", 14 March 2005.
11. *China Daily Online*, "High Water Find on Qinghai-Tibet Plateau", 10 May 2005.

12. World Bank, *Little Green Databook*, 2004.
13. *People's Daily Online*, "China Warned of Water Crisis by 2030", 6 June 2002.
14. *Xinhua News Agency Online*, "China Issues First Guidelines on Water-efficient Technology", 23 May 2005.
15. International Rivers Network, Briefing Paper No. 3, "China's Upper Mekong Dams Endanger Millions Downsteam", October 2002.
16. *International Herald Tribune*, "Sharing the Mekong: an Asian Challenge", by Michael Richardson, 30 October 2002.
17. MRC Press Release No. 15/04, "MRC to Increase Technical Cooperation with China and Myanmar", 26 August 2004.
18. *Far Eastern Economic Review*, "River at Risk", by Barry Wain, 26 August 2005.
19. ADB, "Mekong River Countries to Start Preparing for Regional Power Trading Arrangements", 5 July 2005.
20. "Nu River Background", 24 April 2006 <www.ThreeGorgesProbe.org>.
21. *Reuters*, "China Dam Project Tests New Environmental Policy", by Chris Buckley, 25 October 2005.
22. *Reuters*, "China Says Controversial Dam Plan won't Harm Neighbours", by Chris Buckley, 12 January 2006.
23. *New York Times*, "Seeking a Public Voice on China's 'Angry River'", by Jim Yardley, 26 December 2005.
24. *Times Online*, "Sold Down the River: Tribe's Home to be Valley of Dammed", by Richard Lloyd Parry, 22 March 2006.
25. International Rivers Network, Briefing Paper No. 4, "Damming the Sesan River: Impacts in Cambodia and Vietnam", October 2002.
26. *New York Times*, "China's Reach: The Trouble Downsteam", by Jane Perlez, 19 March 2005.
27. *Associated Press*, "Officials Sounding the Alarm on Southeast Asian Droughts", by Rungrawee C. Pinyorat, 14 March 2005.
28. Mekong River Commission, "Mekong's Low Flows Linked to Drought", MRC 03/04, 26 March 2004.
29. *Reuters*, "Kazakhs may Face Another Aral Sea Disaster, UN says", by Michael Steen, 14 January 2004.
30. UNEP, Lake Balkhash Fact Sheet, 2 November 2004.

31. UNEP, *One Planet Many People: Atlas of Our Changing Environment*, June 2005 <www.earthprint.com/go.htm?to=DEW0657NA>.

32. *Radio Free Asia*, "Xinjiang's Thirst Threatens Kazakhastan", by Antoine Blua, 24 November 2004.

33. The Jamestown Foundation, *Eurasia Daily Monitor*, Volume 2, Issue 178, "Russia Wary of Possible Water Dispute with China", 26 September 2005.

34. *Radio Free Asia*, "Xinjiang's Thirst threatens Kazakhstan", by Antoine Blua, 26 November 2004.

35. *Associated Press*, "Chemical Plant Leaks Waste Water into Chinese River", 14 February 2006.

36. *Reuters*, "China Environment Chief Resigns over Toxic Spill", by Brian Rhoads, 5 December 2005.

37. *Asian Wall Street Journal*, "For Downstream Russians, Pollution Fuels Existing Anger toward China", by Guy Chazan, 16 December 2005.

38. The Jamestown Foundation, *Eurasia Daily Monitor*, Volume 3, Issue 15, "Russia and China Seek to Minimize Political Fallout from Benzene Spill", 23 January 2006.

39. *People's Daily Online*, "No pollution occurs in Songhua River: SEPA", 7 May 2006.

40. *AFP*, "Pollution in Far East Russian River 30 Times above Norm", 1 May 2006.

41. *Interfax*, "Develop and be Dammed — China to Build on Virgin River", by David Stanway, 16 March 2006.

42. *London Daily Telegraph*, "China Planning Nuclear Blasts to Build Giant Hydro Project", by Damien Mcelroy, 22 October 2000.

43. *Xinhua*, "Tibet's Biggest Hydropower Project to Go into Operation", 26 March 2006.

44. PRC Ministry of Foreign Affairs spokesperson at a Press Conference, 9 March 2006.

45. *Xinhuanet*, "China to Continue Electricity Supply to Mekong Neighbors", 5 July 2005.

46. The Jamestown Foundation, *Eurasia Daily Monitor*, Volume 3, Issue 75, "Amid Public Anxieties, Beijing and Astana Boost Ties", 18 April 2006.

Selected References

Economy, Elizabeth C. *The River Runs Black: The Environmental Challenge to China's Future*. USA: Cornell University Press, 2004.

"Environment and Security: Transforming Risks into Cooperation, The Case of Central Asia and South East Europe". Joint report of UNEP, the United Nations Development Programme, and the Organization for Security and Cooperation in Europe, 2003.

Far Eastern Economic Review. "River at Risk", by Barry Wain, 26 August 2005.

International Rivers Network. "Downstream Ecological Implications of China's Lancang Hydropower and Mekong Navigation Project", by Tyson Roberts, 2001 <www.irn.org/programs/lancang/index. php?id=02112.ecoimplications>.

Lohmar, Bryan, Jinxia Wang, Scott Rozelle, Jikun Huang, and David Dawe. "China's Agricultural Water Policy Reforms: Increasing Investment, Resolving Conflicts, and Revising Incentives". Market and Trade Economics Division, Economic Research Service, U.S. Department of Agriculture, Agriculture Information Bulletin Number 782, March 2003.

*New York Time*s. "China's Reach: The Trouble Downsteam", by Jane Perlez, 19 March 2005.

Osborne, Milton. *River at Risk: The Mekong and the Water Politics of China and Southeast Asia*. Sydney: Lowy Institute for International Policy, 2005.

The Economist. Special Report on China's Environment, 21 August 2004.

Three Gorges Probe. "Skyscraper Dams in Yunnan: China's New Electricity Regulator Should Step In", by Grainne Ryder, 12 May 2006 <www. ThreeGorgesProbe.org>.

World Bank, China. *Air, Land, and Water: Environmental Priorities for a New Millennium*. 1st printing, August 2001.

World Water Commission Report. *A Water Secure World: Vision for Water, Life, and the Environment*, 2000.

3

RIVER BASIN AGREEMENTS AS FACILITATORS OF DEVELOPMENT

By Chris Perry

BACKGROUND

The earliest activities of man were influenced — in some cases dominated — by access to and use of water: for drinking, cooking, washing, fishing, irrigation, navigation and, later, the generation of power. The progress of civilization can often be mapped in relation to water, most especially in climates where the reliable production of food and fibre depend on the control of water. Gradually, the cumulative impact of many small interventions, accelerated by the much greater impacts of large-scale consumptive development based on storage eventually meant that interventions at one point in a catchment or basin had a measurable impact on availability elsewhere.

This scenario is increasingly evident in many local catchments, as well as river basins at national and international scales. The implications are now well recognized, and are incorporated in statements that management should be at the basin level, that management should be integrated, that competition should be addressed in management, and so on.

In many countries, the symptoms of competition and scarcity are damage to the environment (declining water tables, salinization of aquifers, drying wetlands and estuaries), inequitable water use (head-end farmers using excessive amounts of water, tail-enders getting little or nothing). Such symptoms are widely observed and widely reported.

It is less widely recognized that many countries in the world have developed and controlled their water resources productively and sustainably over many years to the benefit of their populations, providing essential supplies of water for municipal, domestic, industrial, recreational and agricultural use together with protection from the negative impacts of excess water through drainage systems and flood control works. Literally hundreds of millions of people expect and receive some or all of the following services:

- Potable water, directly from a tap, twenty-four hours a day
- Irrigation services, defined in terms of timing, reliability and quality
- Protection from flood events
- Stability of environmental areas
- Water for recreational purposes — fishing, sailing, or swimming
- Assured stream-flows for navigation.

That is not to say these countries face no problems. At the margin, there are always new environmental concerns, new sources of pollution, and new development priorities to be accommodated. But these constraints have, in many countries, not prevented the specification and delivery of a service that both the providers and the recipients understand, respect and benefit from. Such services are found in countries with vastly differing climates, income levels and water availability per capita.

In parallel with this success story international conferences, research organizations, Web discussion forums and academic journals promote new solutions to the water crisis (privatization, participatory management, stakeholder involvement, treating water as an economic good, livelihood analysis, sustainable development, gender awareness). An objective observer might conclude that sustainable water resources management is one of the great solved mysteries of our time, if only the conferees, researchers and other participants in the debate would analyse the common features and underpinnings of success rather than dissect the symptoms of failure.

THE DUBLIN PRINCIPLES AND INTEGRATED WATER RESOURCES MANAGEMENT

Concern at the poor state of water services in many developing countries has resulted in a large number of international conferences in the last decade or more — Dublin, Rio, Johannesburg, World Water Forum I, II, and III — usually resulting in a new declaration of principles or intent. Perhaps the most widely quoted are the Dublin Principles (see Box 3.1).

Box 3.1
The Dublin Principles

- Freshwater is a finite and vulnerable resource, essential to sustain life, development and the environment.
- Water development and management should be based on a participatory approach, involving users, planners, and policy-makers at all levels.
- Women play a central role in the provision, management and safeguarding of water.
- Water has an economic value in all its competing uses and should be recognized.

Source: Global Water Partnership <http://www.gwpforum.org/>.

It is instructive to note that only one of the four principles is objectively true — that water is a finite and essential resource. The other three principles reflect subjective values — the importance of participatory approaches; the role of women; and the usefulness of economic instruments in management. Such preferences tend to change over time — privatization, for example, was rarely mentioned fifteen years ago, was universally promoted five years ago, but now appears to be in decline. Mixing objective facts with subjective and transient preferences is unhelpful to practitioners.

Practitioners (policy-makers, planners, politicians, managers, donor agencies, etc.) make operational decisions, and want to know the distinction between what must be done and what ought to be done — what is essential and what is desirable. Often, what "ought" to be done will vary depending on local conditions, and the priority given to what "ought" to be done will always be moderated by the progress made on the essential elements.

Perhaps in recognition of non-operationality of the principles, the concept of integrated water resources management (IWRM) has come to the fore (see Box 3.2), stressing the need to recognize the interdependent physical nature of water management under conditions of scarcity, and the social and economic interdependencies that are implicit in successful resolution of these tensions. The full range of issues that have recently been identified is extensive. Box

BOX 3.2

Definition of Integrated Water Resources Management

Integrated Water Resources Management is the process which promotes the coordinated development and management of water, land and related resources in order to maximize the resultant economic and social welfare in an equitable manner without compromising the sustainability of vital ecosystem.

Source: Global Water Partnership <http://www.gwpcacena.org/en/global.htm>.

3.3 lists the themes for discussions proposed at the Third World Water Forum.

It is difficult to determine structure and priorities from such a list. Some topics (water food and the environment; agriculture, food and water; water nature and the environment) appear to overlap substantially. It is striking that all of the "subjective" elements of the Dublin Declaration (gender, water as an economic good, and participatory management) appear in parallel with integrated water management, suggesting they are equal in the hierarchy of dependencies — which in turn brings into question the very concept of integrated water resources management as an organizing framework. The objective element of Dublin — that water resources are finite — is absent altogether. A conclusion might well be that — the fact that water is limited is the organizing principle of integrated water resources management — it is scarcity that forces

BOX 3.3

Themes for Discussion at Third World Water Forum

Groundwater	Floods
Water and Climate	Water and Information
Water and Youth	Water and Poverty
Agriculture, Food and Water	Water, Nature and the Environment
	Water and Gender
Water and Cities	Water and Cultural Diversity
Water Supply, Sanitation and	Water for Peace
Pollution	Water as an Economic Good
Water and Energy	Public Private Partnerships
Water, Food and the	Participatory Management
Environment	
Water and Governance	
Integrated Water Resources	
Management	

Source: WWF III website, March 2003.

integration. The Global Water Partnership definition of IWRM is not inconsistent with this view, focusing as it does on resource management in the context of broadly specified objectives.

In sum, recognition of the complex implications of water scarcity and competition for water is widespread; advice on the practical steps — and especially the relationship between these steps — is poorly defined and difficult to operationalize. Most advice comprises advocacy rather than scientific analysis.

THE ESSENTIAL ELEMENTS OF PRODUCTIVE AND SUSTAINABLE WATER RESOURCES MANAGEMENT

In this section, drawing on the observation that successful and sustainable water resources management does exist, a set of universal elements as they relate to sustainable water resources management is proposed, within which the Dublin Principles and concepts of IWRM may be applied to the extent they are locally appropriate.

A pattern is observable in successful water resources management scenarios, and generally missing in unsuccessful scenarios. A number of essential elements are found wherever water management is effective, and absent, in whole or in part, where water management is ineffective, as manifested by disputes about entitlements, chaotic supply schedules, over-exploitation of resources, pollution, and deteriorating infrastructure.

The elements may be bundled and sliced in various ways. One version consistent with the author's experience,[1] is as follows:

- Clear and publicly available knowledge of resource availability in time and space.
- Policies governing water resources development, including assigning priorities among users for the developed water.
- Translation of those policies into allocation rules and procedures such that the water service to each user/sector are clear for any hydrological circumstance.

- Defined roles and responsibilities for provision of all aspects of the specified water service.
- Infrastructure to deliver the specified service to each user.

It is important to note that there is a hierarchy and interdependence among the elements — roles and responsibilities cannot be defined unless the water service is specified; infrastructure must be consistent in sizing and control features with the service to be delivered; procedures for allocation depend entirely on the assignment of priorities; and the service must be related to the available resource — no point in allocating 100 units if only 90 are available.

Second, this hierarchy and interdependence has important implications for the design of interventions to address unsuccessful management: If everything is in place except the rules are not followed, an intervention that enforced order might be successful. If there are no rules for allocation, then introducing participatory irrigation management will have little chance of sustained success because every other element will be functioning (at best) in an *ad hoc* mode, unrelated to the need for defined responsibilities in system operation and maintenance that participatory management requires.

Third, formulating a successful water management system is a multidisciplinary effort, involving hydrologists and geohydrologists, politicians (and their multidisciplinary advisers, including economists), lawyers, institutional specialists, and engineers. Each discipline has a specialist contribution to make, and it will be rare that a comprehensive solution can be determined without the input of each discipline and concomitant respect for each specialist from the others disciplines.

Fourth, it is clear that theses elements are applicable at various scales: Once the process is resolved at basin scale, each user (for example, an irrigation project) will have its allocation defined, and thus "know" the available resource, but will need to address lower order issues (bargaining between different categories of irrigator, codification of rules and procedures, assigning responsibility for measurement and management of water according to the agreed rules, and installing infrastructure required for management).

As a shorthand, the five component parts identified above are hereafter referred to as:

A. *Assessment* of the available resources;
B. *Bargaining* through the political process over development and allocation;
C. *Codification* of the agreed allocations into laws;
D. *Delegation* of implementation to appropriate institutions and agencies;
E. *Engineering* to create the necessary infrastructure to deliver the agreed services.

THREE CASE STUDIES

In this section, three major international river basins are briefly described, including the situation regarding the allocation of water among the basin states. The A-E framework set out above is then applied to each case.

The Indus Basin

Prior to the partition of India in 1947, the Indus River, and its five tributaries (Jhelum, Chenab, Ravi, Beas, Sutlej) served the largest contiguous irrigation system in the world covering some 16 million hectares.[2] Partition resulted in new borders that bore no relation to hydrological boundaries — as indeed is generally the case in inter-state water issues.

Over the next decade, teams from India and Pakistan worked together with a team from the World Bank (whose offer of its good offices was accepted by both countries) to fashion a solution that would be acceptable and durable. The initial proposal of a single integrated basin authority was quickly rejected. The broad outlines of the final agreement were that Pakistan was assigned full use of the eastern rivers (Indus, Jhelum and Chenab) which accounted for 75 per cent of the available water. India was assigned the water of the Beas and Sutlej, as well as the right to develop hydropower on the rivers flowing to Pakistan — subject to very clearly specified conditions. The final agreement adhered neither to the no appreciable harm principle espoused by the International Law Commission (Pakistan received only 75 per cent of the water for the 90 per cent of irrigated land in its territory, while India received only 25 per cent of the water, in apparent violation of the equitable utilization principle of the International Law Commission, but confirming the pragmatic view that in most cases, international law is used by riparians less to settle disputes than to dignify positions based on individual state interests.[3] As the first president of Pakistan observed, following the conclusions of negotiations on the division of the Indus waters: "We have been able to get what was possible ... very often the best is the enemy of the good and in this case we have accepted the good after careful and realistic appreciation of our entire overall situation."[4]

It is also relevant to note that the system of water management followed in the major areas covered by the Indus Treaty is founded on the fact that the available water supply is finite and scarce, while paying no attention whatsoever to participation at all levels by all actors, the role of women, or the significance of water's status as an economic good.

The system has worked rather successfully over some millions of hectares for more than a century, which does not deny that attention to, for example, gender issues would improve the situation — rather confirms that sustainable and productive use did not depend on that issue in the way that the recognition of scarcity was critical to basic design, operation and management of the water systems in the areas involved.

Since Pakistan was effectively deprived of its historic water use (90 per cent of the irrigated land was in Pakistan; only 75 per cent of the water was allocated to it) a major investment programme was devised, including link canals and reservoirs to transfer and store surplus water from monsoon flows in the eastern rivers to replace historic flows, now utilized in India, from the western rivers. This investment programme was substantially supported by international donors.

Subsequent relations between India and Pakistan have not always been good, including periods of actual conflict. It is a measure of the importance and robustness of the Indus Basin Treaty that the institutions embodied in that treaty (the Joint Rivers Commission, the rules governing basin management and the procedures for dealing with potential disputes in relation to new investments) have survived unscathed and indeed continued to function during conflicts. The investments related directly to the treaty, as well as subsequent investments of similar magnitude in both countries to further develop their water resources are of multi-billion dollar magnitude — as too are the benefits derived.

The Aral Sea Basin

The problems of the Aral Sea have been widely documented for more than a decade. The decline of the Aral Sea started in the 1960s as increasing amounts of water were diverted to irrigation and less, but more saline, water entered the Aral Sea.[5] As of the mid-1980s, only small amounts of water were flowing into the Aral Sea. In 1990 the Aral Sea split into a small northern sea and a larger southern sea as the waters receded. The salinity of the northern sea is gradually decreasing as inflows from the Syr Darya dilute the salt water, and fish have been reintroduced. Today the whole of the former Aral Sea has shrunk by approximately 70 per cent in volume and 50 per cent in area. The water level in the southern body continues to drop and the salinity to increase. In 1997, the southern Aral Sea is biologically dead with salinity levels at around 40 g/l (for comparison, seawater is 35 g/l).

The origin of the above basic problems can be traced in essence to two developments in recent history:

- A massive expansion of irrigation; and
- The breakdown of the Soviet Union and the transition from planned to market economy.

Here, our interest is on the role of inter-state agreements, but to set the context for the current situation in that regard, it is necessary to understand the development context.

The expansion of irrigated agriculture, for cotton and rice production, began under Czarist Russia in the late nineteenth century. By the end of the nineteenth century, about 2.5 million hectares were under irrigation. Expansion accelerated rapidly in the 1920s after the Russian revolution. By 1950 the irrigated area had reached 4.7 million hectares. With the Soviet Virgin Lands Campaign launched in that year, large-scale irrigation projects began, and vast tracts of the Central Asian desert were reclaimed, planted mainly with cotton, and watered from the two river systems. From 1950 to 1990, the irrigated area almost doubled; 3.2 million hectares of new land came under cultivation, bringing the total irrigated area to 7.9 million hectares. Expansion came to a halt only in recent years.

The expansion of irrigation yielded major benefits. The expansion made the Soviet Union independent of cotton imports, and Central Asia became the third largest producer of cotton in the world after China and the United States. It increased and stabilized food production in the region and created a home, a production basis, employment and incomes for some eight million people settled in the newly developed areas. The water control, irrigation, drainage and other infrastructure created by the expansion constitutes today a major economic asset of the region.

However, the quality of the infrastructure is poor, so that irrigated areas take far more water than they actually need, and the excess water either runs to desert sinks and evaporates or contributes to rising water tables and salinization.

Despite these failings, the system functioned at a reasonable level albeit in an environmentally unsustainable, though not necessarily unplanned way.[6]

The breakdown of the former Soviet Union and the transition from planned to market economy, is at the root of the water management and institutional problems. Prior to independence, the upstream states had stored water during the winter season for delivery to irrigated areas in the downstream states during the summer. The net product of this was agricultural production, from which all, including the Soviet Union, benefited. Since the upstream states needed electricity during winter for heating and industrial purposes, and were not generating hydropower because water was being stored for the summer months, the Soviet Union provided oil and power to the upstream states during winter.

This truly integrated water management collapsed with the Soviet Union: At independence, cooperation between the newly created states, each with different positions and interests with respect to water, had to be developed more or less overnight. The states were faced with legacies of the Soviet system, including the neglect of environment and sustainability, and an inherited management structure that required a central authority that was now absent.

In subsequent years, the various basin states adopted a variety of economic/political systems ranging from relatively free market to continuing central planning. Agreement on responsibilities in the management of the basin's resources have yet to be successfully concluded, and while the Aral Sea continues to decline, all basin states profess an intention to expand irrigated areas — in effect states are adopting negotiating positions suited to the period of formulation of development plans, while in fact the development plans are already finalized, the facilities are constructed, and the need is maintenance — which also turns out to be contentious as some upstream facilities were built entirely to serve downstream purposes, in areas that are now different countries.

Donors are active in the basin, but investment is limited by the lack of agreed operating procedures for allocating water among the riparian states. In recent years, final allocations — which are the subject of annual negotiations among the riparian states — have sometimes not been finalized until the irrigation season has commenced, and bilateral non-water issues are sometimes introduced into the negotiating process.

The Mekong Basin

The Mekong is the longest river in Southeast Asia and one of the largest rivers in the world. In terms of drainage area which is 795,000 square kilometres, it ranks the twenty-first in the world and the twelfth in terms of its length (4,800 kilometres). However, its average discharge (15,000 cubic metres per second) ranks it as eighth in the world table of great rivers. Its source is at an elevation of about 5,000 metres in the Tanghla Shua (mountain range) on the Tibetan Plateau. It flows southwards, passing China, Myanmar, and enters its lower basin at the common Myanmar-Laos-Thailand boundary point. Some part is transboundary of Laos and Thailand and flows through Cambodia, Vietnam and finally to South China Sea.

The Mekong drains a total catchment area of 795,000 square kilometres, out of which 606,000 square kilometres is the Lower Mekong Basin (LMB) and comprises almost the whole of Lao PDR and Cambodia, one-third of Thailand in the northeastern region and some provinces in the northern region, and one-fifth of Vietnam (the central highlands and the delta region).

In 1957 the four riparian countries of the LMB, namely Cambodia, Lao PDR, Thailand and Vietnam, have agreed to join their efforts in developing water and related resources of the Mekong River Basin by establishing the Committee of Coordination and Investigation of the Lower Mekong River Basin.

Various studies of the basin were undertaken by the committee, supported by the United Nations' Economic Commission for Asia and the Far East (ECAFE) and the U.S. Bureau for Reclamation. Regional instability interrupted this work and it was only after 1991 that concentrated discussions and negotiations among the basin states led to the eventual transformation of the Mekong committee through the 1995 Agreement on the Cooperation for the Sustainable Development of the Mekong River Basin to which Cambodia, Laos, Thailand and Vietnam are signatories, and China and Myanmar are observers.

No longer under the umbrella of ECAFE/UN Economic and Social Commission for Asia and the Pacific (ESCAP) and the United Nations Development Programme (UNDP), its articles give full management responsibility of the commission to a council of ministers of member countries. Since the 1995 agreement, the member countries have signed sub-agreements on data and information sharing and exchange, a flood management and mitigation strategy, and a formal agreement with China on the exchange of hydrological and other data.[7]

The agreement is a brief but powerful document. It sets out — but does not quantify — key parameters in basin operation (acceptable minimum flows; acceptable reverse flows to the Tonle Sap). It sets out procedures to be used by basin states to advise each other of actual and proposed water use — notification of intended in the case of less contentious uses (wet season, intra-basin use and any intra-basin use on tributaries) and prior consultation in the case of potentially more contentious uses (dry season uses on the main stem; any inter-basin transfers).

The Mekong River Commission (MRC) consists of three permanent bodies: The council, the joint committee (JC) and the secretariat.

The council, comprising one member at ministerial and cabinet level from each MRC member country, convenes annually. The joint committee, comprising also one member from each member country at no less than head of department level, convenes at least twice per year. The secretariat, which provides technical and administrative services to the joint committee and the council, is under the direction of a chief executive officer (CEO) under supervision of the joint committee appointed by the council. The secretariat is located in Vientiane, Lao PDR.

Articles 24 and 26 essentially devolve to the joint committee of representatives of the basin states the responsibility to specify the key acceptable flow parameters, and develop basin plans consistent with these and other possible impacts. The development of these plans is the technical responsibility of the Mekong River Commission.

It is hard to fault the formulation of the Mekong Agreement; it is broad in scope, recognizing that various countries and sectors and have competing interests and providing a framework for discussion and resolution. It allows for participation, incorporation of national political sensitivities and objectives (the countries vary widely in their size, stage of development and political value systems).

Bringing the various countries together, with essentially equal rights in determining what can be done is a substantial achievement, and the acceptance by all the party states of a single hydrological model provides a powerful tool for discussing options and highlighting areas of concern and common interest — for example, Vietnam is an upstream riparian with respect to Cambodia of some left-bank tributaries of the Mekong, but a downstream riparian with respect to Cambodia when the Mekong flows into the delta areas of Vietnam (see <http://www.thewaterpage.com/images/MekongMap.jpg>). The hydrological model clarifies the impacts on Vietnam of its own upstream developments on tributary stream.

However, as is argued below, the essential ability of any nation to veto a development, given that virtually all hydrological developments have some negative as well as positive impacts, presents difficulties to agreeing major investments.

THE INDUS, ARAL SEA AND MEKONG COMPARED

In the first section of this chapter, five essential elements of sustainable water management were defined. They were:

A. *Assessment* of the available resources;
B. *Bargaining* through the political process over development and allocation;
C. *Codification* of the agreed allocations into laws;
D. *Delegation* of implementation to appropriate institutions and agencies;
E. *Engineering* to create the necessary infrastructure to deliver the agreed services.

In Table 3.1, the status of the three basins are compared in relation to these elements. The Aral Sea is assessed twice — first for the situation prior to the break up of the Soviet Union and then for the situation after the break-up.

The proposed sequence of fundamental requirements provides insights into the status of the basins, the constraints and the priorities to be addressed to facilitate further development. In the case of the Indus, massive investment in infrastructure has taken place, both around the time of the agreement between the participating states as well as subsequently in areas served by the river system. In the Aral Sea Basin, investment was enormous and to a degree successful, but the collapse of the Soviet Union has subsequently re-opened the political bargaining process to agree water rights, and while that remains unresolved the scope for successful management — let alone additional investments to modernize and further develop the region — is limited. The international community (as represented by bilateral and multilateral institutions) cannot support investments in the absence of agreements on water sharing, rules of routine operation, and procedures to address extreme flood and drought events.

TABLE 3.1

Elements of Sustainable Water Management — Examples

	Assessment of hydrology	Political Bargaining	Codification into laws and rules	Delegation of powers to agencies	Engineering
Indus	Completed, but relatively simple as division of water was on whole river basis	Completed	Completed and set out in Indus Basin Agreement	Institutions established at Basin and state levels.	Completed internationally (Indus Basin Replacement Works) and nationally
Aral Sea 1	Completed, but based on unsustainable depletion of Aral Sea	Not required as allocation overseen by central authority	Not required	Necessary agencies established	Completed
Aral Sea 2	As above unsustainable use recently accelerated	Underway, but progressing slowly	Dependent on outcome of bargaining	Agencies are in decline with lack of funding and facilities	Completed but no longer operated in accordance with original design
Mekong	Completed and embodied in hydrological model	Underway, but slow due to complexity of agreeing among multiple stakeholders	Principles established but critical numbers still undefined	Limited	Limited

The Mekong is a more complex case: Initial steps and the declaration of principles embodied in the 1995 agreement are comprehensive and well specified. They provide the basis for truly enormous investments to the general benefit of all the countries in the basin. Yet little has happened to date. One interpretation of this situation is that the agreement, effectively giving veto power to each participating state, is comprehensive to the point of paralysis.

The donor community, again moving back into the support of large scale water project, needs confidence that scenarios exist where benefits clearly exceed costs, and which are acceptable to all the parties to the agreement — yet even the specification of scenarios is politically sensitive and subject to the constraints that this implies when four very varied countries are involved.

One critically important point is that the countries have agreed to a specific hydrological model — and agreement that means that each country broadly accepts the results of that model as it portrays the likely outcome of specific interventions. Recently, this allowed a team of external specialists to independently specify a set of potential development scenarios, have these scenarios evaluated by the agreed model, and present the outcome of these analyses to donors as the basis for considering the potential for beneficial development in the basin. To a degree, this short-circuited the process of defining scenarios within the institutional arrangements defined in the 1995 agreement, while exploiting the important steps already taken to establish the basic terms of water sharing, and a technical mechanism for evaluating hydrological impacts.

The results of this exercise have been widely discussed in the donor community and will hopefully result in the initiation of development of the basin with international support — the ultimate inducement to concluding the process of political bargaining and moving forward towards the development that manifests itself in new facilities, properly operated and maintained, to produce benefits to the people of the region.

Notes

1. This section draws on "Non-State Actors and Water Resources Development — An Economic Perspective", *Non-State Actors and International Law* 3, no. 1 (2003): 99–110. For an introductory discussion, see C. J. Perry, "Determinants of Function and Dysfunction in Irrigation Performance, and Implications for Performance Improvement", *Water Resources Development* 11, no. 1 (1995): 25–38 and for a broader analysis, see Harald D. Frederiksen and Rodney J. Vissia, *Considerations in Formulating the Transfer of Services in the Water Sector* (Colombo, Sri Lanka: International Water Management Institute, 1998).
2. FAO <http://www.fao.org/documents/show_cdr.asp?url_file=/docrep/W4356E/w4356e0o.htm>.
3. Undula Alam, "Water Rationality: Mediating the Indus Waters Treaty", Ph.D. dissertation, Durham University, U.K., 1998.
4. Ayub Khan quoted in N.D. Gulhati, *Indus Water Treaty: An Exercise in International Mediation* (Bombay: Allied Publishers, 1973), p. 340.
5. The level of the sea has dropped by 17 metres between 1950 and 1996, mainly due to uncompensated evaporation of the order of 1 metre per year; its surface declined from 67,000 km^2 to 30,000 km^2. The annual inflow used to be about 70 km^3. At the present, no water enters the sea in dry years. In the past decade there are two such years, in the other year inflow was between 5–10 km^3. At that inflow level, the Aral Sea will further decline and stabilize at a size of 13,000 km^2 in about fifteen years. Its salinity will be at about 100 g/l — comparable to that of the Dead Sea in Israel.
6. This was not unrecognized by the designers; a Russian engineer was quoted in 1968 as saying that the evaporation of the Aral Sea was "inevitable" <http://en.wikipedia.org/wiki/Aral_Sea>.
7. <http://www.mrcmekong.org/about_mekong/>.

References

Alam, Undula. "Water Rationality: Mediating the Indus Waters Treaty". Ph.D. dissertation, Durham University, U.K., 1998.

FAO. <http://www.fao.org/documents/show_cdr.asp?url_file=/docrep/W4356E/w4356e0o.htm>.

Frederiksen, Harald D. and Rodney J. Vissia. *Considerations in Formulating the Transfer of Services in the Water Sector.* Colombo, Sri Lanka: International Water Management Institute, 1998.

Gulhati, N. D. *Indus Water Treaty: An Exercise in International Mediation.* Bombay, India: Allied Publishers, 1973.

"Non-State Actors and Water Resources Development — An Economic Perspective". *Non-State Actors and International Law* 3, no. 1 (2003).

Perry, C. J. "Determinants of Function and Dysfunction in Irrigation Performance, and Implications for Performance Improvement". *Water Resources Development* 11, no. 1 (1995).

4

PRIVATIZATION OF WATER SERVICES VIA PUBLIC-PRIVATE PARTNERSHIP AND IMPLICATIONS FOR SOUTHEAST ASIA

Eric Teo Chu Cheow

Privatization and the involvement of the private sector have been definitely important components of many water utilities and public projects in recent years. But the concept of "social goods, services and distribution" has also become resurgent. Is there therefore an alternative formula to "bridge" the private sector and "social goods and services" in the globalized context today, beyond mere outright privatization? However, while attempting to answer this question, it must also be firmly kept in mind, the overarching importance of corporate governance, social distribution and financial viability in public undertakings.[1]

GLOBAL TRENDS IMPACTING ON THE PRIVATIZATION DEBATE

There are several global trends, which have had a direct impact on the privatization debate. The twin trends of neo-liberalism and liberalization have made privatization *à la mode*. Within the context of neo-liberalism, liberalization and globalization, the key globalization elements of goods and services, capital, human resources, and ideas have increased their circulation around the world.

But, a more unstable financial system and unstable financial markets have also ensued, especially in the last decade with the emergence of the U.S. sub-prime crisis. High social costs have also emerged in developing economies, for example, after the Asian financial crisis in 1997–98. As such, a scenario of more political uncertainties, amidst slower economic growth, political upheavals, inter-state conflicts, religious tensions and ethnic violence has thus emerged, with terrorism now deemed the "dark side of globalization". Sustainable socio-economic development and the environment have become *a la mode* today too.

"Unbridled capitalism" is under attack; there is thus an urgent need to re-look at the whole concept of privatization. With an upsurge in democracy and participatory politics, there is thus increased decentralization and more devolution of power downwards. The emergence of civil society and people's power has become a check on both public and corporate sectors' integrity and governance practices. The nexus of the Asian political economy is undoubtedly shifting in Asia, from a bipolar one comprising "big business-big government" to a tripolar nexus of "government-private sector-civil society".

Thanks to the above trends, we have entered a "new" context for privatization, especially when most "privatizable" assets are "in the public domain" or "of a social character". The twin context of social-economic and politico-social must now be seriously considered.

In the new social-economic context, the private sector and privatization are considered "in", although there has been an erosion of confidence in "unbridled capitalism", which in turn has dealt a decisive blow to "pure capitalism". There is therefore a certain distancing from the private sector, as a solve-all panacea to our economic woes, as highlighted by recent crises, like the Asian crisis (1997–98), for us in this region. There is also a recognition of the importance of "social goods and service" (or goods of a social redistribution character), as an imperative to the development, cohesion and stability of post-crisis asian community and society. As a basis for sustainable socio-economic development, infrastructure and utilities development is now perceived as equally critical for social redistribution and development; urban management has thus gained in importance in Asia.

In the new politico-social context, developing Asian countries have had to contend with an enormous post-Asian crisis financial strain; "extra-public" financing for poverty alleviation is urgently needed, especially as its is now seen as a "social good" and even a "right" for the poorest sections of the population, so as to ensure social stability. The shift to a tripolar nexus of the political economy in Asia would mean including the private sector and civil society more effectively at all levels of decision-making; consumer and electoral aspirations will rise, as people's power increases too.

Thanks to the "pressure" of democratization, some Asian governments have had to decentralize governance and their decision-making process downwards to the regions, provinces or municipalities; the private sector has therefore a more crucial "decentralized" role to play, given the inherent weaknesses of local authorities in terms of financial resources, local accountability and technical expertise in water and sanitation management.

INTERNATIONAL EXIGENCIES IN THE WATER AND SOCIAL REFORM SECTORS: FOLLOWING UP FROM THE MONTERREY AND JOHANNESBURG SUMMITS

There are also important international frameworks and decisions taken on water in the first three years of the millennium, which are worth recalling, as in the Second Water Forum of The Hague (March 2000), the UN Millennium Assembly in New York (October

2000), the International Freshwater Conference in Bonn (December 2001), the UN Monterrey Conference on Financing for Development (March 2002), and the more recent Johannesburg World Summit on Sustainable Development (August 2002) and the United Nations World Water Development Report (2002; 2006).[2]

The Second Water Forum of The Hague put the world water crisis squarely on the international agenda, as it called the world's attention to the many urgent water issues.[3] The forum introduced and adopted the idea of "water security" as a noble goal to achieve alongside food and environmental security. Its key message was that "water is everybody's business", with an access to water for all in order to alleviate poverty, thus sharing control over water for all and implying good governance over clean water supply and distribution.

Then came the most important decision taken so far on water at the global level, when the UN Millennium Assembly set in New York an international development target to "halve, by 2015, the proportion of people living in extreme poverty and to halve the proportion of people who suffer from hunger and are unable to reach or afford safe drinking water resources".[4]

Then, the Bonn International Freshwater Conference, with the theme of "Water, Key to Sustainable Development", emphasized the point that there would be no sustainable development without access to water for drinking as well as for productive purposes for all people.

In March 2002, the UN Conference on Financing for Development in Monterrey, Mexico and the concurrent Enron-Arthur Andersen debacle in the United States highlighted the inextricable link between the crucial role of the private sector in the international strategy of financing development (in developing countries) and the critical need for good corporate governance (of the private sector) today. This conference came on the timely heels of four global geo-political factors, which grossly affect international security.[5]

Firstly, 11 September has brought home the long-overdue message that poverty, growing frustrations against the lack of social progress and the growing social inequity found in many developing countries, have helped spawn terrorism. Secondly, globalization, which has the potential to create unprecedented prosperity through liberalized trade, investments and the technological revolution, has also increased inequalities both between and within nations, and thus aggravated economic and social inequities. If not arrested, this trend could lead to more terrorism and instability. Thirdly, in this post-Cold War era, developmental aid is no longer tied to ideological support or allies within the former Western or Soviet blocs. Such aid is now more pegged to criteria other than political or ideological. Fourthly, there is the realization that a sustainable socio-economic development is far more important than development at any cost.

The "Monterrey Consensus" has thus successfully linked these four key global issues of today in a powerful and logical way in the post-9/11 and post-Enron context. Developmental aid is very much depoliticized, as Western-Soviet division has since collapsed; today's aid should be based on merits. 9/11 and the anti-globalization clamour have driven home the message that developed nations could no longer live in security, if poverty is not alleviated and social inequities are not quickly reduced in the developing world. Tearing down trade barriers is therefore imperative, but not sufficient. Developmental aid must flow effectively to developing countries in order to create a more stable and safer world for all. But this aid should now be tied more stringently to recipient governments' anti-corruption clean-ups, democratic reforms, transparency, accountability, domestic private enterprise stimulation within good corporate governance frameworks, and a special focus by developing nations on education, human resource development and health and water services. Above all, developed and developing nations, the public and private sectors must now jointly involve themselves in both institutional and capacity-building exercises in the developing world.

But also according to the Monterrey Consensus, big "clean" corporate businesses should now be closely associated with development, if certain conditions of good public governance are met by emerging economies, to help invest, alleviate poverty, develop infrastructure, utilities, health, water and educational programmes for a sustainable socio-economic development. However, there should also be a clear exigency that the corporate sector must strictly embrace good corporate governance, accountability and transparency. In short, the rampant power and abuse of markets should also be stringently subjected to some forms of control. Furthermore, the "new compact" in Monterrey also highlighted the importance of public-private partnership (PPP), as a model for developing basic infrastructure and utilities, and in the fight against poverty in developing countries.[6] This partnership, which would inevitably come under stricter and more regular public and civil society scrutiny, would be increasingly championed by the World Bank, regional banks such as the Asian Development Bank, and developed countries, as developmental aid donors.

"People power" could be expected ultimately to scrutinize and check both the public and corporate sectors' integrity and governance practices closely. Monterrey has thus focused on the corporate sector's crucial role in international developmental strategies, but only with corporate governance being strictly enforced. In short, the cry today is for the rampant power and abuse of once-omnipotent markets to be stringently checked, curbed and subjected to some forms of international, national and "self" control.

In a certain sense, the Washington Consensus, and especially the prime role of markets and the corporate world, within the context of last decade's "new liberalism", appears to have been dampened and should now be revisited. The Monterrey Consensus thus highlighted the need to rehabilitate the "public economy", a term advocated by Joseph Stiglitz, the former World Bank chief economist. Stiglitz, after his dismissal from the World Bank criticized the markets, the United States and the West, in a series of articles as well as in his famous book, *Globalization and Its Discontents* (2002); his ideas obviously displeased the pro-market liberals in the United States.

The role of the state in economic intervention and a "participatory inclusion" are now back in vogue; new political and social contracts are thus necessary to be renegotiated within developing countries. In the growing anti-globalization climate and the Enron-Arthur Andersen fiasco, markets and big businesses do not necessarily rule the day alone anymore. It is thus only logical that the role of the state be rehabilitated to develop the economy in a more responsible way, perhaps by even playing a key role in helping enforce corporate governance within its borders.

The Enron-Arthur Andersen saga has therefore clearly high-lighted the necessity for the private sector to set its own house in order and strictly enforce good corporate governance, at a time when its contribution is called for in international developmental strategies and in financing development, as contained in the Monterrey Consensus. Such is also now expected of international water companies, like SUEZ, Vivendi Environment, RWE, Thames, etc. As the "Monterrey compact" had already adequately highlighted the necessity for good public governance in attracting developmental aid and investments into emerging economies (on the insistence of Washington and other Western capitals), the corollary of effective corporate governance cannot now be more adequately emphasized as well. Good governance is therefore both a public and corporate exigency by the rising civil society and emerging public opinion. Both governments and the corporate world will now have to measure up to popular expectations.

The economic slowdown has also forced many governments to shift their economic strategies towards Keynesian pump-priming and public spending/works. In this present context of the slowdown and in order to cushion the harsh realities of globalization, there is hence a dire need for big business and capital to partner international and regional financial institutions in order to work with governments more effectively in alleviating poverty and in bridging the social inequity gap that is perceived to have widened with globalization. In fact, water and sanitation are good examples of essential public works, which are of great social value; they could in fact be better developed during this period of economic slowdown and Keynesian pump-priming.

The Johannesburg Summit on Sustainable Development then highlighted the imminent plight of acute water shortages in the world, as it was made known that there is currently no safe drinking water for half a million people in the world, and half the world's total population still do not have good sanitation facilities. Groundwater levels in important aquifers have dropped drastically, thus contributing to the overall "water crisis". It also made known the fact that on a global basis, water withdrawals amount to only 10 per cent to 20 per cent of total renewable water resources. About 40 per cent of the world population already live in river basins with less than 2,000 cubic metres of water per person per year for all purposes. In such areas, water shortages are in fact increasingly limiting development options for these populations. Hence, by 2025, about half of the world's population (or about some 3.5 billion) will live in areas facing such water shortages.[7]

The Johannesburg Summit also highlighted the fact that there is a "crisis of governance" in water, and not a real scarcity of water worldwide. In fact, it advocated changes in the way we manage and develop our water resources and distribution, through four aspects, that is, via a true debate on shared values (especially on an integrated water resources management), the need to come to a consensus on the public-private nexus of water management (not necessarily a privatization of resources, but instead, a privatization of service provision), a new global governance of water (especially in sharing water and in building capacity in water management), and lastly, a wider use of science and technology (for example, in water recycling and research to control the quality of water).

Of particular interest, there was a debate on the public-private nexus in water management and distribution, when Third World countries and activists condemned the international water companies for profiteering from the people in the developing world, when they operate, invest and make money from water projects there. For example, humanitarian groups and NGOs working in the Third World had protested boisterously against such water companies as Thames, Lyonnaise des Eaux, Vivendi and RWE at the Monterrey and Johannesburg Summits, charging that they were reaping hefty profits from supplying water to poor people, especially in the slums of Buenos Aires and Mexico City to Jakarta and Cairo. On the other hand, the developed countries were advocating the greater use of the private sector (primarily international water companies) to alleviate poverty and thus help resolve the current water woes of developing countries. This particular point is worth noting in the current debate on the private sector and the privatization of utilities, especially in the current post-Enron phase and within the growing anti-globalization debate and context.

FUNDAMENTAL OPTIONS IN INFRASTRUCTURE AND UTILITIES PROVISION

But before looking more specifically at the provision of potable water, it is perhaps important to distinguish two basic categories of infrastructural development. Firstly, there is the "hard" infrastructural development, like roads, rail, seaports, airports and roofs over our heads. Then, there is the "soft" infrastructure or "utilities", like water, sanitation, electricity, solid waste collection, telephonic services and cable. These two aspects are both necessary for the development of human communities to live together and to have access, through trade and communication, to other communities.

However, the developmental models of hard and soft infrastructure differ. Hard infrastructure is considered more "passive" in service provision to clients, as they are built and operated for users (that is, consumers) as and when they need them, for example, airports, roads, rail and seaports. In the case of soft infrastructure, the operator plays a more "active" role in service provision as the commodity or service (water, electricity, waste-water and domestic waste management) is delivered on a regular and daily basis to customers; the operator needs the constant daily satisfaction and goodwill of his clients, and these clients pay for the continuous service which is provided. But soft infrastructure or services does not mean that capital investments (or sunken capital) are less important than that of hard infrastructure. For example, in water services (both potable water and sanitation or waste-water), capital cost in distribution/pipe-laying and the treatment plant is enormous, not to mention the cost of maintaining them too.

Developmental models of utilities provision ("softer" infrastructure) could also be divided into two categories, that is, either the private sector becomes the outright owner (totally or partially) of the supply company and the assets (as in the case of a full privatization or a joint venture involving the public sector), or the private sector provides services through a contractual relationship with the authorities (central or municipal), who remain the sole custodian of the assets. But it is becoming clearer today that the asset sale approach is most effective when the public sector entity, that is sold off, is in a field that is, or near being, an industrial activity; an asset sale also works best when there is some alternative form or real competition for the particular service output. However, this approach becomes more questionable when we consider "soft infrastructure" or utilities, which impinges on the essentials of communal existence, or what is now considered a social good.

Utilities pertain to this second category, where it is best for the authorities to retain the outright ownership of such communal assets, and then delegate the management of the services to the private sector over a specific period of time. The production of electricity could be in privatized hands, but well regulated (according to the first option); however, its distribution should best be in state hands. In the case of potable water and sanitation, there are serious doubts today if privatization or "asset sale of water" is indeed the best *modus operandi*. Such "bad" examples would include the outright privatization and sale of nine water companies in the United Kingdom, more than half of which are either bankrupt or need to be re-nationalized, so as to provide affordable water to local communities. After all, water is not a commodity for competition to rule over, but a social good, which should remain in the hands of the state, with the private sector being given the operating rights for a service rendered and paid according to the quality of this service.

KEY ISSUES IN PRIVATIZATION: FAILURES AND EMERGING TRENDS

But in the privatization exercises thus far, there are in general six key issues which must be clearly looked into, whilst privatizing state assets. They include:

- A sound evaluation of the real reason for privatization: Is it to improve efficiency, or is there a need of money to fill public coffers? Is it a "public abdication to the private sector", or is there political mileage or promise of cheap prices, or is it purely for vested interests?
- Determining the "just" price in selling the assets to the private sector, and whether the end justifies the means;
- Which areas to privatize and whether there are possible distortions to the economy, for example, in regulating supply versus demand, especially in the mid and long terms;
- Pricing, or the "just" price, especially for "social goods and services" to both the consumers and the private company/

operator, so as to ensure balance and viability, especially in social redistribution and development;

- A clear and transparent political and governance framework to ensure fair play in the privatization process, as well as to regulate the privatized company's fair play in the economy thereafter; corporate governance is thus key; and
- Long-term financing and a sound financial system to ensure and sustain financial viability are also important prerequisites, especially linked to the high political risks of certain operations.

There have nevertheless been unfortunate examples of privatization that have gone wrong. For example, water privatization in the UK (implemented by Dame Margaret Thatcher in the 1990s) is now leading to a partial re-nationalization today, owing to the bankruptcy of some of its water operators. The collapse of two Californian utilities was a big blow to the 1996 Californian deregulation package for electricity; a serious bridge of the supply-and-demand equilibrium and as well as its projection and its pricing caused this miserable failure.[8]

Deregulation and privatization have thus proven not to be a panacea to the economic woes of scarcity and inefficient management of resources in all the above cases. It is thus strongly recommended that one must duly factor in four new emerging trends in privatization, that is, corporate governance, financial viability of privatization, social redistribution, especially for privatized social goods, and an alternative approach to the privatization of social goods, which is none other than the public-private partnership (PPP).

Firstly, corporate governance can definitely give clear credibility to any privatization process. There must be a private sector that embraces good corporate governance, otherwise, the privatized public assets could be just as well squandered by the private sector. The private sector company that takes over the privatized project must be evaluated to be competent, efficient and upright; otherwise, public opinion (as a watchdog) could react negatively to the whole privatization process. Charges of cronyism and nepotism must be pre-empted, especially when public opinion develops further in Asian countries; the tender process of privatization must be open and transparent, like in Malaysia today.

Secondly, financial viability and a sound financial system must be assured to guarantee the success of any privatization scheme. To ensure financial viability of the privatization process, there must be a viable financial system (banks, insurance and even stock market) to "sustain" the privatized company and its operations. Reforms of the financial system would include the strengthening of balance sheets of banks and financial institutions, ensuring enough circulation of financial liquidity and loans, etc. But it is also indispensable to inculcate good and sound corporate governance into the financial system, whether semi-public or private.

Thirdly, social redistribution must be clearly enacted for social goods and services. For goods and services with a social character or in the public domain, privatization of these goods must "carry" with it the crucial goal of social redistribution within the community. A sound and efficient public service delivery system is thus imperative for such services to be efficiently channelled to the public. These social goods and services would include the provision of water, sanitation, electricity and transport (road, rail and maritime services), which all contribute to social redistribution and development, especially to the poorer segments of the population. There is a need to bring this population segment into the mainstream of economic development and social development, as part of the social contract, especially in the present context of anti-globalization. This in turn guarantees social and political stability. The pricing of such privatized services must be sensitively determined and implemented to ensure some form of social equity and redistribution. The long-term supply-and-demand for such social goods and services must also be clearly looked into.

AN ALTERNATIVE TO "PRIVATIZING" SOCIAL GOODS AND SERVICES: THE PUBLIC-PRIVATE PARTNERSHIP (PPP) CONCEPT

There is another approach to privatizing sensitive social goods and services, and that is, via a public-private partnership (PPP).[9] The social aspect, as stated above, forms the true basis of this approach, besides the economic angle. This partnership should bring together, as integral partners, the local authorities (with the prior blessings of the central authorities), private sector consortia and its subcontractors, as well as financial institutions (both the local private sector and international public ones, which could come in either as guarantors or "part-financiers"). In a PPP, each party brings its own skills and complements those of the others. The end-user of the social services or the consumer will be the final arbiter for the quality of services, its pricing and the good's delivery; the end-user or consumer is also ultimately the electorate, which is gaining political power, clout and influence in Asia. There are thus important political, social, financial, economic and public relations aspects to be seriously considered and managed, in order for a PPP to be truly successful.

PPP is a solution to "deficient" local administrations (that is, deficient financially and technically) in satisfying local utilities or infrastructure demands, especially in the present urban context. Politically, local administrations should outsource the building and management/operation of such infrastructure and utilities works to specialized private companies, through concessions, BOO/BOT (build-operate-own/build-operate-transfer) contracts or delegated management. But pricing as close to the real cost price of the services would be essential to ensure financial viability for a PPP.[10]

In the PPP concept, assets still belong to the state, which also sets the overall developmental strategy and regulatory framework for the private sector to work within. The private sector would build and operate the facilities, so as to deliver these services more efficiently and effectively, according to its best technical, financial and managerial practices. This partnership should clearly establish the quality of service, pricing formula, future tariff increases and duration of concession or contract (ideally for twenty-five to thirty years). The PPP concept could therefore be best described as a privatization of the services, but not its assets.

To satisfy the projected supply-versus-demand curve over the duration of the concession or contract, there is a need to ensure that the private concessionaire or operator abide by his commitment to expand the supply of the services through planned and staged investments throughout the duration of the whole concession, commensurate with projected increasing demand. But financing the expansion of services (according to supply-versus-demand) must be clearly factored into the project over the duration of whole concession, thus involving long-term commitment; project financing will involve both equity and debt financing (usually at 30 per cent–70 per cent ratio) at each and every stage of expansion or investments.

To assure the success of this system, regulatory frameworks must be clear and transparent. The appointed regulator must be fair and neutral, so as to be clearly credible in the eyes of the authorities, operator and consumer. This will also help lower the political risks for the private-sector concessionaire. Developmental banks, multilateral organizations and export credit agencies can provide some confidence to private capital and operators. But crucial to its success would also be the critical issues of good governance, both public and corporate, and a sound financial system.

HAZARDS, ECONOMIC ADVANTAGES AND PR MANAGEMENT IMPERATIVES OF PPPs

There are, however, numerous hazards for the project financing of PPPs in Asia. As stated earlier, project finance must fully integrate the social aspect as much as possible. But the precocity of financing a PPP clearly exposes a PPP to high sovereign risks in the following ways:

- The enormous risks for international operators could be found in high sovereign risk countries like the Philippines, Indonesia (especially in 1997–98) and Vietnam; any pending "collapse" of these economies could set back projected expansion of facilities and the required investments from the private sector, as well as the services tariffs.
- Risks of a massive devaluation are still great, as well as the unpredictability in currency convertibility; they constitute a real financial hazard for project finance.
- With the rise of the civil society (consumer lobbies, NGOs, unions and environmental groups) and against the backdrop of mounting anti-globalization sentiments worldwide, it has become imperative for the authorities and the private sector to cooperate fully in delivering the best "social services" to the population at the lowest price possible. Tariff pricing thus remains a very sensitive issue.
- It is also advisable to closely associate international and regional financial institutions in such PPPs, as these institutions could constitute some form of socio-financial support or guarantee that may be needed from the World Bank or regional developmental banks (like the ADB) to help alleviate poverty.

To summarize, there are five aspects, which necessarily constitute the economic advantages of a successful PPP, beyond the social aspects of necessity. They include better human resource (HR) development and management, better financial management, good technological innovation, better commercial management; and greater customer satisfaction.

But beyond the socio-economic aspects, there is also intrinsically a need for a sound PR management of a PPP, especially in three crucial areas. Nationalistic feelings, fear of unemployment or redundancy and concerns with raising utilities prices indiscriminately could fan protests in the local population. It must be highlighted in the PR that savings could be achieved, as wastage is cut down to the minimum, and the labour force and the operational plants used more efficiently, according to the private sector's best business practices. But consumers should also be made to understand that reasonable price increases must also be expected, in line with inflation, otherwise, the ultimate financial collapse of private service providers may not benefit consumers in the long term.

Eight Points for Private-Public Partnerships

- With the manifold changes in the world (through its ten principal trends enumerated earlier), the private sector and privatization may no longer be considered the panacea to poor economic management and all economic ills of emerging societies.
- The rise of consumer rights and the civil society would give consumers an increasing say in the provision of economic and social services and utilities, whose delivery systems would be increasingly judged at the polls.
- There is clearly an emerging social dimension in the provision of social goods and services, both in terms of poverty alleviation as well as in the sound foundation for a sustainable economic growth. Social redistribution and development are thus crucial, especially in the present anti-globalization context.
- Examples in the United Kingdom and California have shown that full privatization of social services and utilities could lead to unexpected setbacks when they are not properly regulated or if abuses are left unchecked by slackened regulatory bodies.
- But a PPP would only work if both pricing and supply-and-demand are properly factored in, with long-term financing, corporate governance and fair and transparent regulatory frameworks all well locked in too.

- Of late, another facet, which may endanger PPPs, could come from the high risks incurred for such projects in developing countries, especially during wild currency fluctuations and economic crises, like during the 1997–98 Asian Crisis.
- This is where international and regional financial institutions could come in to help play a critical "social" role by supporting governments, the private sector (both the operator and the local financial institutions involved) and the consumers, within a clearly and transparently-established PPP framework.

Public-Private Partnerships in Southeast Asia: Different Rationales and Challenges

Singapore launched into PPPs in a big way when the government announced in early October 2003 a S$1.3 billion package of projects, which would be "farmed out" to the private sector over the next three to five years. This scheme would allow the private sector to operate big public projects and offer public services under a PPP initiative, whose guidelines were first released by the Finance Ministry in August 2003.[11] To date, the latest project would be the completion of the NEWater plant in March 2007, when the Ulu Pandan plant was opened and will produce 32 million gallons per day (mgd) of water per day and supply new customers in areas like Tuas and Jurong.[12] This is the first plant offered to the private sector (Keppel Seghers) to design, construct, and operate in Singapore.

Under the Singapore government's PPP scheme, public sector non-core projects worth more than S$50 million could be outsourced to the private sector to operate and maintain for as long as thirty years. Six big projects have been identified and some open tenders have since been awarded. In fact, Singapore's first seawater desalination project was awarded on 10 October 2004 to home-grown environmental company, Hyflux, and Keppel Engineering has clinched the first of four NEWater plants.[13]

In the region, Indonesia, Malaysia and Brunei are also warming up to the PPP approach, as recent indications have shown. However, unlike Singapore, where the objective of "outsourcing" the maximum of projects to the private sector as possible is to encourage its growth and development, PPPs in Indonesia, Malaysia and Brunei may not have the same rationales or goals; they may also consequently present different challenges to these countries in eventually implementing them.

At the Network Indonesia Forum, organized by IE Singapore in December 2004, Indonesian Trade Minister Marie Pangestu announced that Indonesia would be organizing a huge conference on PPP in Jakarta in February 2005, and hoped that the private sector would invest massively in Indonesia's infrastructure through the PPP scheme. In fact, Minister Pangestu also revealed that her government was hoping to get the private sector financially committed to two-thirds of the country's infrastructure investment needs in the next five years, leaving depleting public coffers to support the remaining one-third. This was clearly reiterated in Jakarta during the summit by Coordinating Minister for the Economy Aburizal Bakrie. Key sectors identified included power, water and sanitation, IT, transport and logistics (highways, ports and airports), and Bappenas would take charge of drafting a masterplan for this national endeavour.

Indonesia is in dire need to develop and improve its infrastructure, after years of wanton neglect and political uncertainties. In 2011, World Economic Forum Global Competitiveness Index, Indonesia ranked 76 out of 142 countries in terms of infrastructure quality. To attract manufacturing and services investments in the country so as to tap its vast natural resources, Indonesia clearly needs good infrastructure to "re-kickstart" FDIs and local investments. In fact, Java faces severe brown-outs, as electricity production capacity is now seriously strained; unclean water and ineffective sanitation threaten big cities such as Jakarta or Surabaya, whereas IT limitations could hamper future FDIs.

Moreover, decentralization in Indonesia could provide a boon to PPPs, as local governments and *kabupatans* (regency chiefs) lack both the financial resources and technical expertise to provide basic infrastructure and public services to the people. It would also be a welcome move for FDIs and the private sector, provided the government can set a clear, transparent and credible framework for PPPs to be implemented at both the central and local levels; the bureaucracy must be equally trained to handle PPPs honestly. Indonesia's financial plight and huge budget deficit are therefore at the core of its decision to turn to PPPs, but its biggest challenge is in its implementation.

Malaysia's interest in PPPs presents another political and economic dimension. Former Prime Minister Abdullah Badawi had pledged to "put some order back" into the private sector, after charges of cronyism had plagued the last administration. As part of his electoral pledge, Abdullah Badawi had also stressed the importance of making Malaysia's delivery system more efficient and people-friendly. These two political reasons would therefore form the basis of Malaysia's current interest in PPPs; unlike Indonesia's financial reasons, Malaysia's attraction to PPPs appears therefore to be more politically and socially motivated.

A report on privatization was commissioned by the National Economic Action Council (NEAC) in 2004 to re-examine and re-evaluate Malaysia's privatization process thus far and recommend measures to improve the present system, especially in corporate governance and what is deemed a failure of its public goods and services delivery system. The balance between financial viability, efficiency and social benefits is being stressed, especially when the Abdullah administration had to deliver on its electoral promises of cleaning up corporate governance in Malaysia, opening up huge infrastructure tenders publicly and transparently, and drastically cutting down waste, inefficiencies and moral hazards in both the public and private sectors. To date, such measures have yet to bear fruit in Malaysia. Presently, the emphasis on building a world-class infrastructure for growth is also very much evident under the Najib Administration (see Tenth Malaysian Plan, 2011–2015).

Another rationale for PPPs could be discerned in Brunei, where a PPP seminar was organized by the Civil Service Institute for senior civil servants in November 2004. Brunei is in dire need to diversify its economy, as concerns mount over the possibility of its oil and gas deposits and revenue running out in the coming years. There is also a second imperative of nurturing an indigenous private sector quickly, as most Bruneians prefer to either work for the government or in the oil and gas sector, which both pay handsomely. The social dimension is therefore key.

Brunei's greatest problem in adopting PPPs would come from the dearth of its private sector and its growing fears that the economy is being kept turning, only thanks to some 70,000 migrant Indian, Filipino and Indonesian workers, whereas some 8,000 Bruneians are "voluntarily" unemployed. The private sector is extremely fragile, as entrepreneurship has never been nurtured, thanks to its oil and gas boom; Chinese businessmen control most of the retail, although Indians are progressively entering this sector in a big way. But with a very small population and market, PPPs would face tremendous difficulties if public services and infrastructure are parcelled out in small packages with no inherent economies of scale, thus posing obvious financial risks to outsourced private operators.

Elsewhere in Southeast Asia, PPP does not appear implementable in the Philippines, as long as the present charter only allows 40 per cent of foreign participation in water projects; as the Maynilad project in Manila has proven, local companies do not have the 60 per cent of financial means to sustain long-term investment projects. Unfortunately, vested interests would always plague the Philippines, as the failure of "chacha" or charter change during ex-President Joseph Estrada's time has shown. The Manilad project needs urgent financial infusion, but as long as displaced nationalism blocks all attempts to reform FDI inputs into an increasingly impoverished economy, PPPs would be in real danger in the Philippines.

Thailand faces a different problem. The powerful stranglehold of the Metropolitan and Provincial Waterworks Authorities, which out of nationalistic fervour, takes on a protectionist posture *vis-à-vis farang* [foreigner] companies and investors in public services. Lastly, in Vietnam, its socialist planning policy (though it could certainly learn from China, which has successfully launched PPPs in water and sewage services) as well as the hazardous monetary policy, do not for the moment favour credible PPPs in water services, as the collapse of the Tu Duc project in Ho Chih Minh City exemplified.

CONCLUSION

A sound PPP is therefore a tripartite enterprise, with:

- The authorities regulating and implementing;
- The private sector operating and delivering the services; and
- The public consuming and "checking" both the authorities and the private operator.

This approach is undoubtedly more viable than pure privatization alone, especially for social goods and services. The PPP is thus advocated as a good social means of privatizing.

PPPs in the region's four insular economies present different rationales, goals and challenges. Singapore's PPPs stress the socio-economic imperative of outsourcing to the private sector, whereas Indonesia needs PPPs for financial and technical reasons. On the other hand, Malaysia has a politico-social imperative of corporate governance and efficient delivery systems, whereas Brunei's dilemma is undoubtedly social, dovetailing PPPs into its diversification and employment policies. Elsewhere, in mainland Southeast Asia, out of vested interests, other philosophical and ideological challenges present themselves. PPPs are hence set to affect regional economies in diverse ways, but challenges remain enormous for their successful implementation in Southeast Asia.

Notes

1. This chapter draws on discussions and materials from an earlier work of mine. Please see Eric Teo Chu Cheow, *Privatisation of Water Supply*, Dialogue of Globalization, Occasional Papers Geneva No. 8, July 2003 <http://www.fes-geneva.org/publications/OccasionalPapers/FES%20OccPapers%208.pdf>.

2. *United Nations World Water Development Report: Water for People, Water for Life* (United States: UNESCO-WWAP, 2003) and also the *United Nations World Water Development Report 2: Water, a Shared Responsibility* (United States: UNESCO-WWAP, 2006).

3. See "And Not a Drop to Drink! World Water Forum promotes Privatisation and Deregulation of World's Water", <www.corporateeurope.org/observer7/water.html>.

4. See <www.unmillenniumproject.org> or <www.un.org/millennium goals/>.

5. See <www.un.orglesa/ffd> or <www.imf.org/external/np/speeches 2003/063003.html>.

6. See <www.uneca.org/disd/documents/privatesectorresolution.doc> as well as the *Jakarta Post*, "Public Accountability now Accepted by Corporations and Development Aid", 25 June 2006.

7. See <www.johannesburgsummit.org/> or <www.un.org/events/wssd> for details on the World Summit on Sustainable Development.

8. There is no book to my knowledge yet published on this, but there is a spate of articles in international newspapers/journals in the late 1990s analysing the "Californian debacle". You could for example refer to <www.erisk.com/Learning/CaseStudies/ref_case_californiacrisis.asp>. We have also seen a re-nationalization of British Rail, given its undoubted failure in private hands.

9. Nick Freeman, ed., *Financing Southeast Asian Economic Development* (Singapore: Institute of Southeast Asian Studies, 2003).

10. For Southeast Asia, see the following links and articles: <http://www.fes-geneva.org/publications/OccasionalPapersShortSummary/occasional_papers_8.htm> or <www.adbi.org/event/333.regional.planning.infrastructure/agenda> and "Marrying Private Initiative with Public Good", *Straits Times*, 12 October 2004; "Deregulating Utilities Without Tears", Singapore *Business Times*, 4 April 2004; and "PPPs in Basic Infrastructure", *Jakarta Post*, 25 January 2005.
11. See <www.pub.gov.sg/NEWater_files> or <www.sph.com.sg/latest/files/hyflux.pdf>.
12. "NEWater to Supply 30 per cent of Singapore's Water Needs by 2011: PM", *Channel NewAsia*, 15 March 2007.
13. See <www.ipfa.org/documents/documents.cgi?t=template.htmanda=390>.

References

"Deregulating Utilities Without Tears". *Singapore Business Times*, 4 April 2004.

Freeman, Nick, ed. *Financing Southeast Asian Economic Development*. Singapore: Institute of Southeast Asian Studies, 2003.

"Marrying Private Initiative with Public Good". *Straits Times*, 12 October 2004.

"NEWater to Supply 30% of Singapore's Water Needs by 2011: PM". *Channel NewAsia*, 15 March 2007.

"And Not a Drop to Drink! World Water Forum promotes Privatisation and Deregulation of World's Water". <www.corporateeurope.org/observer7/water.html>.

"PPPs in Basic Infrastructure". *Jakarta Post*, 25 January 2005.

"Public accountability now accepted by corporations and development aid". *Jakarta Post*, 25 June 2006.

Teo Chu Cheow, Eric. *Privatisation of Water Supply*. Dialogue of Globalization, Occasional Papers Geneva No. 8, July 2003. < http://www.fes-geneva.org/publications/OccasionalPapers/FES%20OccPapers%208.pdf >.

United Nations World Water Development Report: Water for People, Water for Life. United States: UNESCO-WWAP, 2003.

United Nations World Water Development Report 2: Water, a Shared Responsibility. United States: UNESCO-WWAP, 2006.

5

INDONESIA'S WATER MANAGEMENT REFORM

Budhi Santoso

The growing population and economic activities in various regions in Indonesia have caused an intensification of water use, thus increasing scarcity of available water resources, and intensified impacts from adverse conditions. This rising scarcity raises critical issues in the efficient allocation, distribution and control of water resources.

RIVER BASINS

The main problem faced by Indonesia is a deterioration of its river basins in many parts of the country. Damaged river basins are identified when the flow of water from upper to the lower level is now more rapid because of a higher run-off. Because of the higher run-off, less water can be absorbed in the catchment areas. The high run-off results in flooding in the downstream areas which often becomes unmanageable. Catchment areas become short and steep and groundwater recharge potential low. Without adequate containment structures, most wet season discharge flows quickly to the sea. Pollution, mainly from human and industrial wastes, is also serious in many rivers. The concentration of pollution increases dramatically during the dry season, when river flows are greatly reduced.

The water reform as stipulated in the 2004 water law states that in order to reduce damage in river basins, the government has to implement a new approach called "one river one management". By this is meant that solving problems in the downstream areas should take into account forest conservation issues in the catchments areas. The number of river basins in a critical stage has almost doubled every ten years: There were 22 river basins deemed critical in 1984, 39 in 1992, and 59 river basins in 1998. It was reported that in January 2008, the number of critical river basins had increased to about 232.[1]

According to Law No. 41 Year 1999 regarding Forestry, Article 18 states that the catchments areas of a river basin which functions as water absorption and conservation should consist of protection vegetation of at least 30 per cent of the total river basin area. Almost sixty river basins in Indonesia in 1998 can thus be considered to be in a critical condition because the conservation forest at the catchment areas have been severely damaged.

Worsening conditions have arisen due to the unmanageable dynamics of social, economic and natural factors such as sedimentation and land subsidence. With the decentralization of development programmes in Indonesia, regional governments have had to increase regional incomes which have often resulted in land conversion exercises which are detrimental to the environment and also water resource management. The El Nino has also affected flood intensity causing river basin damage in some areas.

In aggregate, there has been no shortage of water, for instance in Java, because rainfall on the island is generally substantial. The problem, however, lies in seasonal and annual rainfall variations. Increasingly, as urban areas expand and industries grow, conflicts between competing agricultural, industrial and municipal water uses have also grown, so have conflicts between surface and groundwater use in urban areas. Many of the aquifers in urban centres are already being over-extracted and have been experiencing saltwater intrusion and ground subsidence.

In Jakarta, water has traditionally been supplied by three sources: Private connections to the municipal system, standpipes (or hydrants), and vendors. Based on the 2004 data provided by PAM JAYA (province government-owned company) authorized as drinking water regulator, only 20 per cent of the twelve million people in Jakarta live in homes that are connected to the municipal water system. By 2015, it has been predicted that there may still be about 31 per cent of the people in Jakarta without access to piped water (Lanti 2009). The non-municipal sources of water include neighbourhood standpipes or door-to-door vendors, albeit at a significantly inflated price.

The impoverished people of Jakarta have had limited access to water because the available non-municipal standpipes are located quite far from their homes. As a result, the portion of their incomes devoted to buying non-municipal sources of water would naturally have to be increased in situations of water scarcity during the drier seasons of the year. One might thus suggest that the Jakarta government must take further steps to improve the availability of water within the city. Indeed, the government has been attempting to connect all houses to the municipal water system, but many households still cannot afford the cost of connection or do not connect because they think that they need water only on a day-to-day basis and not on a long-term perspective.

As shown in Figure 5.1, water availability has been high during the rainy season, but low in the months of July and August. The graph also shows that water balance has been below that of the level of water demand between June and August. In terms of economic value and pricing, the scarcity of water has usually been followed

FIGURE 5.1
Water Balance in Jakarta and West Java, 2000

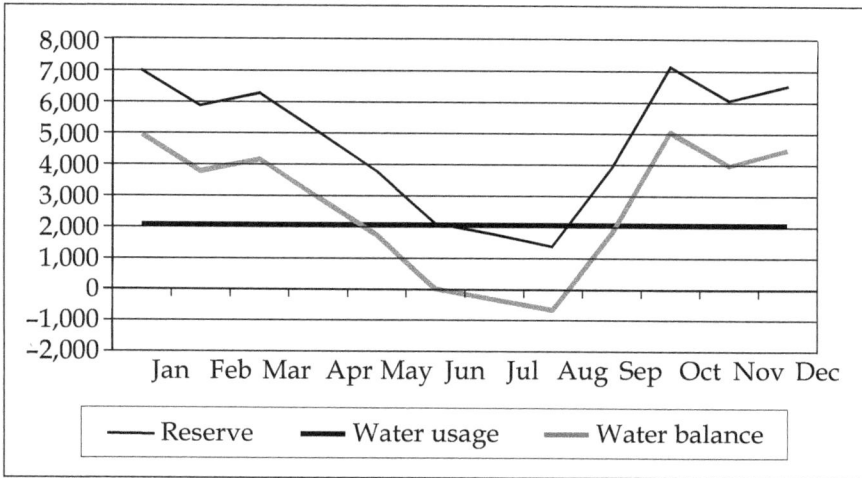

Source: BAKOSURTANAL (Coordinating Agency for National Survey and Mapping), 2004.

by water price increase in Jakarta. Such conditions have remained prevalent even at the present.

Java island comprises 7 per cent of Indonesia's total land area; however, water potency is only about 4.5 per cent of the national average. On the other hand, about 65 per cent of the total population of Indonesia live in Java. Water availability is 1,750 cubic metres per capita per year (m³/capita/yr) which lies below the normal standard of 2,000 m³/capita/yr. If no action is taken, it has been estimated that water availability will fall to 1,200 m³/capita/yr by the year of 2020. During the dry seasons, water flowing to the main rivers drop to about 20 per cent of annual flow, and even lower to 10 per cent in an exceptionally dry year. Irrigation accounts for some 57 billion cubic metres per year (m³/yr) in a one-in-five low-rainfall year. Irrigation water has largely been derived from run-off river supplies. Dams impound about 8 billion m³/yr

(5 per cent of total river flows). Rain is heavily concentrated during the six to eight months wet season.[2]

Java as an area has experienced the most severe damage caused by flood disasters and landslides in recent years.[3] In early January 2008, 32 people had been admitted to hospitals and 24,893 outpatients were treated due to floods and landslides in the Central Java province. In the East Java province, 15 people were admitted to hospitals and there were 361,098 outpatients, according to the Department of Health.[4] In order to successfully manage such occurrences, which for some areas in Indonesia has become recurring, there is a need to manage the long-term maintenance of the river infrastructure including rivers weirs, flood protection embankments, river training works, drainage outfall etc.

Due to the nature of environmental disasters, high and uncertain risks are associated with the construction of such infrastructure, and there has been a need to allocate sufficient funds for preventive maintenance. The early identification of river sourcing, for example, the adoption of alleviation measures, can save considerable future expense. Operational procedures can also have a significant impact on the reduction of the risks associated with infrastructure, for example flood warning systems can provide early warning to systems downstream and timely deployment of measures for flood protection.

However, it is important to understand that the main cause of flood disasters in Indonesia is due to inconsistent spatial planning implementation. In this regard, land use for specific purposes such as conservation or forest area, industry and living have been agreed and issued a decree for it by each regional/provincial government. However, contraventions have occurred with villas built in con-servation areas, illegal logging taking place in the catchments areas, and communities living along the riverside. These activities have affected water absorption capacity in the catchment areas and along the riverside by increasing water run-off during rainy periods, which in turn have stimulated flooding disasters.

Irrigation

Currently, agriculture accounts for about 97 per cent of total water demand, while industrial and municipal use together account for 3 per cent to total water demand. However, industrial and municipal use will double during the next two decades, and as there are few additional storage sites that can be developed without incurring high economic, social and environmental costs, water resources would have to be shifted out of the agricultural sector for industrial use.

Increasingly, urban demands are being met at the expense of dry season irrigation water, that is, irrigation water available during summer season which is now used to support raw water demand in urban areas. Two kinds of diversions are taking place: From rural to urban areas and from agriculture to land that had been recently converted to urban and industrial use. The land use conversion process is proceeding at the rate of about 15,000 hectares per year. By the year 2010, 10 per cent of Java's irrigated paddy will have been converted to urban and industrial use. The water requirements of the new users are not expected to be any greater than those of agriculture. The challenge will be to manage both diversion processes in a way that minimizes the economic and social costs to farmers while maintaining the agricultural output.

Indonesia has achieved self-sufficiency in rice, that is, the ability to fulfil its demand for rice consumption from domestic production in 1985. However, in the years following, Indonesia started to import rice again. There are many reasons behind this trend. At least three main factors can be identified, namely: Population increase, price competition between domestic and international producers, and domestic production decreases. The price competition with imported rice has resulted in lower incentives for the domestic farmer to increase their rice production level. With regard to the domestic production, the availability of water has been the main problem constraining rice production in the dry season. Less water has been available for farmers (compared to ten or fifteen years ago) due to sedimentation and damage to the existing water infrastructure. According to the latest data from the Ministry of Public Works, the damaged water infrastructure in 2001 has reached 30 per cent of its total asset.

Figure 5.2 shows that the irrigation infrastructure was in critical condition because, of the total of 6.7 million hectares of irrigated land, 1.5 million hectares were severely damaged. Within 23 per cent of the damage, 73 per cent are located in Java and Bali and the water available all year long is only 11 per cent of the total area. The situation has worsened because Operations and Management (O&M) fund provided by the government only meets 35–45 per cent of the total requirement each year. Overall, land conversion and irrigation infrastructure has worsened by about 15,000–20,000 hectares per year in Java island alone.

FIGURE 5.2
Condition of Irrigation Infrastructure, 2001

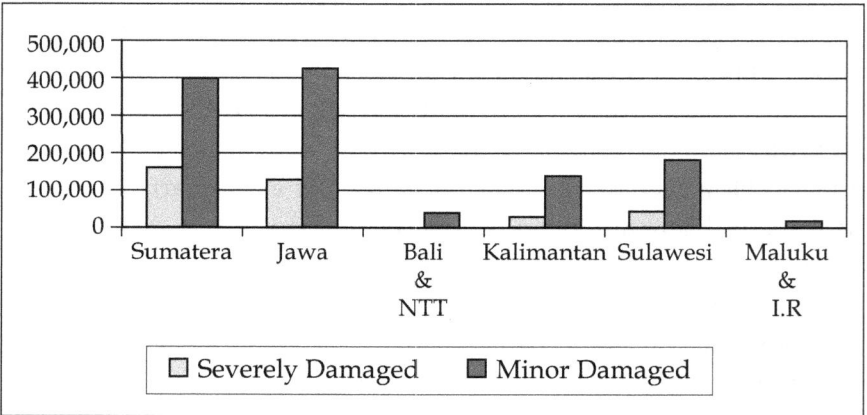

Source: Directorate for Water Resources and Irrigation, BAPPENAS (National Development Planning Agency), 2004.

THE ORIGINS OF WATER SECTOR REFORM

Indonesia comprises 17,508 islands divided into 31 provinces and more than 200 districts. These divisions serve as the administrative frame of the fourth most populous country in the world, having a population of 215 million that is immensely ethnically diverse, with approximately 500 tribes and 583 languages and dialects. Despites its size, geography, and diversity, Indonesia's bureaucracy and economy has traditionally been highly centralized. Provision of quality services in the water, sanitation, and irrigation sectors to its burgeoning population has been a daunting task that has not been realized to the satisfaction of urban and rural water users. The financial crisis of 1997, the overthrow of the New Order regime, and the continuing less-than-satisfactory provision of basic services has heightened the nationwide demands for reform in the various sectors of developments including the water sector.

The Need for Reform

The origins of the current reforms can be traced to a series of seminars and discussion sessions initiated by the Government of Indonesia (GOI) in September 1997. BAPPENAS, the national planning agency, had earlier concluded that despite having a national programme which laid out a strategy for efficient and productive water utilization, implementation by the various agencies responsible for water allocation had been severely deficient. It believed that:

- The legal and institutional arrangements for water allocation and management were inadequate;
- That water quality and the environment had been severely degraded;
- That due to unclear regulations and procedures, the private sector was not able to participate fully in water sector development; and

- That investment in infrastructure development was being hampered by a lack of policy re-orientation towards it.

It is widely accepted that the water sector in Indonesia was unable to meet the growing and varied demands placed upon it by a rising population. Industrial usage, farm usage, and home usage were the competing interests whose needs were not being met by the range of government agencies responsible for the clean and adequate supply of water.

Indeed, water provided in urban centers by PDAM (Perusahaan Daerah Air Minum), the municipal water companies, was considered suitable for cleaning purposes only; while wealthy families could afford to buy bottled water, most families in cities resorted to a daily routine of boiling water for drinking purposes. Even, the quality of water in Jakarta and other big cities was not guaranteed for drinking because supplies were polluted.

A slowdown in rice production in part due to the inability to extend irrigation schemes is cited as another critical factor driving the reforms. It is said that 80 per cent of the water used in Indonesia is for irrigation purposes. Thus, to support the food demands of a growing population and to overcome the decreasing function of the existing irrigation schemes, completing partially built irrigation should become a priority programme including to build new irrigation infrastructures. It was also noted, however that the traditional approach to irrigation management whereby the government alone is responsible for operations and management would not suffice; sustainable irrigation could be achieved if farmers and other water users were included in the management and operations of the schemes directly benefiting them. Moreover, the collection of government subsidized irrigation dues accruing from water development costs were never fully realized. Deemed to be fiscally unsustainable, beneficiary contribution towards cost recovery (another term for user fees) was thought to be the answer. The broad principles of the reform process were as follows:

- The role of central government would be limited to that of an enabling and regulatory one;
- Public-private partnerships will be promoted at the regional and local levels;
- Resources will be transferred to the local and regional levels. Implementation authority would also be devolved to provincial, district, and local government;
- Public consultation and stakeholder participation will be encouraged by creating institutions which would facilitate such dialogue and inclusion; and
- A participatory irrigation management system will be put in place so that responsibility of irrigation management is transferred to water user groups.

With these principles in mind, Indonesia embarked upon an ambitious and rapid restructuring of the water sector, one that would decentralize operations and oversee responsibilities. Reform efforts of the scale envisaged in the water sector in Indonesia is expected to overcome any number of political, bureaucratic, and financial obstacles in order to achieve their objectives. Lack of political will on the part of the government to promulgate required laws, a reluctant bureaucracy that resists reforms from within, lack of coordination between government agencies, unreliable data and diagnosis are but some challenges on the road to institutional reform. Problems such as these have already taken a toll on the pace of the implementation of water sector reforms in Indonesia.

THE WATER RESOURCES LAW

The Water Resources Law (WRL), passed by Indonesia's Parliament on 19 February 2004, effective to the present moment, introduced basic reform principles to underpin water resources management. First, there was a need to balance social, economic and environmental values, that is, that even if water is utilized as an economic resource, its optimum added value is to be sought by observing its conservation and maintenance costs. Second, management must also consider principles of: (a) provision of effective and efficient public benefits; (b) balanced development meeting the principles of integration and harmony in balancing different interests; (c) sustainability, justice, autonomy; and (d) the principles of transparency and accountability that imply development and management are regarded as an open and publicly accountable process.

The law is aimed at promoting a coherent, integral, sustainable and open approach to water resources management. The WRL is also participative in that, non-government organizations, businesses, individual citizens and communities are given the option of participating in the process of planning and implementation of water resources management. The act also includes new subjects, such as community participation, a water resources information system and, investigations. Along with its social function, the economic function of water now also takes an important place in law as all users, except farmers in public irrigation schemes whose water use is considered a basic need, are to bear the cost of water resources management services. A major deficiency of previous law (Law no. 11/1974 regarding Irrigation) was rectified whereby modalities for conflict resolution have been introduced along with stronger enforcement provisions.

The WRL is a true management law as it focuses primarily on the creation of conditions for sensible, sustainable water resources and irrigation management based on integrated water resources management principles. The act's scope aimed at integrated water management with regard to quantity and quality of surface water and groundwater. A strategic plan drawn up for each river basin in which all relevant aspects are considered and weighed together. Furthermore, along with water's social function, its economic and conservation functions are now also emphasized as functions that need to be implemented in a balanced manner. The conservation function emphasizes that water quantity and quality needs to be preserved for the future as well as present needs. Although the government remains responsible for the equitable allocation of water for its various social purposes, the option for joint ventures with the private sector has been opened up as indicated in Figure 5.3.

The WRL stipulates the tasks and responsibilities of national government, the provinces, and the districts/municipalities must be in line with decentralization legislation. It also provides for an arrangement that gives the provinces the option of transferring part their task to the national government under circumstances of poor management, conflicts or disaster. Similarly, if the district government lacks capacity to fulfill some of their tasks, they may also request their provincial government to take them over.

The authority and responsibilities of provincial and district/municipal governments are similar and based on the river basins under their jurisdiction. A provincial government carries out its tasks in river basins, aquifers and/or basins crossing districts boundaries and its policy and management considers the interest of surrounding provinces. It issues licences for surface water utilization; resolves disputes between districts and provides them with technical assistance and guidance; and establishes a provincial

FIGURE 5.3

Delegation of Authority and Responsibility

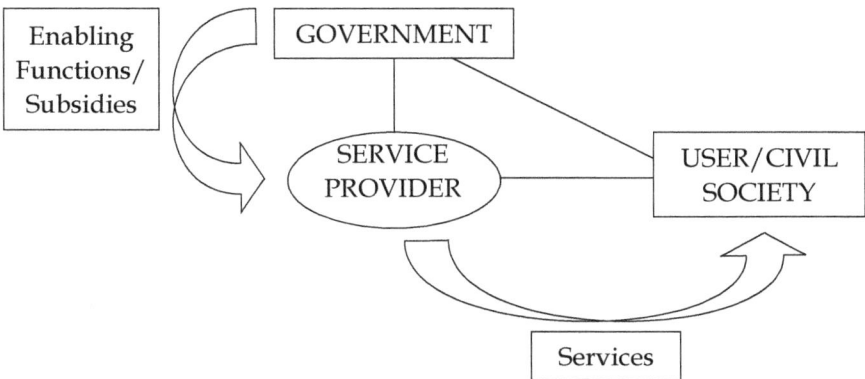

water resources council and/or basin water resources councils. Districts have similar tasks except that they are only carried out for basins within their administrative boundaries.

The authority and responsibility of the national government includes:

- Determination of the water resources management patterns (policies), management and development plans for basins crossing provincial boundaries and specifically nationally strategic water resources areas;
- Determination of the water resources national policy;
- Determination and management of water resources protected areas and conducting water resources management for basins under its jurisdiction;
- Organization, determination and issuing of licenses for supply, usage allocation and exploitation of surface and ground water for basins under its jurisdiction;
- Establishment of a national water resources council;
- Facilitation and resolution of disputes among provinces in water resources management;
- Determining standards, criteria, and guidelines for water resources management in river basins under its authority; and
- Giving technical assistance and services to provinces and districts according to needs.

SUSTAINABLE WATER SECTOR DEVELOPMENT PROGRAMME

In order to be consistent with the reform agenda, the GOI has been engaging in a major programme of policy, legal regulatory, and administrative reforms of the water resources and irrigation sector aimed at improving the sector governance and management of water resources and public irrigation scheme. The main target of the policy programme includes:

- Facilitating efficient and environmentally and socially sustainable water resources development and management by establishing national and provincial policies, institutional, regulatory and decision support frameworks;
- Strengthening the institutional and regulatory frameworks for integrated and equitable river basin management;
- Establishing effective regulatory institutions and implementation arrangements for water pollution abatement and regional water quality management; and
- Improving the performance and sustainability of irrigation system by establishing an institutional framework for the transparent and accountable delivery of irrigation services and participatory fiscal support to democratic farmer organization empowered with governance and financial authority to manage irrigation network under their control.

WATER SECTOR DEVELOPMENT AND PROGRAMME

Basically, reform programme in river basin planning is being implemented in Indonesia with the principal objectives of optimizing resource use and mobilizing user involvement. Implementation of this planning requires the setting up of the appropriate institution which prepares and maintains the basin plan, which interacts with other agencies and provides communication on river basin development issues with stakeholders. In recent years river basin planning is being implemented in response to this communications system. The objectives are to improve regionalized planning by:

- Focusing on the problems and processes of a particular region: these are interrelated and will be tackled at a regional scale; and
- Mobilization of user involvement. The involvement of stakeholders in planning and implementation is generally accepted as an effective way of improving planning and effectiveness

of implementation as well as a prerequisite for generation of financing through cost recovery.

The main requirements for implementation of basin planning in Indonesia including: (i) definition of appropriate river basin units (large single basin or combination of smaller basins); (ii) setting up the relevant institutions; and (iii) setting up the planning process.

As regards river basin development principles consist of four aspects, namely: (i) conservation of river, lake and other water resources under one management unit (one river one management); (ii) improving the management of irrigation, swamp, and other water related infrastructure and (iii) strengthening flood control and coast protection.

As stated in the National Medium Term Development Plan 2004–2009, to conserve and secure water supply, currently the government has conducted an operation and maintenance programme for fourteen big dams, rehabilitation of fourteen small dams, and built twenty new small dams. In addition, there were four big dams built including Batutegi in Lampung, Pelaperado and Batubulan in Nusa Tenggara Barat, and Tilung in Nusa Tenggara Timur.

Meanwhile, to increase the service of irrigation infrastructure providing water for agriculture production (food security), there were approximately 662,000 hectares of irrigation land that has been rehabilitated and upgraded, 138,000 hectares of irrigation infrastructure that has been newly built, new paddy field totalling 4,000 hectares were developed, fifty-six village dams rehabilitated, two new dams under construction locating in South Sumatera and South Sulawesi, and ground water irrigation for more than 10,000 hectares developed, as well as swamp infrastructure for almost 100,000 hectares upgraded. To secure raw water supply, seven raw water reservoirs were rehabilitated, and thirty-seven raw water reservoirs developed, also the rehabilitation and development of drainage canals.

PARTICIPATORY IRRIGATION AND MANAGEMENT

In line with the new paradigm of development that is to involve the stakeholders in development, the GOI has started a series of discussions with government agencies and non-governmental organizations to formulate participatory irrigation management programme (PIM). The agenda for irrigation management policy reform programme implies the following shifts:

- Authority and responsibility over water management and irrigations system management are decentralized from central government agencies to district governments. The district governments subsequently hand over governance, and responsibility over water allocation and the use and improvements of the canal infrastructure to the Federations of Water User Associations (WUAFs), with one WUAF managing one system. The District Public Works Department remains responsible for large and complex components of the infrastructure and for assisting the WUAFs.
- WUAFs are large, autonomous and legalized entities. Different from the period before 1999, they now represent 2,000–5,000 farmer-irrigators, elect their leadership more democratically, and collect and retain fees. They are better able to pool resources and information, represents the scattered farmer-irrigators in negotiations, for example with the District Public Works Department, and take entrepreneurial initiatives.
- WUAFs are now to participate in the selection, design, implementation and supervision of any physical (rehabilitation) works. Typically, in the past only contractors carried out such works. Now, WUAFs can engage in construction themselves.
- Cost sharing. Before the reform, nearly all finance schemes originated from the national budget. With the reform, WUAFs collect fees and organize contributions in the form of labour to (1) carry out all routine operation and maintenance, and

(2) share the costs of all periodic repairs and maintenance, and of replacement. The district budget finances some infrastructure components that are very complex, and co-finances all other repairs and replacement on a "matching fund" basis.

CONCLUSION

The Indonesian economy is now operating at close to full capacity in many sectors, paving the way for continued growth in investment and overall growth. The current growth performance will not deliver the sustained, quality growth that Indonesia's requires without fundamental reforms to the investment climate, improvements on governance and urgent attention to infrastructure.

Water is an integral part of sustainable development. Policies for all aspects of water has to continue to be clearly linked to policies for poverty reduction and economic growth. The government has to review the priority given to water (and sanitation) and to productive water infrastructure in national and international programmes to tackle poverty. Water infrastructure and services must continue to be pro-poor (and gender sensitive).

Poverty in Indonesia is mainly found in the rural areas, where agriculture production averages half of rural households' total income. A meaningful strategy of rural poverty reduction must therefore integrate agriculture as a major element for development. To achieve an agricultural growth rate of 3.9 per cent as stated in the Medium-Term Development Plan (Government Decree No. 25 Year 2004) will require strong measures to boost agricultural productivity through expenditure on research, demand-driven approaches to extension, dry land area development, strengthening regulatory capacity, and improving rural infrastructure including irrigation infrastructure.

In general, the water sector road map in Indonesia has been executed through the following actions: Securing equitable access to water for all Indonesian people, the primary responsibility for ensuring equitable and sustainable water resources management has rested with the government. However, this requires the participation of all stakeholders who use to protect water resources and their ecosystems. To ensure that water infrastructure and services are delivered to the poor, the investment plan in water infrastructure has to be realistic and targeted to the needs of the poor, and include targets and indicators of progress at all levels. In appropriately allocating water among competing demands, the water plan directed has to be equitable and sustainable, firstly to human needs and then to the functioning of ecosystems and different economic uses including food security.

Allocation mechanism plans to balance competing demands and take into account the social, economic and environmental values of water are important. In managing water at the lowest appropriate level, people at all levels have to be involved in the management and governance decisions concerning water resources. Local stakeholders have to be in plans to develop mechanisms for collaborative management of local needs and resources.

Regarding funding required for water sector infrastructure, public budgets are now, and will continue to be the biggest source of investment in water. Public funds will generally be needed to support complementary investments. External financing in the form of loan and grants will be used for investment in water for productivity whose priority will be given to meeting the basic needs of the poor and to preserving the integrity of ecosystems.

Notes

1. See "Government to Restore River Basins", Planet Mole: Indonesia in Focus, 17 January 2008 <http://www.planetmole.org/indonesian-news/government-to-restore-river-basins.html>.

2. Data acquired from "National Medium Term Development Plan Year 2004–2009" and The Directorate of Water Resources and Irrigation, BAPPENAS/National Development Planning Agency, 2004.

3. See for example, "Indonesia: Floods and Landslides in Central Java and East Java Provinces, OCHA Situation Report No. 3", 3 January 2008 <http://www.reliefweb.int/rw/rwb.nsf/db900sid/YSAR-7AHML2?OpenDocument>.
4. Ibid.

References

Achmad Lanti, Firdaus Ali, et al. "The First Ten Years of Implementations of the Jakarta Water Supply 25-Year Concession Agreement (1998–2008) (A Draft Translation)". Jakarta Water Supply Regulatory Body, 2009.

Arif, Sigit Supadmo, ed., et al. "Initiating Sustainable Water resources Development". Directorate for Water Resources and Irrigation, National Development Planning Agency/BAPPENAS, Jakarta, 2003.

Dikun, Suyono, ed. "Indonesian Infrastructure". State Minister of National Development Planning (BAPPENAS), Jakarta, 2003.

Government of Indonesia Regulation No. 20 Year 2006 regarding Irrigation.

Huppert, Walter, Mark Svendsen, and Douglas L. Vermillion. "Governing Maintenance Provision in Irrigation". Universum Verlagsanstalt GmbH KG, Federal Republic of Germany, 2001.

Law of The Republic of Indonesia No. 11 Year 1974 regarding Irrigation.

Law of The Republic of Indonesia No. 7 Year 2004 concerning Water Resources.

President of Republic Indonesia Regulation No. 7 Year 2005 concerning National Medium Term Development Plan 2004–2009.

Santoso, Budhi. "Perencanaan Pengelolaan Sumber Daya Air Terpadu". Perencanaan Pembangunan 01/Tahun XIV/2008, National Development Planning Agency/BAPPENAS, Jakarta, 2008.

_____, ed. Proceedings: "Asset Management for Hydraulic Infrastructure". Directorate for Water Resources and Irrigation, National Development Planning Agency/BAPPENAS, Jakarta, 2002.

6

WATER RESOURCE MANAGEMENT ISSUES IN MALAYSIA

Salmah Zakaria

INTRODUCTION

Water is of vital importance in sustaining life in this world, in various forms. The hydrological cycle in nature involves the evaporation of water, and its precipitation and flow, which is life-supporting. The rise and fall of great civilization such as in the valleys of the Indus and Tigris and Euphrates have been attributed to changes in the hydrological cycle, both natural and artificial. In recent years, human activities have exerted greater influence on the hydrological cycle. This has resulted in the emergence of serious and considerable damage not only to water systems, but ultimately, unless arrested, will impact on the economic and socio-political activities of the people. The ASEAN region and Malaysia in particular, have not been isolated from this phenomenon.[1]

The ongoing process of urbanization the world over, has worsened our vulnerability to water disasters, and many countries have been afflicted by repeated cycles of floods and droughts. The excesses of human activities, solid waste and untreated waste-water, released into the environment, are apt to worsen the water quality of our water bodies, both at and below the surface, causing widespread concern over our health and safety, and threatening the earth's ecological system.

Malaysia is signatory to the Johannesburg World Summit on Sustainable Development (WSSD) declaration of August 2002, which includes the commitment to halve by 2010 the proportion of people unable to reach and afford safe drinking water and by 2015, to halve the proportion of people who do not have access to basic sanitation.[2] At the WSSD, agreement was reached on launching a programme of action to achieve these goals, and this includes the development of integrated water resource management (IWRM) and water efficiency plans by 2005.[3]

Integrated water resources management (IWRM) as defined by the Global Water Partnership (GWP 2004) is a process which promotes the coordinated development and management of water, land and related resources, in order to maximize the resultant economic and social welfare in an equitable manner without compromising the sustainability of vital ecosystems. This includes the coordinated development and management of, land and water, surface water and groundwater, the river basin and its adjacent coastal and marine environment, and upstream and downstream interests. IWRM is not just about managing physical resources; it is also about reforming human systems to enable people to reap sustainable and equitable benefits from those resources.

For policy-making and planning, taking an IWRM approach requires that: Water development and management takes into account the multiple uses of water and the range of people's water needs; stakeholders are given a voice in water planning and management, with particular attention to securing the participation of women and the poor; policies and priorities consider water resources implications, including the two-way relationship between macro-economic policies and water development, management, and use; water-related decisions made at local and basin levels are in-line with, or at least do not conflict with the achievement of broader national objectives; and water planning and strategies are integrated into broader social, economic, and environmental goals.

Integrated river basin management (IRBM) is an integral part of IWRM, where the river basins constitute the management unit. IRBM is defined as the coordinated management of resources in natural environment (air, water, land, flora, and fauna) based on the river basin as a geographical unit, with the objective of balancing human need with the necessity of conserving resources to ensure their sustainability. The river basin is defined as the area within the whole catchments of a specific river system. It is divided from other adjacent basins by the catchments' divides (or hydrological divides), the highest points of the area, the hills and mountains. Alternatively, depending on the area of specialization and the country of usage, the river basin can also be known as the total catchment area, and the total watershed area, etc.

IRBM looks at the management of human activities in the river basin, on an integrated basis. It deals largely with issues of water allocation, pollution control, flood control, and is a subset of integrated water resources management (IWRM), which addresses the broader issues of food self sufficiency, tariffs, cross subsidies, institutional roles, etc. (Jonch-Clausen 2000). The river basin (or sub-basin/basin of tributaries) provides the appropriate and logical physical management unit for the application of IWRM principles and practices.

The IRBM approach recognizes the physical constraints within a river basin, and looks at all components in an integrated manner. These include the social/cultural infrastructure, natural fauna and flora, its landscape and soil, as well as development plans and the accompanying impacts from agriculture, commercial and industrial activities. The IRBM, besides recognizing the optimum availability of water and other resources within a basin, should also identify the optimum carrying capacity of the rivers in terms of discharge volume as well as pollutant loadings within the basin. IBRM looks at appropriate location of housing areas, business centres, industries and recreational areas, *vis-à-vis* the river basin and its flood plains. The methods and pattern of waste disposals within the whole basin to ensure the waterways remain relatively clean are also studied as well as the need for river riparian areas to sustain biodiversity to ensure that the river environment remains vibrant and living.

WATER RESOURCES STATUS[4]

Malaysia is within the equatorial zone with a climate that is influenced by an alternating northeast monsoon and southwest monsoon and is rich in water resources with an average annual rainfall of 3,000 millimetres (mm). The average annual rainfall over the Malaysian land mass amounts to 990 billion cubic metres (m³), of which 566 billion m³ becomes surface run-off, 64 billion m³ recharges the aquifers and 360 billion m³ returns to the atmosphere through the process of evapo-transpiration. The groundwater resources in Malaysia, the volume of water stored in the aquifers is estimated at 5,000 billion m³. Although groundwater accounts for 90 per cent of the freshwater resources, 97 per cent of the raw water supply in Malaysia originates from surface water sources.

The first National Water Resources Study was completed in 1982 (Department and Irrigation and Drainage (DID)/Japan International Cooperation Agency (JICA), 1982). A second National Water Resources Study (Economic Planning Unit (EPU)/Jabatan Kerja Raya (JKR), 2000) was completed in March 2000. Amongst the recommendations of this study and other subsequent studies is the need to formulate a masterplan for water resources management and development and in the process, to reorganize Malaysia's water sector.

With average annual rainfall of 3,000 mm, with daily rainfall that frequently exceeds 100 mm during the wet season, and the high tidal ranges and generally flat coastal and river plains, flood occurrences in Malaysia are quite common. Occurrence of major floods have been recorded in the years 1925, 1949, 1967, 1971, 1073, 1979, 1983, 1985 and late 2006 to early 2007.

EMERGING ISSUES

The population growth, rapid urbanization and industrialization over the past decades (Malaysia's urban population: 26.8 per cent in 1970, 60 per cent in 2000, 72.2 per cent in 2010), have imposed rapid and growing demands and pressures on Malaysia's water resources. This land based developments, besides contributing to the escalating floods and rising water pollution, have also resulted in diminishing biodiversity in its riverine and riparian areas. With development, the competition for water has continued to rise from increasing number of users and greater demand by each user. For example, new industrial areas, requiring domestic and industrial water supplies, developed in predominantly agriculture areas lie in the Muda River Basin. New agriculture areas and plantations were also established in the decades after independence. Demand for alternative power, which looks at harnessing the available huge hydropower potential within the country, also places demands on water resources.

Yet each of the country's 189 river basin management units has water supplies limited by the amount of rainfall and have limited flow-carrying capacity constrained by the size of the channel that carries the water to the sea. In each river basin, upstream developments have discharged increasing flood waters downstream, complete with the pollutants, both dissolved and solids. Many natural retention and detention areas and other water bodies in the flood plains have been reclaimed for industrial and housing areas. Not only has the water supply situation in Malaysia changed from one of relative abundance to one of relative scarcity, but increasingly, environmental problems such as floods, pollution, forest fires, diminishing biodiversity, has become more common. Economically, the country has and is paying a very heavy price to these incidences, both tangibly and intangibly.

The water demand for the year 2004 was 11.62 billion m^3, of which 7.3 billion m^3 was for irrigation and 2.4 billion m^3 and 1.90 billion m^3 was for domestic and industrial uses respectively.[5] The overall water demand has been growing at the rate of 4 per cent annually, and projected to be about 14.5 billion m^3 by 2025. The annual domestic and industrial water demand will grow to 4.2 and 3.9 billion m^3 respectively, and the irrigation water will be at about 6.3 billion m^3 in 2025.[6] Collectively, this is less than 2 per cent of annual runoff, but due to the variations of rainfall both in time and space, some regions of high water demand are approaching the limits of readily available water and water stress has become more prevalent, in tandem with the rapid growth of the country over the past few years, culminating in the water crisis affecting some parts of the country in early 1998.

In 2005, the state of Negeri Sembilan was already rationing water supply to their customers. The percentage of water consumed by the irrigation sector is expected to decrease with time and this is mainly due to the increase in demand by the domestic and industrial sectors. However, unless there is a change in the National Agriculture Policy, the present irrigated rice cultivation areas is not expected to increase in the years ahead.

The frequency and severity of flooding have escalated over the years and physical damages were estimated to be RM100 million (US$28.33 million) per year in 1982 (DID/JICA 1982). Recent studies have updated this figure to RM1 billion per year for the year 2002 (DID/MAMPU 2003). Accounting together the economic "drag" effect, some economies have indicated a possible loss in the region of RM3 billion per annum.

Data compiled by the Department of Environment (DOE) points to a trend of a slow but steady deterioration in the water quality of sampled rivers. The various sources of pollution include untreated sewerage, untreated wastewater discharge and waste disposals from municipalities, factories, squatter areas, hawkers, agriculture fertilizer and pesticides residuals, as well as sediments from land clearance and construction sites.

Landslides are common occurrences during the wet season around the country and are increasingly reported in the media. Not only have they resulted in increase sedimentation in rivers, thus choking the rivers and aggravating flood conditions, but lives have also been lost. An example is the infamous Highland Towers event. The worst was a repeated occurrence very near the Highland Towers, at the Hill View, some years later.

Forest fires are an increasing occurrence, and in many cases occur in peat swamp areas, particularly in drained peat swamp areas. Peat swamps are generally made of 90 to 95 per cent organic materials and have void ratios of around 90 per cent, formed as a result of net deposition due to humid and/or inundated condition more then 6,000 years ago. With rapid development and man's incessant hunger for land, peat swamps have been drained for economic activities such as agriculture, industry and housing. Peat swamps in its natural form is a flood detention and retention area. With drainage, not only does the floodwater have to flow and flood elsewhere, but the drained peat becomes a dried, and excellent source of burning and combustible material. A cigarette butt or sunlight reflected from glass surfaces can trigger peat burning and create an unhealthy shroud of haze over the land.

MANAGEMENT ISSUES

The inadequate integration between development initiatives is a legacy of a developing country, where sectoral development is the norm. Not only was this development the prevalent trend when Malaysia gained its independence, but it also made sense as demand for development projects was small and human and financial resources were limited. The development of irrigation, drainage, municipal and industrial water supply, and river conservancy was planned and carried out unilaterally by each agency concerned.

Generating from the concept of sectoral development is the formation and setting up of various agencies within the water sector. Over the years numerous new departments have been created to regulate, manage and provide services related to water. In carrying out the duties and responsibilities assigned to them, agencies have carried out planning; implementation of projects; operation, maintenance and management of schemes; extraction of river water; discharging of wastes and effluents; issuance of licences; formulation of rules and regulations; enforcement of regulations and laws; and prosecution; either individually or in cooperation with other agencies. Some agencies are responsible for more than one such function, and overlaps in responsibilities are not uncommon. It is also not unusual to find agencies having the technical expertise but no legislative or enforcement powers; and *vice-versa*. Many agencies have also suffered from inadequate funding, the lack of expertise and a shortage of manpower.

As the development of the country progresses, demand has also been picking up for more development projects. Yet there has been insufficient awareness of the negative impacts of such activities on the natural ecosystem in general and the water sector in particular. This can be seen from the rapid and inadequately co-coordinated development initiatives of the previous decades. As such, advocacy in these areas have been largely recent.

All activities in each river basin will affect a river and its water quality. This is evident from the pristine river water quality near the river source and the subsequent quality deterioration as the river passed through man's habitats. The current situation in the country is one where there is either insufficient understanding or coordination and consideration for the river in the many development initiatives and activities that are carried out in each river basin.

Naturally, by the time the country awakens to the problem and issues faced, there would have been inadequate capacity both technically as well as financially. Admittedly, it probably took some time to realize the looming issues that could backfire on a country's development initiatives. There will certainly be a required gestation period and the need for time before things can fall in place. As highlighted above, these activities have been under the purview of many ministries, departments, and agencies; and awareness of the needs for coordinating development, both land and water base together, within a river basin to control escalating flood occurrences and pollution, has been still largely lacking among the practitioners.

The absence of an enabling environment is a natural development of a country that has developed incrementally. The enabling environment is a function of the development itself. As the country prospers, such issues have become more complex and challenging with more water-related laws being passed. Some gaps may remain and this has also resulted in overlaps. To date Malaysia has an abundance of sectoral-based water laws at both the federal and state levels but lack comprehensiveness and integration in such laws.

With rapid economic development of the country the overlaps and gaps in the land-water base development have become more apparent. As negative impacts of water stress, escalating floods, increased pollution, and diminishing biodiversity emerge, conflict areas and confusion have also been created. At the federal level, the enforcement of water laws and legislations are carried out by the various water-related agencies. Many of these laws are outdated, redundant or ambiguous. These diversified water legislations have focused on limited aspects of water resources and services that are directly related to the responsibilities of the respective government agencies. Because they have not been formulated to cater for the current new challenges, they have not been easy to enforce effectively and are also inadequate from an IWRM perspective.

The other constraint faced by the federal agencies is the absence of legal jurisdiction, due to the fact that in the Constitution, water and land is largely a state matter. Until recently, the existing institutional linkage mechanisms between these agencies have also been generally weak as there is no single specific authority that has been made responsible for the management of rivers and water resources in the states.

CURRENT INITIATIVES

In recent years, there have been a number of initiatives in the country to help redress the issues highlighted above. The Malaysia Water Forum from 7–12 June 2004 explored initiatives taken to date on the IWRM processes in Malaysia, recording the achievements, challenges and reservations and the way forward in areas such as policy, legislative and institutional framework, financing and incentive structure, water consumption and demand, water allocation and conservation, pollution control and management, information management and research and development (R&D) and capacity-building.[7] These observations were made by the various stakeholders from the non-governmental organizations (NGOs), academia, and the public and private sectors. The focus has been on integrating development initiatives, and on implementing these initiatives using and incorporating the concepts of IWRM and IRBM.

The Economic Planning Unit in formulating the National Development Policy documents for the Third Outline Perspective Plan (OPP3) for the years 2001–10 describes development thrusts for a sustainable environmental development as:

> A major environmental and natural resource concern includes improving water quality, efficient management of solid waste and toxic and industrial waste, developing a healthy urban environment and the conservation of natural habitats and resources. During the OPP3 period, emphasis will be placed on addressing environmental and resource issues in an integrated and holistic manner. The challenge will be to identify prudent, cost-effective and adaptive management approaches that yield

multiple benefits for a more sustainable future. These approaches will, among others, be geared towards addressing the challenges of providing access to clean water, providing adequate food and energy services without environmental degradation, developing healthy urban environments, and conserving critical natural habitats and resources.

One of the key strategies of the Eighth Malaysia Plan (8MP) for the years 2001–05, the first phase in the implementation of the OPP3 (2001 to 2010), include "Adopting an integrated and holistic approach in addressing environmental and resource issues to attain sustainable development". The plan recognizes the need for the formulation of a national water policy to ensure adequate and safe drinking water, as well as clean rivers and minimal flooding. This policy will provide the framework for water conservation and management. It will also address several challenges, including managing water resources and floods effectively and efficiently, and emphasizing the need to keep development to a level that is within the carrying capacity of river basins, while protecting and restoring the environment. In the most recent Tenth Malaysia Plan (2011–2015), three areas of four were put in place: developing a long-term strategy for water management to achieve water security, continuing efforts to restructure the water services industry, and protecting rivers from pollution.

Following the water crisis of 1997, a National Water Resources Council (NWRC) was set up under the Ministry of Public Works (MPW). The Department of Water Supply (DWS), which provided support to the NWRC, has since been moved to the Ministry of Energy, Water and Communication. A National Water Policy was drafted with the general objective to promote national economic development, enhance regional development, upgrade environmental quality and improve the social well-being by meeting water resources needs and alleviating water resources problems. In formulating the National Water Policy (NWP), two guiding principles were recognized:

- *Water must be managed holistically.* Water resources planners must consider interdependencies among sub-sectors and uses; and they must at the same time conserve aquatic ecosystems and the wider biophysical environment. This requires coherent policies, consistent laws and regulations, collaboration among water sector institutions and carefully targeted government actions.
- *Water must be managed efficiently.* Water is an increasingly scarce resource in several regions in Malaysia and the best available management tools are needed to use if efficiently. In the final analysis, water sector management must be business-like, while observing the standards of integrity and transparency expected by the public at large.

There are other national policies and plans developed for respective sectors which will have impact on water resources management such as the Industrial Master Plan, the National Agriculture Policy, the National Environmental Policy, the National Energy Policy, the National Forestry Policy, the National Physical Plan, etc. Within each individual agency and department are also various plans and initiatives supporting IWRM. The various sectoral guidelines and policies from the various agencies such as DID, Jabatan Perancangan Bandar and Desa Semanunjung Malaysia (JPBD), Department of Environment (DOE) and others have been recorded as important initiatives and milestones.

In line with the overarching policy in IWRM incorporated in OPP3 and Eighth Malaysia Plan, there was consolidation towards integrated and holistic water-based institutions with new legislation and institutional rearrangements. These can be seen in the setting up of the Sabah Water Resources Department, the Selangor Waters Management Authority (LUAS) and the various relevant committees at state levels. The setting up of the National Water Resources Council (NWRC) and the drafting of the National Water Policy as well as the endorsement for integrated river basin masterplans for all 189 river basin management units (RBMUs) were also seen as important initiatives. The re-engineering of government machineries and the creation of the Ministry of Natural Resources and Ministry of Energy and Water and Communication was a milestone, and seen by many as an attempt as a separation of the responsibilities of resource planning and service provision.

Capacity-building is defined as training, education and information dissemination, both formal and informal. Among the initiatives highlighted have been the workshops, seminars and conferences organized for all stakeholders, curricular and co-curricular activities in environmental education in primary and secondary schools, the Masters programme in Environmental Science (IWRM) from the Open University and EPU's study on awareness and best management practices in IWRM. In information management, the development and setting up of the Registry of River Basins (RRB) for Sg Padas, Sabah, the National River Basin Information System (RBIS), the Integrated Shoreline Management Plan (ISMP) for North Pahang and West Coast Sabah and the Integrated Coastal Zone Management Plan (ICZM) for Penang, Sabah and Selangor were important initiatives. In research and development projects in Malaysia, initiatives related to IWRM are many, such as rainwater harvesting, mini wet pond, contact gravel and crystal carbon for river-water purification and treatment, water quality modelling, constructed wetlands, etc. Concurrently awareness and advocacy programmes were identified in the various capacity-building programmes and studies.

With the overarching policy in place, increased financial allocation for water-based projects such as for water supply, flood mitigation, sanitation, pollution abatement were noted. Funds were also made available for resource planning and management studies as well as awareness programmes. Alternative sourcing for funds from the private sectors were explored. Encouragements were given to developers to draw maximum and multiple benefits from mitigating structures (such as flood structures) and in the process increase added value to their properties. This can be the result of the provision of recreational facilities and enhancement in the aesthetic value of the properties. Public and NGOs' voluntary participation were also encouraged and aided.

WHAT LIES AHEAD

Both the IWRM and IRBM concepts are processes. As the country develops and moves on, continuous adjustment of these processes, for a better integration of development initiatives will be required, adapting and modifying along the way to meet the needs of the times. These will include a review of policies, financing and incentive structures and the legislative framework, and in the process creating a better enabling environment. As it is, Malaysia has yet to have a holistic and integrated water law although much progress in this direction has been seen.

Efforts at awareness and advocacy will need to be continued at the various levels and subsidiarity, so that there will be an increase in stakeholders' participation in water resource management in Malaysia. This will enable requirements of all users be accounted, considered and negotiated for, allowing for a greater chance of acceptance of development initiatives as well as pre-empting negative impacts.

There will always be a need for better and more accurate information as well as developing best management practices, particularly as the country continues to develop and change, in line with its objective to attain a developed-country status by 2020. Current capacity-building is inadequate and needs to be developed further, and there is a need to share and integrate the knowledge archives in the various agencies. This knowledge should be collated, analysed, archived and periodically updated in each of the 189 RBMUs, and be made available for planners and decision-makers. When the next review of the National Physical Plan is carried out, this invaluable information should be considered and used where applicable. There is also the need to build and explore new and cutting edge technology.

CONCLUSION

Managing water resources in an integrated manner has to be looked together with the management of the land resources of each specific area. Since the river basin is a natural physical unit on the ground, it is therefore natural and logical to manage these two natural resources, and other related resources such as human resource and finance, in an integrated manner within each river basin or a manageable sub-basin, in each development initiative.

No man is an island and no river basin is totally isolated. Managing each of the river basins is not only influenced by the needs of stakeholders within the basin. External constraints must be taken into cognizance. These include not only national overarching policies on water-related issues but also on related international agreements.

Ultimately an integrated management of the land and water resources is the management of national heritage. It is very much influenced and affected by the governance within each of the specific river basins (or sub-basins) and the country. The land use planning (location, intensity and pattern of urbanization, industrialization and type of agriculture), the planning, design and management of infrastructure projects and construction methods (including the land clearance), the management of waste disposals, the required legislation and institutional arrangement, the monitoring and enforcement of the issues and challenges, if not done carefully and if not fully integrated within the specific needs and constraints of each river basin or sub-basin, may give rise to negative impacts such as induced drought conditions, floods, pollution and diminishing biodiversity. Ultimately this will have an impact on sustainable economic development and the socio-political stability of the area concerned.

Notes

1. See Le Huu Ti and Thierry Facon (2001) and Third ASEAN State of the Environment Report (2006).
2. For more information on the WSSD, see <http://www.un.org/jsummit/>.
3. See also *United Nations World Water Development Report 2: Water, a Shared Responsibility* (United States: UNESCO-WWAP, 2006).
4. See ibid. and also *State of Water Resources Management in ASEAN.* (Jakarta: ASEAN Secretariat, October 2005).
5. Ibid., p. 5.
6. Ibid.
7. MyWP, Proceedings of First Malaysian Water Forum, Kuala Lumpur, 7–12 June 2004.

References

Awgwrm Draft Report. Draft Report of the State of Water Resources Management in ASEAN (restricted), 2005.

DID. Proceedings of the International Symposium on Management of Rivers for the Future, 1993.

DID/JICA. "National Water Resources Study, 1982".

DID/MAMPU. "DID Institutional Study" (restricted), 2003.

EPU. "Eighth Malaysia Plan 2001–2005", April 2001.

———. "The Third Outline Perspective Plan 2001–2010", April 2001.

EPU/JKR. "Master Plan for the Development of Water Resources in Peninsular Malaysia 2000–2050", March 2000.

GWP TEC. "Catalyzing Change: A Handbook for Developing Integrated Water Resources Management (IWRM) and Water Efficiency Plan", 2004.

———. "Policy Brief", 2004.

INTAN. "Malaysian Development Experience". National Institute of Public Administration, Malaysia (INTAN), 1994.

Jonch-Clausen, T. "Current Trends and Thinking in Integrated Water Resources Management". Proc Nat Conf on Sustainable River Basin Management in Malaysia, DID/MyWP, 13–14 November 2000.

Laws of Malaysia. "Federal Constitution". Kuala Lumpur: MDC Publications, 1998.

Le Huu Ti and Thierry Facon. "From Vision to Action, a Synthesis of Experiences in South East Asia". FAO and ESCAP, Bangkok, 2001.

Lee Jin. "Sector Review 2 — NGO". First Malaysian Water Forum, Kuala Lumpur, 7–12 June 2004.

MyWP. Proceedings of First Malaysian Water Forum. Kuala Lumpur, 7–12 June 2004.

Salmah Zakaria. "Country Paper — Development of National Water Resources Management in Malaysia". UNESCAP Ad-Hoc Expert Group Meeting on Policy Options and Planning in Sustainable Development of Water Resources in Asia, Bangkok, 18–20 November 2002.

_____. "Sector Review 1 — Public Sector". First Malaysian Water Forum, Kuala Lumpur, 7–12 June 2004.

Shahrizaila Abdullah. "Country Dialogue on Water, Food and Environment, Concept and Process — A Malaysian Experience". International Water Conference, Hanoi, Vietnam, 14–16 October 2002.

State of Water Resources Management in ASEAN. Jakarta: ASEAN Secretariat, October 2005.

Third ASEAN State of the Environment Report. "Towards an Environmentally Sustainable ASEAN Community". Jakarta: ASEAN Secretariat, November 2006.

United Nations World Water Development Report 2: Water, a Shared Responsibility. United States: UNESCO-WWAP, 2006.

Zelina Z. Ibrahim. "Sector Review 3 — Academia". First Malaysian Water Forum, Kuala Lumpur, 7–12 June 2004.

7

PRIVATIZATION ISSUES IN WATER SUPPLY IN MALAYSIA

Syed Danial Syed Ariffin

INTRODUCTION

One of the growing trends in the global water industry is the transfer of the production, distribution, and management of water services from public entities into private hands — a process commonly known as "privatization". The privatization of water encompasses a wide variety of possible water management arrangements. Privatization could be partial, leading to so-called public/private partnerships, or to the total elimination of government responsibility for water supply systems except for its regulatory role. This chapter presents, in part, case study undertaken by Puncak Niaga in mid-2005.

As a measure of importance of privatization, the Second World Water Forum in March 2000 gave special emphasis to the need to mobilize new financial resources to solve water problems and called for greater involvement by the private sector.[1] The "Framework for Action" released at the forum called for US$105 billion per year in new investment to meet drinking water, sanitation, waste treatment, and agricultural water needs up to year 2025. The framework also called for 95 per cent of this new investment to come from private sources.

In Malaysia, the National Water Resources Study Report produced in year 2000, which covers the planning needs up to year 2050, have recommended sixty-two water projects costing US$13.66 billion. The projects include the construction of forty-seven dams, large treatment plants and the transfer of water from one state to another.[2]

The need for new development programme and investments coupled with the need to improve current condition of assets and service definitely requires substantial capital expenditures (CAPEX),[3] which has become a fundamental problem in all privatization endeavours. In some cases, the rate of return in investment is not even adequate to even cover the operating cost, resulting in the accumulation of huge debts.

Such enormous tasks covering the aspect of developing, financing, managing and operating the water supply services have made it inevitable for private water operators to be more involved in the industry. New and innovative financing tools available to the private operators have also made it possible for them to undertake the transfer of responsibility for developing, managing and operating water supply services. The financial capabilities coupled with technological expertise have equipped private operators to tackle the enormous challenges in the water supply and services sector.

Overall, the participation of private operators in the water supply and services sector has significantly reduced the burden on the government to provide the necessary funding required to develop and improve this sector. In fact, the water sector is now a much-coveted area of participation by the private operators, mainly due to the sector being recession-proof and not affected or controlled by the fluctuations of the market.

PRIVATIZATION POLICY IN MALAYSIA

Historical Development

The Government first announced privatization as a national policy in 1983. This represented a new approach in national development policy and complemented other national policies such as the Malaysia Incorporated Policy, which was developed to underscore the increased role of the private sector in the development of the Malaysian economy.

This approach was to facilitate economic growth of the nation, relieve the financial and administrative burden of the government, reduce the government's presence in the economy, decrease public spending and to allow market forces to govern economic activities and increase efficiency and productivity in line with National Development Policy.

In respect of the ownership of wealth, privatization policy forms an integral part of the government's strategy in realizing active participation by *bumiputra* in the corporate sector to correct the imbalances in socio-economic structure. The privatized entity should allocate 30 per cent of its equity to *bumiputra*. Foreign participation in a privatized entity is limited to a maximum of 25 per cent of its share capital.

In order to ensure that privatization effort is channelled to the appropriate priority areas and to maximize the impact of the policy implementation in terms of achievement of the policy objectives, the government published the Malaysian Privatization Master Plan (PMP) in 1991 followed by the Guidelines on Privatization. The PMP explained the implementation of the policy as well as the progress achieved, and addressed the future direction of the programme. The Guidelines on Privatization detailed, among others, the objectives of the policy, the methods applicable, and the implementation machinery.[4]

Several developments have taken place since the policy was first announced. The significant changes that have been introduced include the amendments of the various laws in order to allow for privatization to take place and the commissioning of a study to help in the drawing up of a privatization masterplan.

Privatization can be implemented by several methods, namely sale, lease, management contract, build, build-operate, build-operate-transfer (BOT), build-operate-own (BOO), build-lease-transfer, land development/land swap, and management buy out. Either a single method or a combination may be chosen depending on the merits of each case. As a general rule, the methods that results in the maximum practicable degree of private sector involvement will be aimed for. In addition, the methods to be used will reflect the requirements of national objectives and the constraints in each case. In order to facilitate the implementation of the privatization programme, the Malaysian government has amended a number of laws such as the Pension Act 1980, Telecommunication Act 1950, Port Act 1963, and Electricity Act 1949.

PRIVATIZATION ACHIEVEMENT

There are 474 privatized projects as of 31 December 2003, as reflected in Figure 7.1, which shows the percentage by sectoral distribution. During the period 1996–2000, the construction sector topped the list with 27 privatized projects, followed by the service sector (20) and the transportation sector (16). Some of the public utility services already privatized are the provision of electricity which has been taken over by Tenaga Nasional Berhad and telecommunications by Telekom Malaysia.

A total of fourteen projects were approved by the government for privatization between 2001 and 2003, including four projects privatised through the build-operate-transfer (BOT) and three projects through land swap method. Table 7.1 shows the list of implementation of major privatized projects in Malaysia in 2004 and 2005 as approved during the Eighth Malaysia Plan (2001–2005).

FIGURE 7.1
Sectoral Distribution of Privatized Projects, 1983–2003
(% of Total)

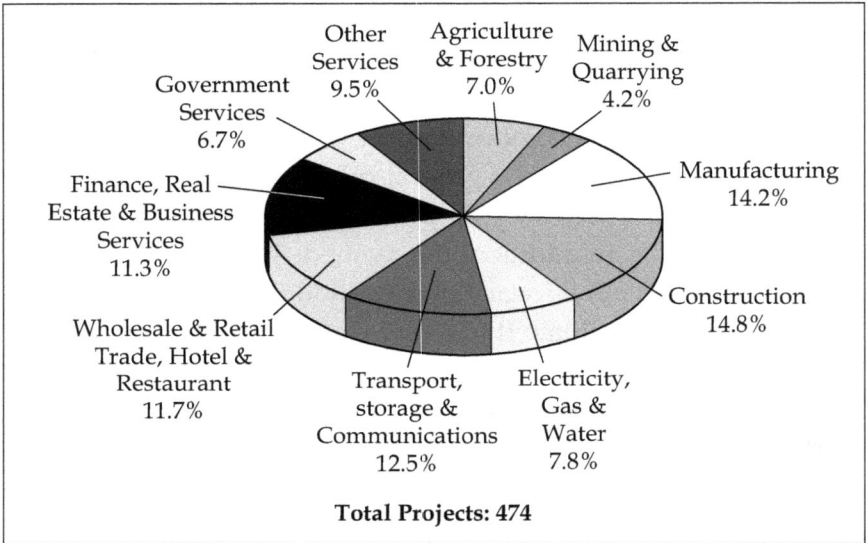

Other Services 9.5%

Agriculture & Forestry 7.0%

Mining & Quarrying 4.2%

Government Services 6.7%

Finance, Real Estate & Business Services 11.3%

Manufacturing 14.2%

Wholesale & Retail Trade, Hotel & Restaurant 11.7%

Transport, storage & Communications 12.5%

Electricity, Gas & Water 7.8%

Construction 14.8%

Total Projects: 474

Source: Malaysia Plans (various years)

Between 2001 to 2005, thirty-five projects were approved for implementation, of which ten were existing entities and services while the other twenty five were totally new projects.[5] The number of privatized projects under the "electricity, gas and water" sector in 2005 as reported in the Ninth Malaysian Plan (2006–2010) was eight. In terms of the privatization of water supply services in Selangor, it was undertaken to meet the high capital expenditure required to build dams, reservoirs and water treatment plants as well as replacing old pipes to cater to the increase in demand for water. A total of RM3.4 billion (US$0.96 billion) of capital expenditure was committed for capital works. Under the Ninth Malaysian Plan (2006–2010), the strategies for privatization include: Strengthening approval procedures, emphasizing performance standards,

TABLE 7.1
Implementation of Major Privatized Project in Malaysia in 2004 and 2005

Entity/Project	Mode of Privatization
Construction of Road Tunnel from Kg Pandan to Sungai Besi	BOT
Construction of Jalan Travers Police Stataion	LS
Construction of Marine Police Base in Lumut, Perak	LS
Construction of Immigration complex in Shah Alam	LS
Construction of Government Complex and quarters in Limbang, Sarawak	LS
Corporatisation of Malacca Water Authority	COR
Corporatisation of Malaysia External Trade Development Corporation	COR
Corporatisation of Radio Television Malaysia	COR
Management and operations of Carcosa Seri Negara, Kuala Lumpur	MC
National Solid Waste Management	MC
Privatisation of Negeri Sembilan Water Supply Department	—
Kuala Lumpur North-East Express (KLNEE)	BOT
Penang Outer Ring Road (PORR)	BOT
Senai-Desaru Highway	BOT
South Klang Expressway (SKVE)	BOT
West Coast Highway (Taiping-Banting)	BOT

Note: BOT = Build-Operate-Transfer   LS = Land Swap
        COR = Corporatizaton   MC = Management contract
Source: Malaysia, Mid-term Review of The Eighth Malaysia Plan 2001–2005, p. 161

streamlining the implmentation process, enhancing viability through risk distribution, strengthening the institutional and regulatory framework, and increasing *bumiputra* participation.

The government is expected to continue to foster greater partnership with the private sector in the implementation of development projects as well in the delivery of public services. This is expected to encourage greater contribution by the private sector in financing development projects, ensure cost effectiveness and value for money in the utilization of resources as well as improve operational efficiency.

PRIVATIZATION OF WATER SERVICES IN MALAYSIA

Currently, various authorities such as the state Public Works Department, state Water Supply Department, state Water Supply Board, corporatized entities and private companies manage water supply in the various states in Malaysia. The share of private-public responsibility for water supply in Malaysia is as shown in Table 7.2.

In Malaysia, privatization of the water supply system has made its presence felt in several states. Johor, Penang and Kelantan have privatized the construction, operation and maintenance of source works, treatment plants and distribution systems, as well as billing and revenue collection. Selangor has recently privatized its water treatment plants and distribution aspect of the water supply system including billing, revenue collection and consumer services. Other states are in various stages of corporatization and privatization of their water entities.

In line with the National Privatization Policy, more and more states are moving towards privatization to lessen the burden of high development cost of water supply programmes. Privatization is looked upon as the way forward as it will bring enhanced financial capabilities to the water supply industry. As a logical

TABLE 7.2
Share of Private-Public Responsibility for Water Supply in Malaysia

Water Supply Entities	Water Supplied (m3)	Population Served (in 2000)	Expenditure in 2000 (RM mil)	Revenue in 2000 (RM mil)
Privatized				
Selangor/ Wilayah KL	3,436,500	5,235,778	599.78	701.79
Pulau Pinang	1,049,544	1,222,994	80.74	126.37
Johor	1,285,409	2,547,162	205.37	299.16
Kelantan	213,700	683,595	30.64	31.80
Corporatized				
Terengganu	510,523	712,215	37.08	67.74
LAKU	221,380	683,595	27.07	40.98
Government				
State Public Works Department				
Kedah	987,805	1,543,205	103.54	124.04
Perlis	91,232	194,397	12.28	10.47
Sarawak	186,000	1,535,438*	43.11	20.44
State Water Supply Department				
Negeri Sembilan	527,542	826,345	42.36	68.95
Sabah	718,488	1,788,178	178.05	51.68
Pahang	762,044	1,142,382	107.43	88.05
State Water Supply Board				
Melaka	386,364	600,898	69.02	88.89
Perak	969,419	1,022,158	161.68	176.93
Kuching	380,000	-	49.78	51.44
Sibu	130,650	-	16.53	19.51
Federal PWD Headquarters				
Labuan	60,454	70,517	22.88	9.62
TOTAL	**11,917,054**	**20,518,489**	**1,787.34**	**1,895.52**

* includes Kuching and Sibu

Sources: *Malaysia Water Industry Guide 2002*; *Malaysian Business, 1–15 January 2003*; Strategic Resource Centre, Puncak Niaga, 2005.

development, the future trend is to move into a more holistic approach, covering both the treatment plants and the distribution system.

Penang and Johor have registered the highest figures of water revenues over expenditure of 57 per cent and 46 per cent respectively. This compares to the state water supply departments of Sabah and Pahang which registered a deficit of 71 per cent and 18 per cent respectively. Selangor, under its corporatized entity, registered a strong revenue over expenditure of 17 per cent.

CAPITAL INVESTMENT FOR DEVELOPMENT OF WATER SUPPLY INFRASTRUCTURE

It is a fact that the water supply industry is capital intensive and, to a certain extent, has prevented several new companies from venturing into the industry. This scenario has indirectly given the impression that this is a "closed" industry, therefore limiting the number of players to only a select few established operators and only allowing the entrance of new players which are stable and have already established themselves in other sectors of the economy. This has caused the industry to be viewed upon as an unexciting sector and given less importance by the media.

However, things have changed since 2001. The Klang Valley water crisis in 1998 and several high-profile water supply projects have managed to elevate the industry to a higher profile and this can be seen by the recent entries of several major corporate players into the industry. In the Eighth Malaysia Plan, the federal government has increased its allocation for the development of water supply infrastructure by 43 per cent as compared to the allocation in the Seventh Malaysia Plan. The big increase is indicative of the federal government concern over the need to ensure a continuous and efficient supply of treated water, both to urban and rural areas. Thus, it is expected that the private sector will play a leading role in the development of the water supply industry in the years to come.

On the part of the government, in the Ninth Malaysia Plan, it has allocated RM1.48 billion to rehabilitate the distribution the distribution network and to reduce the rate of non-revenue water.[6]

THE NEED FOR PRIVATIZATION

There are many fundamental issues in the water supply industry, among them are:

a. Escalating Cost of Water Supply Expenditure

In most state water authorities in Malaysia, water revenue is barely adequate to cover the operating cost and insufficient to finance the development of new water supply facilities. Most of the states have difficulty in carrying out major water supply infrastructure projects and fulfilling their payment obligations to the private water operators. Undoubtedly, the state needs to turn to the federal government for assistance to settle the outstanding payment issue. This situation is also prevalent in other Asian countries.

b. Increasing Rate of Non-Revenue Water

TABLE 7.3
Percentage of Non-Revenue Water: Selected States

State	% of NRW (Year 2000)
Selangor	41.64
Melaka	31.00
Negeri Sembilan	44.61
Johor	31.72

There is a need for effective water demand management to reduce non-revenue water (NRW) losses as indicated in Table 7.3. The Eighth Malaysia Plan sees the continuing replacement of existing asbestos cement pipes as well as old pipes to reduce water losses, which currently stand at 36 per cent nationwide. This clearly reflects the need for intensive capital requirement in order to develop the water supply sector. In the Ninth Malaysia Plan, NRW losses are expected to fall from 38 per cent in 2005 to 30 per cent by 2010.[7]

c. Deterioration of Raw Water Quality

TABLE 7.4
Reported Cases of Pollution in Selangor

Year	Number of cases	Types of Pollution
1999	809	Diesel/oil, odour, turbidity and colour
2000	1044	Diesel/oil, odour, turbidity and other chemicals
2001	957	Diesel/oil, turbidity and colour
2002	909	Diesel/oil, odour, turbidity and other chemicals

The lack of environmental awareness has contributed to higher investment needed in water supply projects. Table 7.4 shows the number of cases and types of pollution in Selangor, Malaysia. For example, pollution has significantly deteriorated the quality of Malaysia's rivers and this has made the task of using the river as a water source much more difficult. Therefore, in order to treat the water to an acceptable standard, the most up-to-date and expensive water treatment process has to be installed. This inevitably pushes the treatment cost higher and higher.

In Malaysia, the riverwater quality in year 2000 showed that only thirty-four out of 120 rivers can be classified as clean and free from pollution. In the Ninth Malaysia Plan (2006–2010), RM510 billion has been allocated to cleaning, preserving, and beautifying rivers.[8] This clearly shows that more effort is required to protect our raw water sources from pollution, encroachment of water catchment areas and illegal activities. This problem is not only confined to this country, the Asian region as a whole is experiencing rapid economic activities which at times are carried out at the expense of the environment. The private sector's expertise and financial capabilities are needed to adopt the latest technologies required to overcome the problem of raw water pollution.

d. Insufficient Fund to Improve Assets and Finance Further Capital Expenditure

It has now become increasingly difficult for the government to provide sufficient funding for the development of the water supply system because the financial resource requirement is enormous. *The Malaysia Water Industry Guide 2002* shows that the water supply operating expenditure exceeded revenue at the national level for the year 1998–99. Only in year 2000 did the revenue exceed expenditure by 6.1 per cent. Moreover, some of the current assets and services are not in an acceptable/working condition. Huge capital investment is required to improve infrastructual and operational efficiencies. This goes to show that privatization is the only option to cope with the rising water demand and production costs.

e. Ensuring Water for the Future

In 1997, the then Prime Minister Dr Mahathir Mohamad pointed out that the water industry must be privatized in total. It means that the private company which undertakes privatization must be responsible not only for water treatment and processing but also for the distribution, billing and other parts related to the water supply services. This is vital to ensure that the development and sustainability of the industry is maintained.

The federal government has initiated several long-term measures to meet the ever-increasing domestic and industrial demand. The National Water Policy also supports the formation of the National

Water Resources Council (NWRC) and Water Commission. In addition, the National Water Master Plan covering a planning horizon up to the year 2050 has been formulated to lay out the strategic directions, and forms the basis of the future development of the industry.

According to the NWRC, US$13.66 billion worth of water resource projects will be implemented to meet the water demand until 2050. Some major projects include the Jelebu and Batu Hampar dams in Negeri Sembilan, the Perak-Penang Raw Water transfer and the RM4 billion Pahang-Selangor Raw Water Transfer project (PSRWT). This scenario reflects the strong commitment of the federal government in facilitating the privatization programme to ensure the sustainability of water for the future.

PRIVATIZATION OF WATER TREATMENT SUB-SECTOR BY PUNCAK NIAGA (M) SDN BHD

The management of water supply services in the State of Selangor and Federal Territories of Kuala Lumpur and Putrajaya is split into two sub-sectors; firstly the water treatment sub-sector which has been privatized beginning with the taking over and management of existing water treatment plants by Puncak Niaga (M) Sdn Bhd (PNSB) in 1994. In 2008, other than PNSB, which operates twenty-nine water treatment plants and manages three dams, three other water treatment plants are operated by Syarikat Pengeluar Air Selangor Sdn Bhd (SPLASH) and Konsortium ABASS.[9]

The second sub-sector is the water distribution sector and it has been privatized to Syarikat Bekalan Air Selangor Sdn Bhd (SYABAS) on 15 December 2004. This entity is now responsible to distribute water treated by the three water treatment operators to more than 6.4 million consumers in the state of Selangor and the federal territories of Kuala Lumpur and Putrajaya.

In 2008, PNSB is the largest water supply concessionaire in Malaysia. It operates, manages and maintains twenty-nine water treatment plants with a total average production capacity of 1,929 million litres per day (mld).[10] This is equivalent to 56 per cent of the treated water requirement in Selangor and the federal territories of Kuala Lumpur and Putrajaya.

The privatization programme was principally implemented through two major concession agreements, as follows:

a. Privatization Cum Concession Agreement (PCCA)

This agreement signed in 1994 involved the taking over, operating, managing and rehabilitating of twenty-six water treatment plants (WTPs) for a concession period of twenty years until 31 December 2020. The total capacity of the works was approximately 907 mld.

b. Construction cum Concession Agreement (CCOA)

Under this agreement signed in 1995, PNSB financed the construction and is currently operating and managing the Sungai Selangor Phase 2 (SSP2) WTP. The concession will run until 2020. The RM1.3 billion project (equivalent to US$342 million) for the development of the 950 mld treatment plant was completed in December 2000.

c. Other Projects Awarded as follows:

i.   Build-operate-transfer: Wangsa Maju WTP

This fast-track project, completed within six months, was for the construction of a WTP with a design capacity of 45 mld, necessitated by the water crisis in 1997. This WTP has been operated by PNSB since July 1998.

ii.   Distribution Supply System Contracts I and II

This involved the award of two turnkey contacts at a cost of RM317 million (US$84 million) and RM294 million (US$77 million) respectively. It was for the construction and installation of pipelines, reservoirs and pumping stations to deliver the treated water from the newly constructed SSP 2 WTP[11] to water-stressed areas.

FINANCING THE PRIVATIZED PROJECTS UNDERTAKEN BY PUNCAK NIAGA (M) SDN BHD

The capital costs incurred in the privatized projects undertaken by PNSB is as shown in Table 7.5:

TABLE 7.5
Capital Costs of Privatized Projects

Privatized Project	Costs
1 Refurbishment cost for the existing 27 WTPs under the PCCA	US$39.5 million (RM150 million)
2 Design and construction of the SSP2 WTP	US$342.1 million (RM1,300 million)
3 Construction of the Wangsa Maju WTP	US$33.9 million (RM129 million)
TOTAL	**US$415.5 million (RM1,579 million)**

The total project cost included design, construction, development costs, bank charges, taxes and interest servicing during construction.

The projects was financed by a combination of the following:

- Funds generated from operations;
- Equity funds; and
- External borrowings.

The 1997–98 financial crisis had left the company exposed to the interest rate hike and high exchange rate when purchasing chemicals, machines and equipment. In undertaking these privatization programmes, the cash flow evaluation and projections at the beginning of the programmes have to be detailed and as accurate as possible. If not carefully projected, it could have brought adverse effects to the company's revenue projection.

Hence, in any privatization programme careful planning has to be given to the following factors:

- Increase in future interest rates;
- Increase in operational costs, such as chemical costs, equipment and machine costs, automated waste disposal, etc.; and
- Technological advancements.

a. Equity Financing — Flotation of Puncak Niaga Holdings Berhad (PNHB)

The funding for the privatization projects was also raised through the flotation of Puncak Niaga Holdings Berhad (PNHB), the holding company of PNSB on the KLSE main board in July 1997. The flotation project comprised the acquisition of the entire share capital of PNSB by PNHB, a rights issue and a public offering.

The rights issue and the public offering collectively raised gross proceeds of RM406.94 million (US$107 million), of which RM281.23 million (US$74 million) accrued to PNHB from the rights issue and the public issue of new shares in PNHB, and about RM125.71 million (US$33 million) accrued to shareholders pursuant to the offer for sale of existing shares in PNHB.

From the proceeds raised from the rights issue and the public issue accruing to PNHB, RM250.0 million (US$65.7 million) was applied towards part-fulfilment of the required equity contributions to PNSB's projects, RM22.23 million (US$5.8 million) towards working capital requirements and RM9.0 million (US$2.36 million) was used to cover the company's expenses for the listing exercise.

Public listing has allowed the company to obtain additional capital more easily and in larger amounts than a private company, not only through issues of shares and bonds but also other short-term lending as lenders will have greater confidence. Its quoted shares are also acceptable as consideration in merger and takeover transactions. This allows the business of the company to expand more quickly.

b. External Borrowings — Project Financing

It is a common practice in Malaysia for all major infrastructure projects to be financed via project financing. Such financing is to be raised for a particular project in a single purpose company. Project financing is different from conventional financing in that it is raised against future receivables from the project rather than raised against the strength of the balance sheet. The financing includes interest servicing during the period of construction of the project and it is usually for periods of ten to fifteen years.

PNSB have gone through two rounds of financing; the first during the early years, followed with a refinancing exercise which took advantage of favourable current interest rates:

i.   Initial Financing

In order to finance the capital expenditure required for the existing and new facilities, PNSB initially secured a combination of fixed and floating rate financing facilities amounting to RM1.28 billion (US$336.8 million), signifying one of the largest non-recourse project financing facilities to undertake a water project.

A total of RM980 million (US$257.9 million) of the fixed and floating rate facilities was replaced by a RM800 million (US$210.5 million) revolving underwritten facility (RUF), which has a lower interest cost. The remaining RM300 million (US$78.9 million) financing facility was made available to PNSB on a fixed rate basis from a government pension fund. More recently, PNSB secured a RM140 million (US$36.8 million) bridging loan to be used for financing the remainder of SSP2 Stage 2.

Financing was put in place in 1996 and repayment commenced in year 2001 and to be fully repaid in 2007.

Financing for the development of the Wangsa Maju WTP was via a Government soft loan.

ii. Refinancing

Recent developments in the Malaysian economy have resulted in reduction in the cost of borrowings. PNSB has taken advantage of the situation to refinance its existing loan facilities through fixed rate borrowings for its debts at low interest rates through the avenue of Islamic financing. This mitigates the risk of interest rate fluctuations. In line with this, the company has refinanced its existing debts through the issuance of :

- RM1,020 million (US$284.6 million) ten-year Al-Bithaman Ajil secured serial primary bonds together with non-detachable secondary bonds; and
- RM350 million (US$90.1 million) Al-Murabahah Commercial Papers/Al-Murabahah medium terms notes.

PRIVATIZATION OF TREATED WATER DISTRIBUTION BY SYABAS

Issues Prior To SYABAS's Privatization

i. Indebtness — Amount owing to WTP Operators

Under PUAS, the State Government of Selangor owed money to the WTP operators. The State Government of Selangor's ageing of outstanding receivables to PNSB as at 30 April 2004, had amounted

FIGURE 7.2

Ageing of Outstanding Receivables at 30 April 2004

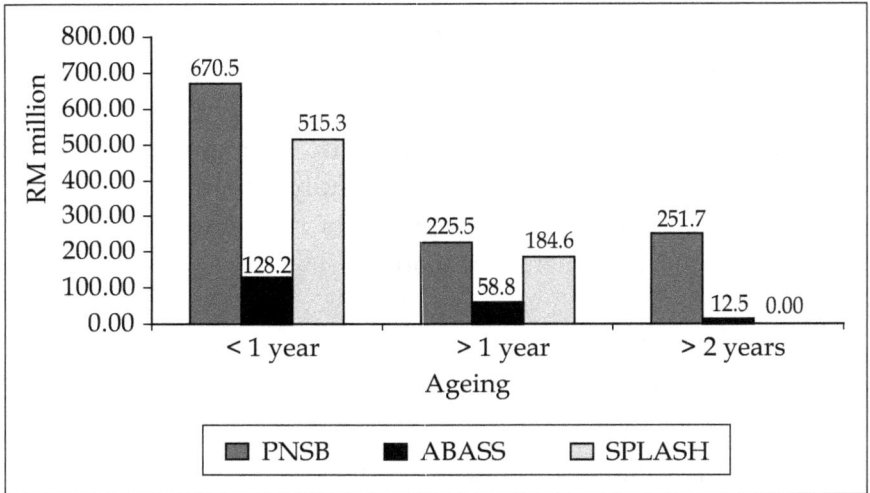

FIGURE 7.3

Amount Owing to the Water Treatment Operators

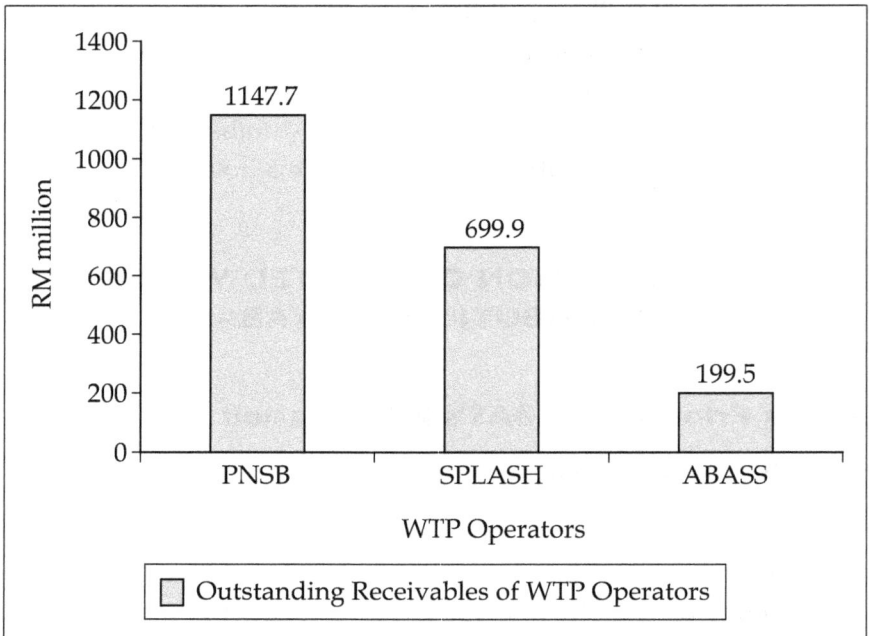

to RM670.5 million for one year and less, RM225.5 million for more than one year and RM251.7 million for more than two years (see Figure 7.2).

Among the reasons for the failure to pay the WTP operators were as follows:

a. Bleeding by the consistently high non-revenue water (NRW).
b. Long privatization negotiation process and changes in policy.
c. Wrong planning on CAPEX works.
d. Inconsistent tariff reviews.
e. Substantial increase in operating cost elements when Jabatan Bekalan Air Selangor was corporatized on 15 March 2002.
f. Poor billing and collection of revenue.
g. Poor planning in capacity development.

The amount of financial debts of PUAS Bhd /State Government of Selangor to water treatment operators is reflected in Figure 7.3.

Amount Owing to the Federal Government

Selangor State Government/PUAS Bhd had not been able to pay back the federal government's loan with a total amount outstanding at RM772.5 million.

Amount Outstanding to the Contractors for Works-In-Progress and Supplies

PUAS Bhd has committed works and supply contracts, which are in progress. The total outstanding amount committed and payable when the works are completed was about RM700 million as at November 2003.

Amount Owing to the Consumers

PUAS Bhd has used up all its consumer deposits, amounting to RM276.7 million as at December 2003, to pay for CAPEX and operating cost. This deposit is refundable to consumers.

Summary of Debt

Table 7.6 shows the summary of debts of PUAS/State Government of Selangor to the water operators, the federal government and the consumer prior to privatization of PUAS to SYABAS.

TABLE 7.6
Summary of Debts

Party	Amounts Owing (RM million)	%
Water Treatment Operators	2,047.1	53.88
Federal Government	772.5	20.33
Works-In-Progress	700.00	18.43
Consumer Deposits	279.5	7.36
Total	3,799.1	100

FIGURE 7.4
Summary of Indebtedness

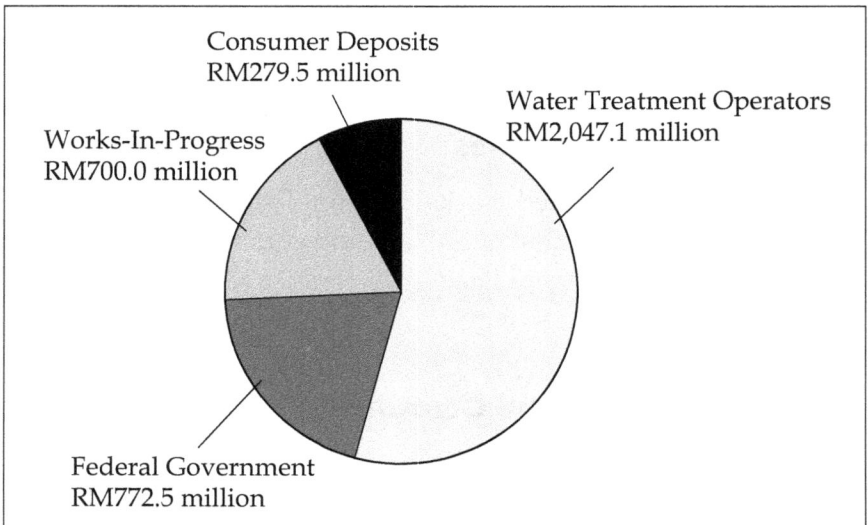

Consumer Deposits
RM279.5 million

Water Treatment Operators
RM2,047.1 million

Works-In-Progress
RM700.0 million

Federal Government
RM772.5 million

ii. The Problem of High NRW

The problem of NRW has already been there since 1990s, but limited works programmes have been planned or committed to reduce NRW. See Figure 7.5.

FIGURE 7.5

NRW Level from 1992 to 2003

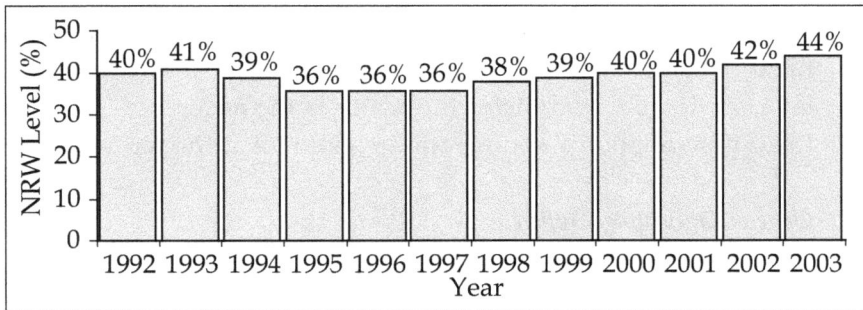

iii. Wrong Planning on CAPEX Works

The SPLASH scope of works included the development of the Rasa WTP (250 MLD) as indicated in Table 7.7.

TABLE 7.7

Development of Rasa WTP

30 Jan 2002	Completion of Rasa WTP (Stage 1)	125 MLD
31 Jan 2004	Completion of Rasa WTP (Stage 2)	125 MLD
	Total Capacity	**250 MLD**

On the development of the Rasa WTP, it was the fact that:

* Completion of Rasa WTP Stage 1 attracted a fixed capacity charge of RM2.07 million per month of RM24.84 million per year.
* Completion of Rasa WTP Stage 2 attracted an additional fixed capacity charge of RM2.24 million per month or RM26.88 million per year.

- Currently, the completed Rasa WTP (both Stages 1 and 2) are only operational at about 50 mld, which is only 20 per cent of the developed capacity.
- Despite the low production level at Rasa WTP Stage 1 after completion, the Stage 2 works were not deferred.
- The monthly capacity charge is being paid without consideration on over-planning in capacity for this project.
- Unfortunately, the extra capacity at Rasa WTP cannot be used to divert surplus water to be used in Klang Valley (which is in need of more water) due to the long distance and the cost to lay the pipeline to transfer the water is too excessive.
- It is a case of poor planning and investment at the wrong place.

iv. Overall Operating Deficit

Another issue is that SYABAS has to take over the substantial increase in operating cost elements when Jabatan Bekalan Air Selangor was corporatized on 15 March 2002. See Figure 7.6.

FIGURE 7.6
Overall Operating Deficit

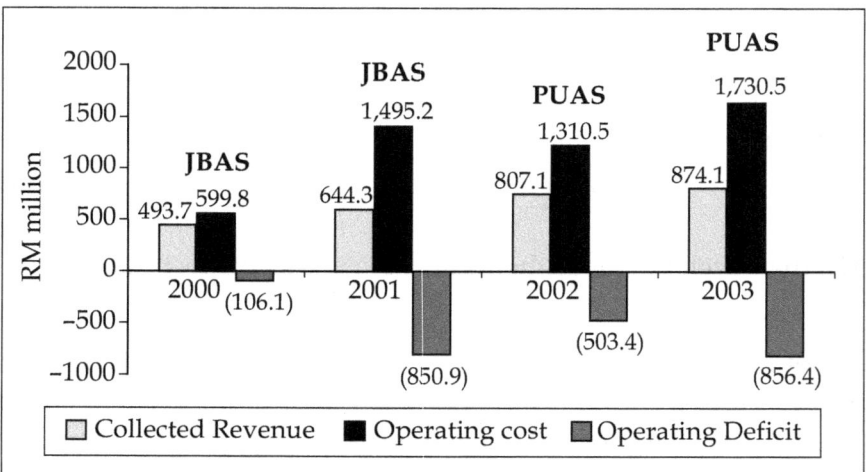

FIGURE 7.7(a)

Overall Operating Deficit:
Emoluments and Allowances Expenses

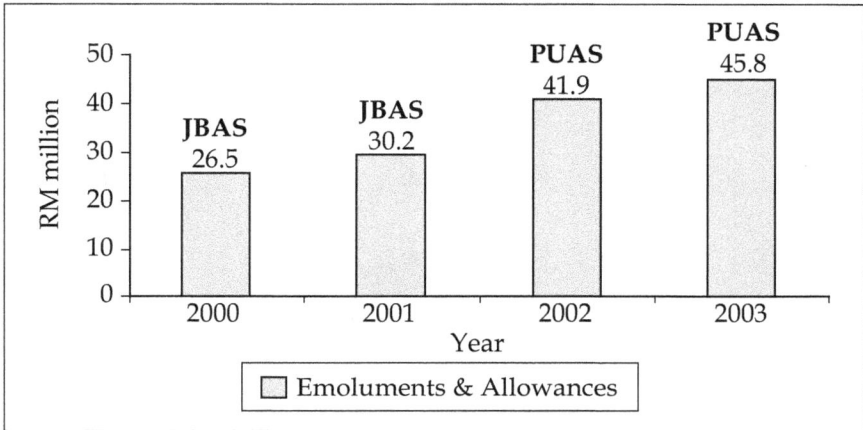

Note: Costs for emoluments increases significantly when JBAS was corporatized since March 2002.

FIGURE 7.7(b)

Increases in Various Operating Cost Elements:
Repair and Maintenance

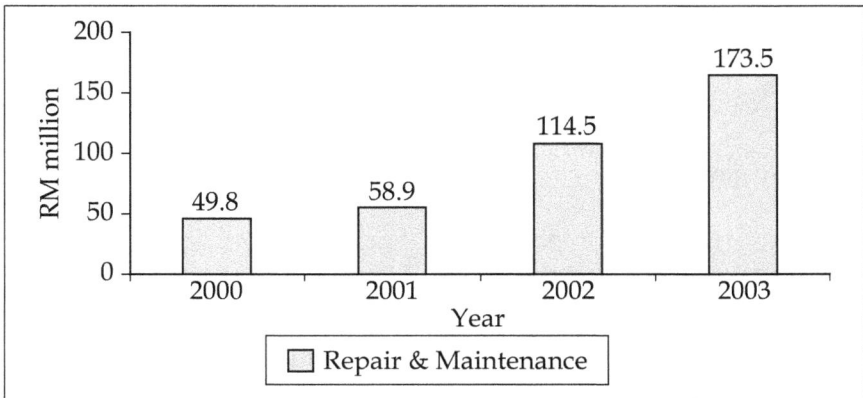

Note: Cost for repair and maintenance has also increased significantly when JBAS was corporatized since March 2002.

FIGURE 7.7(c)
Capital Expenditure

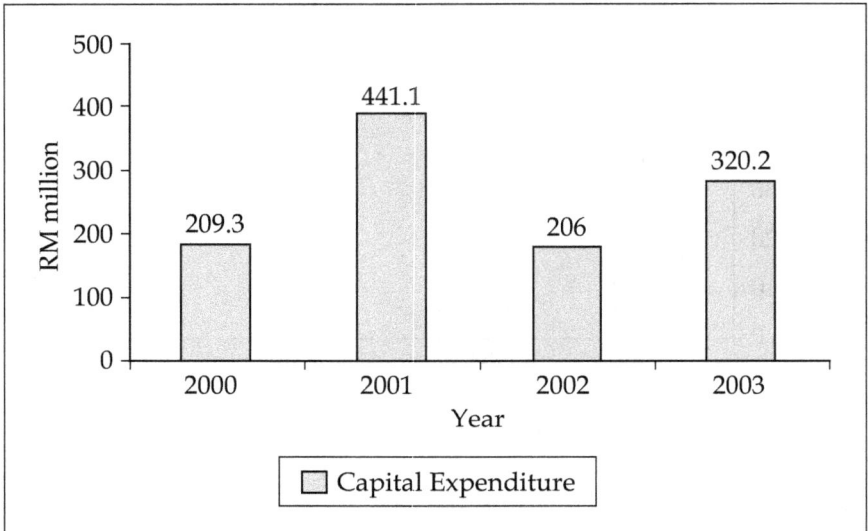

Note: Substanstial CAPEX continue to be incurred despite huge operating deficit.

The cashflow deficit (including payment for CAPEX works) for year 2003 was RM939.1 million. This means that the operating deficit has increased significantly since 2001.

v. Poor Billing

There was also a poor billing management. Efficient billing should be at least 99 per cent of account billed but there were occasions when it dropped to 38 per cent only. See Table 7.8.

There was also a substantial amount of RM176 million (70 per cent) due from consumers exceeding one month up to twenty-four months. See Figures 7.8 and 7.9.

TABLE 7.8

Percentage of Account Billed, Jan–Dec 2004

Subject	Active Accounts	No. of Account Billed	% of Account Billed
Jan	1,367,801	808,467	59.11
Feb	1,366,835	514,483	37.64
Mar	1,371,350	554,950	40.47
Apr	1,376,806	1,206,759	87.65
May	1,329,951	1,199,510	90.19
Jun	1,333,703	1,160,360	87.00
July	1,339,098	1,084,606	81.00
Aug	1,345,678	1,231,723	91.53
Sept	1,349,925	1,161684	86.06
Oct	1,347,148	1,191,277	88.43
Nov	1,350,954	1,150,941	85.19
Dec	1,347,292	1,324,048	98.27

FIGURE 7.8

Ageing of Active Consumers

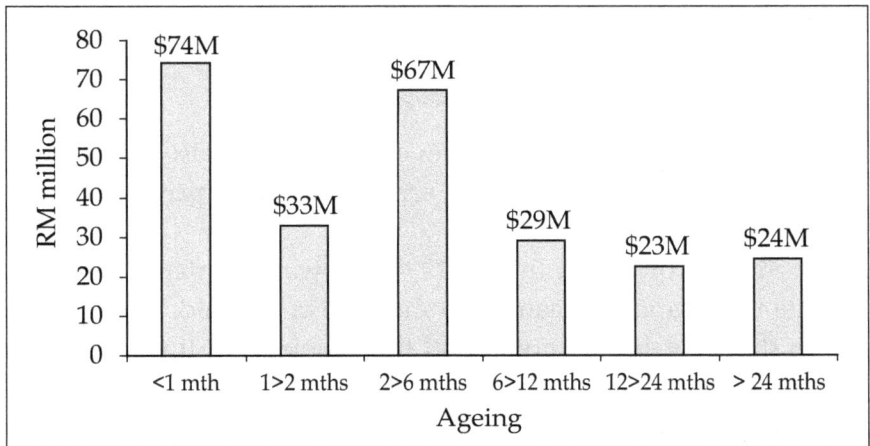

FIGURE 7.9

Ageing of Terminated Consumers

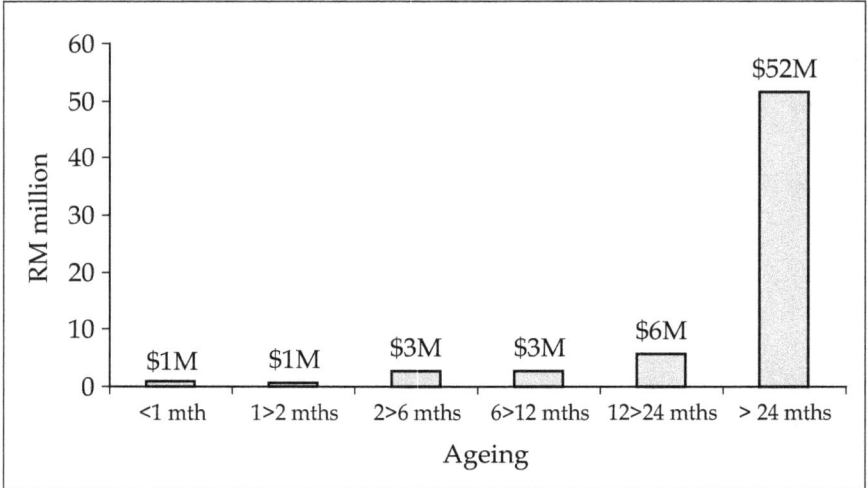

A significant amount of receivables (RM52 million) was from consumers with account closed for more than twenty-four months. It is difficult to recover this amount.

There was about RM40 million (95 per cent) from amount owing exceeding two months. See Figure 7.10.

vi. *Poor Planning in Capacity Development*

Poor planning in capacity development was also evidence of poor management of water services prior to privatization to SYABAS. See Table 7.9.

It was observed that in 1998, the water demand exceeded the WTP capacity, leading to shortage of 105 mld. The drought in that year has compounded the problem leading to a water crisis. The accelerated completion of SSP2 WTP Stage 1 (475 mld) in October 1998 has provided the relief and reduced suffering by consumers caused by the crisis. If NRW Programmes were

FIGURE 7.10
Ageing of Disconnected Consumers

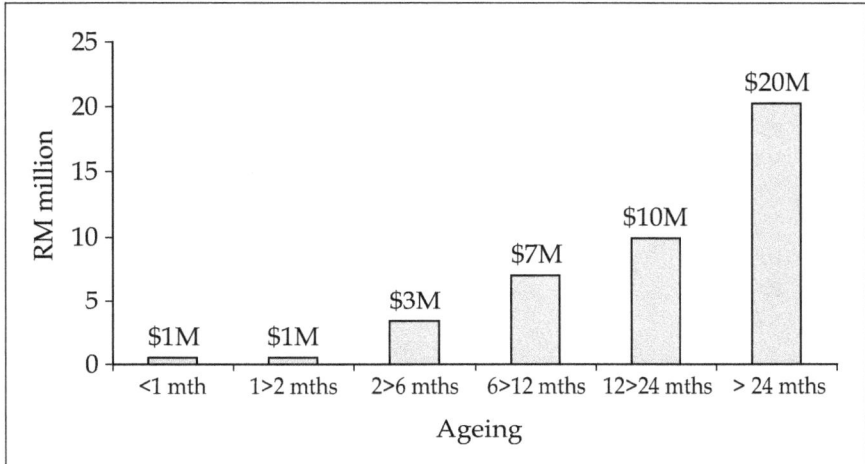

TABLE 7.9
Demand and Supply of Water (mld), 1995–2005

YEAR	DEMAND (mld)	SUPPLY (mld)	REMARKS
1995	1,920	2,078	—
1996	2,250	2,553	475 MLD — SSP1 Stage 1
1997	2,454	2,553	—
1998	2,658	2,553	105 MLD deficit
1999	2,811	3,028	475 MLD — SSP2 Stage 1
2000	2,973	3,503	475 MLD — SSP2 Stage 2
2001	3,144	3,503	—
2002	3,326	3,717	125 MLD — Rasa 1
2003	3,519	4,117	400 MLD — SSP3 Stage 1
2004	3,723	4,242	125 MLD — Rasa 2
2005	3,940	4,624	400 MLD — SSP3 Stage 2

FIGURE 7.11

Water Supply Planning

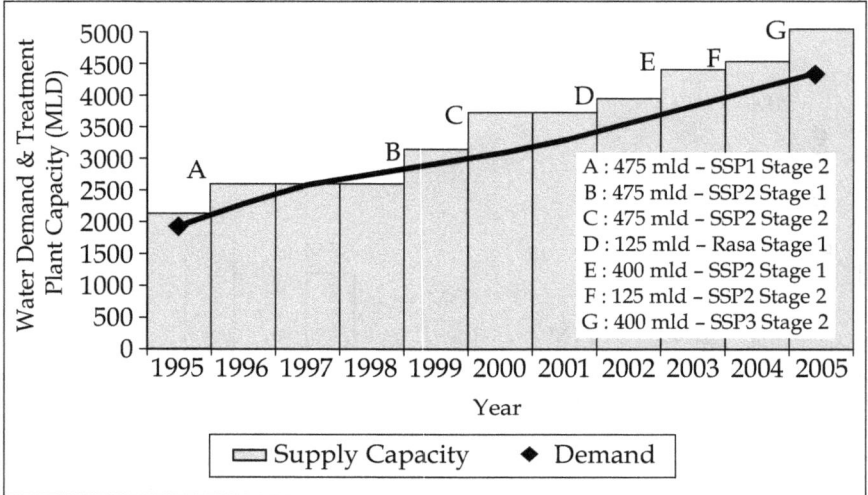

to be implemented, the construction of new water treatment plants would have been deferred. See Figure 7.11.

COMMITMENTS TO UNDERTAKE THE PRIVATIZATION OF WATER DISTRIBUTION

a. Financial

i) SYABAS will implement capital expenditure (CAPEX) works programmes amounting to RM10.7 billion to ensure that there will be an overall upgrading of water supply services via the development and upgrading of the distribution system, asset management and replacement, NRW reduction and the provision of land matters.

ii) SYABAS will spend RM99.3 billion for operating expenditure (OPEX) on water purchases, raw water royalty, NRW recurring cost, payment to the state government, repayment of loans, operating cost, payment for moveable assets and development expenses.

iii) federal government to assist in the implementation of the privatization by granting loans amounting to RM2.9 billion. This includes a RM250 million grant for SYABAS to carry out NRW reduction works.

b. Mandatory Levels of Service

For the first time in Malaysia, the concept of penalty was imposed on the privatization of water distribution services in situation of non-compliance. This was non-existent in the already privatized water companies such as in Penang and Johor.

i) SYABAS is to provide the following principal levels of service relating to the quality and quantity of treated water to consumers, failing which a penalty will be imposed.

- Quality of treated water complying with the National Drinking Water Quality Standards (revised 2000) issued by the Ministry of Health.
- Maintain adequate pressure of supply at the point the communication pipes with the following minimum residual gauged pressure during the peak flow (rural 10 metres, urban 22 metres)
- Water supply levels of coverage shall be 100 per cent for urban areas; whereas for rural areas, the director shall set a target for each operating period so as to achieve a level of coverage of at least 98 per cent by 2010.

ii) SYABAS to reduce NRW level to 15 per cent by 2015.
iii) To provide relief water for areas with water supply interruptions exceeding twenty-four hours.
iv) Failure to provide the above services will attract a penalty ranging from RM500 to RM50,000 for each failure.

c. Client Charter

i) SYABAS is to strictly observe a client charter for various consumer services covering:

- Counter service
- Response time to application
- Recovery period of interruption
- Billing schedule
- Notices and sending relief water to consumers during supply interruptions
- Response time to complaints
- Others

The government can revise the levels of service in the client charter from time to time.

d. Regulation by Government

i) The operation of the Concession Agreement is regulated by the director, a government officer as provided under the Water Supply Enactment 1997.

The director acts as the regulatory body on behalf of the state government and federal government in accordance with the concession agreement and reports to the state government in relation to works undertaken in the state of Selangor, and liaises with and reports to the federal government in relation to works undertaken in the Federal Territories of Kuala Lumpur and Putrajaya.

ii) The director is to approve the programme of works for each operating period as proposed by SYABAS.

iii) The director shall have unrestricted access to existing and new infrastructure to monitor, inspect or oversee any works.

iv) The director shall have full access to all documents relating to any works.

v) The federal and state government must also approve all tariff review documents, which are subject to vetting and verification by the government auditor.

vi) The federal government holds a golden share under Clause 24.3.

vii) The federal government or state government shall be entitled to carry out audits on the company's operational and financial matters throughout the concession period.

viii) The federal government and the state government may at least once every five years undertake a review of the terms and conditions of the Concession Agreement, and the parties may, following such review mutually modify, vary or amend the terms and conditions of the Concession Agreement.

ISSUES AND CHALLENGES

As a holistic water services provider in Selangor and the Federal Territories of Kuala Lumpur and Putrajaya through PNSB and SYABAS, the following issues and challenges have been identified to be most prevalent in implementing the privatization of the water supply services in specified areas.

Issue 1: Regulatory Environment

Under the Constitution, matters pertaining to natural resources such as land, mines, forest and water fall under the jurisdiction of the states. Water becomes a federal matter only if a dispute arises in the case of a river basin, which crosses state boundaries. State governments are responsible for water management including the gazettement of water catchments. In the country, there are fifty-six water supply dams and only eleven dams catchments have been gazetted for water supply purposes.

Water resources developments are sectorally based whereby the development of domestic, industrial and irrigation water supplies and hydropower are undertaken unilaterally by the respective agencies. Water legislations are contained within the laws that are enforced by the various water-related government agencies and are focused on limited aspects of water resources that are under the jurisdiction of the respective agencies, and there are gaps and overlaps in legislation.

Water issues are high on the political agenda. At the federal level, a National Water Resources Council (NWRC) was set up in 1998 to pursue effective water management and services. In 2003, in order to improve the national water sector, NWRC proposed federal government involvement in the formulation of an Integrated River Basin Management Master Plan for all river basins nationwide, based on priority.

The political will to improve the water sector was again manifested with the formation of the new cabinet after the Eleventh General Election on 14 March 2004. The national water sector is now being addressed with respect to improving services and conserving resources, through the formation of the Ministry of Energy, Water and Communications (KTAK), and the Ministry of Natural Resources and Environment (MONRE), respectively. The Water Supply Branch in the Public Works Department, within the Ministry of Works and Department of Sewerage Services in the Ministry of Housing and Local Government are transferred to the Ministry of Energy, Water and Communications.

The Department of Irrigation and Drainage in the Ministry of Agriculture that is responsible for surface water resources which include the management of National Hydrological Network, rivers, floods, urban drainage/stormwater run-off and coastal zones, has been transferred to MONRE. The Department of Mineral and Geosciences that is responsible for groundwater resources, Department of Environment that is responsible for raw water quality and Forest Department that is responsible for forest management are also in MONRE.[12]

Issue 2: Raw Water Pollution

Malaysia's raw water supply continue to be polluted with each passing year. The Malaysia Environmental Quality Report, various years, highlighted the following figures as shown in Table 7.10.

Table 7.10
Water Quality in Gombak and Klang Rivers, Malaysia

River basin	2002	2003	2004	2005	2006
Clean	63	59	58	80	80
Slightly polluted	43	52	53	51	59
Polluted	14	9	9	15	7

Source: Malaysia Environmental Quality Report, various years.

In Selangor, there are eleven rivers that fall under the "slightly polluted" and "polluted" categories. Among them are the major Gombak and Klang rivers that run through Kuala Lumpur city.

It is clear that the public still resorts to treating the rivers as their rubbish dumping ground. SYABAS has long established activities and programmes such as the River Rescue Brigade, educational outreach programmes to schools and factory visits to raise the awareness on preserving the rivers and its surrounding areas. However, more needs to be done in a concerted manner by all parties involved in preserving Malaysia's rivers and environment.

Issue 3: Non-Revenue Water (NRW)

An area where the public needs to be educated is the practice of stealing water. Pilferages of water have contributed 12 per cent of the NRW rate for the year 2003, which stands at 44 per cent. In Selangor and the Federal Territories of Kuala Lumpur and Putrajaya alone, there are approximately 6,000 kilometres of asbestos cement pipes which need to be replaced as they are subjected to frequent bursts and leakages.

As such, SYABAS has committed to reduce NRW to a level of 15 per cent by the year 2015 through an investment of RM2.7 billion. Failure to reduce NRW would lead to:

- Loss of revenue collected over the concession period;
- Additional cost in purchasing water; and
- Additional investment in manpower and financial resources are required to repair the burst pipes and maintain the distribution system.

Issue 4: Financial Commitments

The water services sector is a capital-intensive sector as it requires huge amounts of funding to implement water supply development works. As mentioned earlier, billions of ringgit are required to undertake the pipe replacement programme in the Klang Valley alone.

On the issue of preserving Malaysia's raw water supply, it has been mentioned that it would require more than RM1 billion to clean the Klang and Gombak rivers. The same amount was also mentioned for cleaning the three most polluted rivers in the state of Johor.

Therefore, it is clear that an enormous amount of funding is needed for maintaining the upstream and downstream activities of providing clean treated water to the public.

Issue 5: Technological commitments

Under the privatization proramme, PNSB was entrusted with the responsibility to develop the Sungai Selangor Phase 2 water supply project at a cost of RM1.3 billion. In its undertaking this exercise, Puncak Niaga evaluated numerous water processing technologies with the view to importing one which will guarantee the quality of treated water to be produced by the plant.

PNSB finally decided to introduce into Malaysia the "Actiflo" system that allows for a faster process as well as having the ability to treat water with a very high level of turbidity. In the continuing effort to try out new technology, PNSB also introduced the Dissolve Air Flotation System (DAF) for the Wangsa Maju WTP, based on technology imported from the United Kingdom.

For SYABAS, there was a need to upgrade the levels of service by introducing new technologies in the following areas:

*   Fully-integrated SCADA, GIS and telemetry system;
*   Fully-integrated call centre linked to the operation, billings and collections;
*   Fully digitized maps of the distribution system for fast access to information necessary for remedial works; and
*   Pipe-laying works to prevent the pollution of water supply and to speed up works by using a no-dig system.

There is a need to conduct intensive R&D to determine and resolve the problem of dirty water supplies and for increasing efficiency of water distribution system.

CONCLUSION

Privatization has had the benefits of:

*   Allowing market forces to drive economic activities;
*   Developing sectorial industries with a high level of professional, financing and technical managerial skills;
*   Facilitating the acceleration of economic growth, corporate expansion, efficiency and productivity;
*   Improving and enchancing competition between similar sectors; and
*   Opening the opportunity of public and institutional participation by way of investment in public listing of shares.

Some of the challenges faced by PNSB and SYABAS are as follows:

- The need to have a strong and effective regulatory framework to ensure compliance by concessionaires, and healthy competition in the industry and protection of consumers interests;
- Higher public/consumer demand for better, more competitive and satisfactory level of services and water quality with afford-able charges;
- Ensuring a sustainable tariff structure and its viability due to the long gestation period of water supply projects;
- Reducing the rate of non-revenue water (NRW);
- Having sufficient private sector financial resources particularly, which require high investments; and
- Improvement in efficiency and performance, as well as to keep pace with technological advances.

Notes

1. See <http://www.nunc.com/gb/secWWF.htm>.
2. EPU, National Water Resources Study (2000–2050), Malaysia.
3. CAPEX are capital expenditures creating future benefits. It is used by a company to acquire or upgrade physical assets.
4. See also the Eighth Malaysian Plan (2001–2005) and Ninth Malaysian Plan (2006–2010) at <http://www.epu.jpm.my> for recent updates on privatization.
5. Details from Ninth Malaysian Plan (2006–2010).
6. Speech by the Prime Minister YAB Dato' Seri Abdullah Ahmad Badawi at the Tabling of the Motion on the Ninth Malaysia Plan, 2006–2010 Dewan Rakyat, 31 March 2006 <http://www.networkmalaysia.com/subtitle/articles_9thMalaysnplan.htm>.
7. Ibid.
8. Ibid.
9. See brochure of Puncak Niaga (M) Sdn Bhd, "6th World Water Congress and Exhibition", Vienna, 6 to 12 September 2008 <http://www.iwa2008exhibitors.org/pdf/Profile%20Puncak%20Niaga.pdf>.

10. Ibid.
11. Sungai Selangor Phase 2, Water Treatment Plants.
12. See Malaysia National Report, IWRM 2005 Southeast Asia Project, United Nations Environment Programme (UNEP), September 2006.

8

TROUBLED WATERS:
Rehabilitating the Pasig River, the Philippines

Donovan Storey

INTRODUCTION

Urban Southeast Asia is experiencing an environmental crisis in which there have been few triumphs. The Asian Development Bank (ADB) considers Southeast Asia's water pollution to be "severe", more severe than China and East Asia. In particular faecal coli forms, low levels of oxygen and high levels of lead are seen as very severe; suspended solids as severe; and nitrates as a moderate but rising threat.[1] ASEAN too sees "the management of environmental problems arising from a rapidly expanding and highly diversified industry sector is one of the most important issues confronting ASEAN today".[2]

Despite widespread concern over water pollution by governments, donors and civil society there have been few examples of partnerships developing to turn the region's cities into more sustainable entities. Instead, there have been acknowledged failures in both state-led and private sector strategies. The limitations of past and present responses have resulted from, and also now contribute to discord over an urban vision and disaffection over who is responsible for pollution and what actions need to be taken. These conflicts, in turn, are the product of economic and social polarization in many Southeast Asian cities, which makes consensus over issues such as pollution and policy responses increasingly difficult. As a result, environmental conflict is becoming a new social and political fault line in the region's industrializing cities.

In surveying a number of policy responses to environmental problems in urban Asia, an inherent tension is immediately evident between the science and the politics of pollution. While pollution lends itself to measurable and quantified data, the causes and solutions are to a great extent more socio-political in origin and nature. As such, there are clear limitations in government and development agencies approaching urban pollution with immediate technical solutions.[3] McGranahan[4] has remarked that "the notion that local environmental problems can be engineered away" is a convenient fiction, suppressing the inherent tensions between social groups around the framing of environmental problems and their resolution. Pollution may be biophysical but responses often reflect strategic decisions which are based on an uneven quantity and quality of data. Invariably, policy choices reflect and result in both "winners" and "losers". These outcomes often reproduce the political ecology of individual environments.[5] Just as environmental change and ecological conditions are the product of specific political processes, these too are mirrored in policy formulation. In the context of urban planning in Southeast Asia, such dynamics need to be better understood in policy-making if planning interventions are to be supported and take root.[6]

This chapter outlines and critiques the Pasig River Rehabilitation Project (PRRP), the latest in a history of efforts to clean the Pasig River and its catchment areas. It is based on fieldwork conducted in Metro Manila over 2004–2006. It argues that in order to bring about more opportunities for progressive environmental policies in the (urban)

Philippines, there needs to be greater attention given to the wider causes of environmental degradation and increasing opportunities for policies to emerge which transcend confrontation and instead create innovative, inclusive and sustained change based on partnership and co-responsibility. This necessitates a shift away from financial and bureaucratically-driven agendas and programmes, which reinforce elite framing of the environment, towards forms of sustainability based upon progressive possibilities that exist in all cities. Carley[7] has referred to such openings as "eco-innovations", which explore new ways of fashioning citizens more effectively into participating in urban development and which involve "active partnership between business, local government and civil society at both neighbourhood and citywide level". These are not necessarily unique to the region. "Bottom-up" urban environmental projects have been successful in Thailand, Indonesia and in provincial cities in the Philippines.[8] They provide examples of how environmental policy can both succeed and be inclusive of community claims for creating socially just and sustainable cities.

PHILIPPINES:
THE LIMITATIONS OF STATE AUTHORITY

Waterways throughout the Philippines are highly polluted by any standard. Nationally, there are over 400 principal rivers, 7 major river basins, 6 major and 52 minor lakes, and a number of significent swamplands. Of these, a Department of Environment and Natural Resources (DENR) study has recently documented that 180 of the country's 421 main rivers and other bodies of water are so heavily polluted that they may soon be declared biologically dead. Fifty of these major rivers are already considered biologically dead. They include four rivers each in Metro Manila, Cebu and Negros Occidental.[9]

Chronic water pollution in Manila dates back to the nineteenth century with *esteros* (artificial and natural estuaries) and the Pasig

River being described as cesspools which were unfit for even washing clothes.[10] More recently serious policy attention did not emerge until post-war concerns over industrial pollution were expressed in the 1950s and 1960s. From this point legislative response has not been lacking. Indeed the Philippines offers a plethora of environmental legislation dating back several decades. Congress enacted Republican Act (RA)3931 in 1964 to protect air and water of the country and also created the National Water and Air Pollution Control Commission (NWAPCC), to maintain "reasonable standards of purity for the waters and air of this country" and to

> adopt, prescribe and promulgate rules and regulations for proper implementation of the Act; to make or modify orders requiring discontinuation of air and water pollution; to issue, renew, permits for the discharge of sewerage, industrial wastes or other wastes as a means of preventing/abating pollution; and to hold public hearings with respect to the violation of this Act, before the Commission.[11]

This later became the National Pollution Control Commission (NPCC) which was responsible for the regulation and enforcement of pollution control and setting standards, though initially it had no powers to either ensure compliance or punish polluters.

Following these initiatives, Presidential Decree (PD) 1151 (the Philippine Environmental Policy) and PD1152 (the Philippine Environment Code) came into effect in 1977. PD1151 outlined "that it is a continuing policy of the State to create, develop, maintain and improve conditions under which man and nature can thrive in productive and enjoyable harmony with each other".[12] It also recognized the right of people to a healthy environment. PD1152 then set the standards for this, including prohibiting solid waste disposal into the sea, including shorelines and river banks.[13]

A further key piece of legislation, PD984 (the Pollution Control Law of 1964), allowed the NPCC to enforce rules and regulations and impose penalties and fines, which included the threat of closure. However, some regulations gave no thought to enforcement capabilities and even bordered on the absurd. For example, on air pollution the NPCC prohibited:

> any person from causing or allowing emissions of smoke from gasoline-powered vehicles on any street, highway or other public roadway that is visible within the proximity of the engine exhaust outlet for a period of more than ten consecutive seconds...; any person from allowing emission of smoke from diesel powered motor vehicles and other moveable sources on any street, highway or public roadway of a shade or density greater than 20 per cent capacity for more than ten consecutive seconds; and any persons from causing or allowing emission of carbon monoxide from motor vehicles on any street, highway or other public roadway that is greater than 40 per cent by volume.

In the mid-1970s greater effort was made to create inter-agency institutions to deal with environmental pollution. This led to the creation of the Inter-Agency Committee on Environmental Protection (IACEP) within the Department of Natural Resources. However, the establishment of a Ministry of the Environment as such was resisted, as it would cross-cut twenty-two separate government agencies and this would not work "in view of the Filipino trait of non-interference among equals".[14] One outcome was that the IACEP banned heavy industries from operating within 50 kilometres of Metro Manila and industrial designations were made distinguishing polluting/non-polluting and hazardous/non-hazardous businesses. Nevertheless, the implementation of restrictive regulations in a period of rapid growth and industrialization in which the political elite had an economic stake, meant that few serious impediments were put in the way of even highly polluting factories.

Despite the creation of a number of environmental codes factories continued to openly pollute the environment with little fear of punishment. The main problem was seen to be coordination, so the National Environmental Protection Council (NEPC) was established in 1977 through PD1121 to rationalize government functions; formulate policies and issue guidelines (especially on environmental quality standards and impact assessment); to undertake research; check environmental assessments of projects submitted for government approval; and to monitor projects. The Solid Waste Management Act (RA9003) and several administrative orders sought to control waste. However, key tensions apparent in environmental legislation throughout this period were to be found in the "trade-off" between development and the environment. Nowhere was this tension more evident than in the environmental legislation that emerged during the Marcos dictatorship, which on the one hand espoused the importance of community involvement and claimed to have "a new orientation on community and public participation in environmental protection",[15] yet on the other maintained that environmental policies should not impede development; "development can and must continue ... Environmental standards and conditions need not stand in the way...".[16] A number of these apparent contradictions, between development, community participation and environmental policy, continue to exist today. Consequently while the Philippines may be considered to have comprehensive legislation on the environment, it nonetheless remains "rule burdened but not rule bound". As Ohmachi and Roman have summarized, "Government leadership regarding environmental issues in Metro Manila is weak, the financial means available for environmental management meagre."[17] What is not lacking is the quantity of legalisation as well as the number of "stakeholders" involved in policy and implementation. At present around thirty government agencies are currently involved in water resources management and approximately fourteen water-related acts of legislation exist, dating back to 1938.[18]

INCOMPLETE DECENTRALIZATION AND LOCAL-CENTRAL GOVERNMENT CONFLICT

Of the manifold governance challenges facing the Philippines, tensions between the state, national bureaucracy, local authorities and communities remain central. Governance conflict, which occurs within institutions as much as between them, is a serious impediment to sound and consistent environmental policy. It emerges in the form of confusing jurisdictions and powers of litigation; a lack of coherent policy development and implementation (especially on issues which require inter-agency collaboration); and inconsistent monitoring, evaluation and consensus building.

For those who argue that decentralization offers a cure for poor environmental regulation and enforcement, the Philippines offers only lukewarm support.[19] While the 1991 Local Government Code (LGC) decentralized many functions from central to local government units (LGUs),[20] a culture of patrimonialism and the financial weakness of local government has ensured that true power has remained largely in traditional (individual and institutional) hands. In the case of environment policy and agencies, decentralization has been incomplete, which has resulted in muddled and blurred responsibilities and actions between the centre and local government. This tension is illustrated in Section 3 of the LGC which states that "LGUs shall share with the national government the responsibility in the management and maintenance of ecological balance within their territorial jurisdiction, subject to the provisions of the Code and national policy." Yet, Section 17 of the code adds that any local action is "subject to national policies and subject to supervision, control and review of the DENR".[21] This is made even more complex in terms of an already somewhat chaotic governance structure of Metro Manila, with mayors, urban government agencies, NGOs and the governor of Metro Manila all vying for control and influence over policy.

Pollution control laws and other laws on the protection of the environment are pursuant to national policies and also subject to the supervision, control and review of the Department of Natural Resources (DENR).[22] Yet, city mayors and *sangguniang* [councils] are expected to adopt adequate measures to "protect the environment and impose appropriate penalties on acts which endanger the environment" including "activities which result in pollution, acceleration of eutrophication of rivers and lakes, or of ecological imbalance".[23] This creates a situation in which ultimate responsibility is ambiguous at best. Expertise in the form of human resources but also key data is also still primarily held at the centre. For example only 4 per cent of DENR staff were devolved into local bodies in the 1990s (other departments reached as much as 50 per cent). Though given greater responsibility, LGUs remain weak in terms of revenue, resources, and recruits. LGUs tend to be given service responsibility, but not the appropriate authority or human resources necessary to effectively respond to a raft of difficult and pressing challenges. This is especially so regarding the "brown sector" (pollution sector), covering industry and large-scale development, which receives the least amount of DENR personnel and resources. Indeed Chua and Coronel[24] regard pollution control as the DENR's "poor cousin". A lax attitude to pollution is not aided by LGUs being generally welcoming of high-pollution industries for investment and employment, but vulnerable to the financial and political power owners' wield.

Some have even claimed that it is the DENR itself which poses the greatest threat to the environment. Chua and Coronel[25] have argued that "the DENR is not an independent scientific institution; it is an agency of government with a strong political and economic agenda". The DENR is a somewhat schizophrenic agency. Its role as one of the country's most powerful "development" agencies has lead to corruption in several forms: "field personnel have been known to distort land survey results, decrease reported volumes of confiscated logs, fake inspections, approve permits without basis, or simply look the other way in the face of violations of environmental regulations".[26] Given the small penalties imposed for breaching environmental laws (fines are typically P50,000 (about US$1,000) or less) many firms prefer to pay fines rather than comply with environmental regulations. This is especially the case if compliance requires the purchase and maintenance of technology which may run into millions of pesos.

The Philippines case clearly illustrates the limits of State and even local government power in enforcing policies towards sustainability through environmental legislation. The failure of a planning approach which has relied on a traditional "study, plan, execute" model,[27] while not unique to the Philippines, demonstrates the weaknesses of an approach which depends upon a centralised and top down form of governance. Nowhere is this more evident than in the unexceptional gains made in addressing the Pasig River's chronic pollution over a number of decades.

THE PASIG RIVER

The Pasig River is a tidal estuarine ecosystem 27 kilometres in length, averaging 91 metres in width yet only four metres in depth (see Photo 8.1). These averages conceal great seasonal variations with dry season stagnation of the river (March to May) in contrast to flooding and high flows in October-November. This latter period provides an essential annual "flushing" of the river system. The Pasig passes through nine cities of Metropolitan Manila and acts as an outlet for thirteen major river tributaries as well as playing an important role in the health of Laguna de Bay (Laguna Lake). Its geographical catchment is sizable, encompassing five river basins and 215 square kilometres, which constitutes one-third of Metro Manila's total land area.[28]

As such the Pasig receives a myriad and substantial amount of waste. An estimated 1,000 tonnes of solid and liquid waste are dumped into the river daily, of which 200 tonnes is recovered (see Photo 8.2). At least 300 factories operate along its banks and a further 12,000 industrial and commercial establishments are located in the Pasig River's catchment area. In addition, approximately 175,000 urban poor live alongside the Pasig River's banks; a similar number also live along its major tributaries in the catchment area; while more than 50,000 more live alongside and on top of *esteros* (estuaries).[29] With a sewerage and sanitation system that reaches only 5–10 per cent of the city's 12 million residents, there are an estimated 1.1 million septic tanks in use in Metro Manila, many of which are old, unserviced and subsequently leak substantial amounts of human waste in the wet season. In short, in the absence of services and infrastructure, canals and rivers act as open sewers for large numbers of businesses, urban poor and non-poor alike.

In the early 2000s there were an estimated 5,345 tonnes of solid waste generated each day in Metro Manila, with approximately 75 per cent of this collected. These estimates (which are perhaps conservative) suggest that 475,000 tonnes of solid waste is not collected each year.[30] Much of this waste finds its way into the city's major river systems directly or through its *esteros*. Feeder rivers into the Pasig River are heavily polluted. For example, the Navatos-Tullajan-Tenejeros River system receives waste from over 100 large industrial and 200 smaller industrial and commercial firms.[31] A 1999 study showed Dissolved Oxygen (DO) to be almost zero at the junction of the San Juan and Pasig Rivers, the result of pollutants in the river being greater than the capacity for natural decomposition. While dredging is occasionally carried out, sludge is often toxic. In the past, this has been dumped in Manila Bay, which has further contaminated sea life and led to increased problems of "red tide". This "footprint" of river pollution has been devastating for the fishing industry, with yields declining by a substantial amount in Laguna de Bay from the 1970s.

There are of course significant threats to human health from highly polluted waterways.[32] As McGranahan et al. have noted "neither people nor pathogens act within well-defined boundaries".[33] This is manifested in substantial cases of diarrhoea and the threat to ecosystem integrity at local and regional levels. Coliform bacteria, which indicates sewerage contamination, shows very high levels in coastal waters. In the late 1990s faecel bacteria counts in three sites of the Pasig system (Navatos, Bacoor and Luneta) were recorded as being 240 to 17,000 times the limits for safe bathing (1,000/100 ml).[34] Diarrhoea, intestinal worms, typhoid

**PHOTO 8.1
The Pasig River**

Source: *Photo taken by the author*

**PHOTO 8.2
Solid Waste**

Source: *Photo taken by the author*

and cholera from poor sanitation and hygiene still menace urban residents, particularly the poor and children, but water pollution also includes a financial health cost to all (estimated by the World Bank at US$134 million annually).[35]

SOURCING POLLUTION

Far from being a technical exercise, identifying the source and responsibility of pollution is a highly sensitive and political act. Estimates vary considerably depending upon the agency involved or the measurement used. The DENR estimated pollution sources in 1997 as 60 per cent domestic; 35 per cent industrial; 5 per cent municipal.[36] Other calculations have put the breakdown at 45 per cent industrial waste; 45 per cent domestic sewerage; and 10 per cent domestic solid waste, while Hingco[37] has reported that in the Navatos feeder system 48 per cent was domestic sewerage; 35 per cent industrial waste and 17 per cent solid waste. These estimates clearly identify domestic sources as the principal origin of non-industrial waste but there are wide variations on measuring pollution.[38] As an example, popular media outlets regularly cite domestic sources as representing anything between 70–90 per cent, though Greenpeace Southeast Asia has noted that many forms of toxic pollution are not even assessed.[39]

Sources of pollution are clearly related to class. About half of Metro Manila's population live below the income poverty line, and 55 per cent of these urban poor earn less than the food threshold alone.[40] For example a 1995 World Bank report showed that 91 per cent in the lowest 30 per cent income bracket had no access to solid waste disposal, whereas those in the top 50 per cent had a 74 per cent regular collection rate.[41] While the poor may contribute the greatest amount of solid and liquid domestic waste into rivers and estuaries, they also are exposed to the greatest health risks as a result of limited access to services and infrastructure.

The logical outcome of these inequalities is that it is the urban poor who are responsible for much of the river pollution in Metro

Manila. For example, Charifa[42] has stated that "the continuing urbanization of Metro Manila coupled with the illegal construction of squatter shanties in esteros and other waterways ... contribute to the deterioration of our water system". Similarly, the NPCC contended that most pollution was caused by general public (70–80 per cent) rather than industry (20–30 per cent) "because of domestic sewerage and the indiscriminate disposal of garbage in the esteros and rivers".[43] However, to date very few of the river system's 12,000 industrial and commercial establishments have participated in waste minimisation and control programmes, casting some doubt on what we know about industrial pollution and revealing a lack of political commitment to holding private sector polluters accountable.

Measuring pollution is weighted towards measuring domestic sources of pollution, and therefore gives greater account to the impacts of the poor on water quality. Heavy metals are less regularly and rigorously tested, or in the case of some forms of toxic pollution (such as nickel) are rarely tested, if at all. Waterways are mostly monitored for colour, temperature and pH, dissolved oxygen (DO), BOD, solids and total coliform.[44] Yet a 1993 report on the Pasig River and Manila Bay cited high and fluctuating levels of lead, cadmium, zinc and copper.[45] While it is assumed that the urban poor are responsible for the high levels of organic waste, other key sources of DO-lowering industries are sugar mills and distilleries, pulp and paper mills, markets and food manufacturing plants.[46] Thus, the Pasig River is used by a range of actors as an open gutter. Today only six fish species and two plant species survive in its dark and often stagnant waters.

REVIVING THE PASIG RIVER:
A NEW BEGINNING?

It is within this context that the most recent project to revive the Pasig River has emerged and is best understood. The challenge is not an envious one. As Constantino-David[47] has noted, "every previous administration for the past 40 years has tried to revive the river, and each has failed".

The current initiative to revive the Pasig River has a number of possible starting points, but the most contemporary is the interest shown during the presidency of Fidel Ramos (1992–98) and the creation of the Presidential Taskforce on the Rehabilitation of the Pasig River (PTRPR) (AO 74, 1993). The taskforce aimed to upgrade water quality by 2005, but met with limited success. This was complemented by the "Peso for the Pasig" fundraising drive chaired by the First Lady and which continues today. These initiatives were subsequently given a new sense of momentum by the ill-fated administration of President Josef Estrada (1998–2001). President Estrada's ambitions were more wide ranging and ambitious, namely "to resurrect the river (dredging, revetment walls, minimising water pollution, etc.); relocate the settlers within the ten-metre easements; restore it as a viable means of alternative transportation, and create open spaces along the banks".[48] A revised deadline of 2014 was set. Rehabilitation was driven by a mission and vision "to restore the Pasig River to its historically pristine condition by applying bio-eco engineering and attain a sustainable socio-economic development" which reflected "the country's noble history and socio-economic progress".

A commission of cabinet ministers was created in January 1999 with project funding coming from a number of donors and sources, the most significant being DANIDA (in terms of research) and the Asian Development Bank (ADB).[49] From that point the ADB played a key role in the financial and administrative support for the project, with total support comprising US$175m for Phase One (2000–08). To a great extent the current effort to rehabilitate the Pasig River is portrayed as an ADB initiative and staff initially saw wider opportunities through successfully addressing river pollution. It was believed that the Pasig could be "the jewel of the city" within the fifteen-year timeframe. Successfully addressing the plight of the Pasig would also be a catalyst for wider environmental change and of urban renewal. This latter responsibility however, in developing nearby Urban Renewal Areas (URAs) for relocated communities, would remain the responsibility of national and local government agencies.

The Pasig River Rehabilitation Commission

In order to coordinate the various stakeholders associated with efforts to revitalize the Pasig River system the Pasig River Rehabilitation Commission (PRRC) was formed in 1998 under the Estrada presidency and created through EO54 on 6 January 1999 "to promote policy reforms and physical improvements to enhance the water quality of the Pasig River, its tributaries and *esteros*" to a water quality of Class C (a water quality level acceptable for recreational use; fish and wildlife habitat; agricultural and industrial supply and other legitimate uses including navigation). In so doing its target was to "transform the Pasig River and its environs into a showcase of a new quality of urban life" through:

- Improving the water quality of the Pasig River through strategic investment on proper waste collection and waste treatment structures;
- Improving the level of awareness in Metro Manila residents on the value and function of the Pasig River and its tributaries;
- Increasing local revenue by improving the planning and management capabilities of local government units;
- Ensuring sustained management of the Pasig River through riverfront development based on sound land valuation.[50]

Initially the PRRC intended to be inclusive of those both heading the project as well as commuinities (including NGOs) affected by it, but in effect it primarily included government and private sector interests. This representation has morphed over time. In 2004, seventeen government and non-government agencies were represented but in 2006 the PRRC fell under the orbit of the DENR with co-chairing from the Metro Manila Development Authority (MMDA). The PRRC today is comprised of thirteen national government agencies, the Metro Manila Mayor's League and three "others"; Clean and Green Foundation (an NGO chaired by former first lady Amelita Ramos), Unilever Philippines and a media outlet, GMA-7 Network. Hence by 2008, PRRC composition had essentially narrowed to government, business interests and a mainstream NGO.

While in theory the PRRC is the coordinating body of the Pasig River Rehabilitation Project, in practice it has suffered from division and weakness in relation to more powerful government agencies and businesses. These weaknesses also derive from the dysfunctional relationships which exist between and within key organizations represented on its board. Before coming under the direction of the DENR, the PRRC was predominantly staffed by young professionals, and suffered from a lack of political clout and a clear mandate. Against departments, such as the Department of Public Works and Highways (DPWH), the DENR, Metro Manila mayors and even some NGOs, the PRRC failed to establish either consensus or respect. This meant that even progressive ideas made little headway into patrimonial systems which permeate Philippine environmental politics. In particular, the PRRC remained on the sidelines of wider political turf battles between LGUs, the MMDA and government departments. Given that the PRRC had no significant powers of its own, it remained weak and therefore gave the impression of a fragile project with ephemeral political commitment.

More recently former Manila Mayor "Lito" Atienza has taken over the chair's role. While this has arguably given the PRRC greater political clout and experience, it has essentially moved it into the orbit of government, reflecting powerful interests and elite views. A more politically powerful PRRC may be better funded and staffed but it also ensures a distance between the project and those affected. In particular it has acted to further marginalize voices of critical NGOs and CBOs, many of which work with riverside communities.

The Ten-Metre Easements — a.k.a. Environmental Preservation Areas (EPAs)

One of the more contentious "achievements" of the Pasig River rehabilitation project to date has been the emphasis placed on creating ten-metre easements. Drawing in part upon legislation initially dating back to the Marcos Martial Law period, the creation of ten-metre easements is seen by those directing the project as critical to allow room for public access and enjoyment of the river, and also maintenance. The space created through easements is then developed into "linear" or "people's parks" (there will be twenty-nine in all). By mid-2008, fifteen parks had been completed, covering an estimated 24.5 kilometres along the Pasig River. Though it has taken an enormous effort to create and secure riverside parks, they are nevertheless seen as an important move in creating accessible and picturesque environments along the Pasig River's banks.

Though an integral part of the project, even ADB staff have admitted that the EPAs have created "terrible, terrible problems" between stakeholders. For others though, including the government which is "comfortable" with a ten-metre easement, the project "necessitates" the clearing of areas for parks. Criticisms have been levelled at the cost of essentially aesthetic constructs which will have little or no impact on water quality. For example, the cost of the initial fifteen parks was estimated at US$5.8 million. The cost of one promenade alone, Muelle del Rio was P51.6 million (see Photo 8.3). Though considered financially "impossible" at the time, this would have funded in-city land for 287 families (approximately 1,500 people).

PHOTO 8.3
Meulle del Rio Linear Park

Source: Photo taken by the author

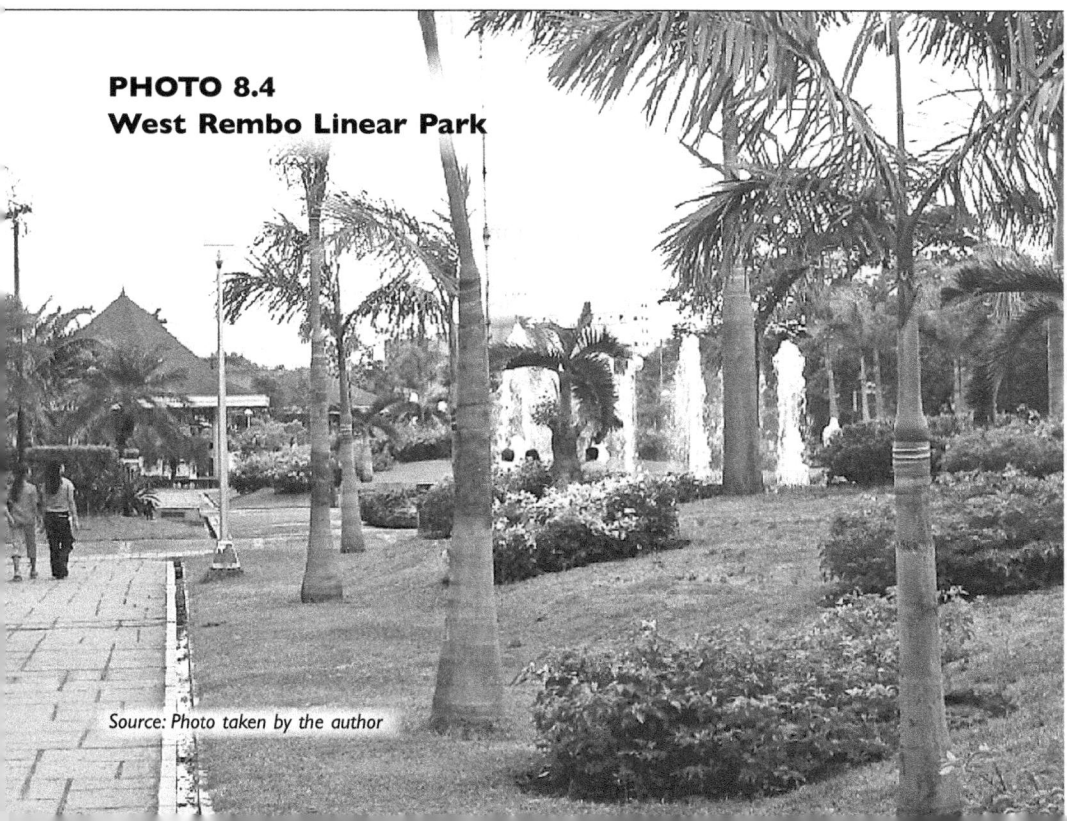

PHOTO 8.4
West Rembo Linear Park

Source: Photo taken by the author

Despite continued resistance, parks have been developed as "neighbourhood lungs" and "aesthetic additions to the urban landscape". One PRRC official commented that "we don't necessarily want to be in the business of building parks ... but the linear parks are to prevent people going back"; it is "a strategy" to ensure clearance. Others involved in the environmental components of the project are more hard-line: "the ten meter strip will be cleared. ... If we make one exception the whole thing will be a waste of time". Stilted houses on or near the water were seen as "unmanageable". Resistance to these easements from the urban poor was put down to problems of a national "culture of squatting".

Perhaps no other objective highlights the chasm which exists between donors, government and the poor than the creation of EPAs. For the DENR, Environmental Preservation Areas represent the ideals of planning. For those affected by river rehabilitation, EPAs represent an elite and exclusive representation of both space and nature. This essentially aesthetic and arguably elitist ideology of space is captured in one submission to the PRRC's own magazine, *The River Post*, entitled "A Glimpse of the Vitality that is Pasig River":

> Serene, calm and captive. Peaceful and yet ever changing and full of life ...
>
> The environmental protection areas of Pasig River, completed and on-going linear parks, walkways and greenbelts. They show a lot of promise in fulfilling the vision. Especially the recently inaugurated Meulle del Rio park, now clear and orderly, beautiful and refreshing, providing a needed respite to the ever present noise of urban life, enhancing and inviting one to nearby Arroceros Park, so full of trees, so green, so alive.
>
> Such is the Pasig River Park experience, a reality, a glimpse of the future — of what it could be. Find an answer to why man, after achieving tremendous progress, has to go back to Mother Nature. Experience a feeling of rest, of contentment — feelings that perhaps could not be explained but by the oneness of man and nature.[51]

Relocation and Resistance

The creation of twenty-nine EPAs will officially require the removal of at least 10,000 riverbank dwellers, though this estimate is a gross undercount of the number of urban poor that would likely be affected.[52] By mid-2008 approximately 6,300 people had been relocated to five resettlement sites. However, according to one NGO which works in relocation areas, many have returned to informal settlements back in the city and few have benefited from planned livelihood initiatives, increased tenure security or better quality shelter which were offered as part of the social objectives of the project. Thus Pasig River rehabilitation, or more accurately, its aesthetic redevelopment, continues an unfortunate and essentially negative history of forced eviction and failed relocation policy in the Philippines.[53]

The eviction and relocation of riverside communities has proven contentious and a source of conflict between communities, NGOs and institutions coordinating and executing the project. For those who have lived through a number of "good" reasons given for demolition in the past, eviction for whatever reason is viewed as part of a historical demonisation of the poor and hostility toward their right to space.[54] Given that urban poor communities constitute only 10 per cent of settlement along the Pasig River (90 per cent is privately owned, and is too expensive for government to acquire), poorer communities often protest that it is they who must make way for parks for others to enjoy. Community leaders and residents have increasingly taken the view that environmental rehabilitation is a less likely reason for the project than a "land grab" by the elite, a point supported by the development of expensive highrise houses alongside the river, few of which effectively treat waste which enters into the river system.

Relocation, and resistance have dogged the project and provided significant "bad press" for those involved. To some extent this represents the failure of project governance, as social housing and livelihoods (in the form of Urban Renewal Areas) were largely the responsibility of local government rather than donors and central agencies. PRRC and ADB officials regularly concede that relocation sites have been a problem. Many are distant (in some cases more than 50 kilometres from the city centre), lack livelihood options and have little in the way of infrastructure and services. Given that there is little or no provision for alternative land acquisition and development in the project (this is left to government departments and LGUs which have a poor track record) resistance to relocation has been strong and the poor have painted the project (somewhat successfully) as an eviction campaign.[55] In short, NGOs and communities have largely dug in.

Environmental Impacts

The impact of the Pasig River rehabilitation project on the environment after a decade is not yet clear. While ADB officials feel that industrial pollution is better regulated now than before others admit that monitoring remains "spotty". Over 400 factories have been summonsed under tighter enforcement of the regula-tions, many of which have been fined, cleaned up their activities, have moved elsewhere, or have closed down. While pollution loads have stabilized or improved since the mid-1990s these gains remain fragile, dependent on the annual flushing of the river system by rains or, according to one senior official involved in the project "on issues and events outside our control".

The PRRC's own data and indices over the 1999–2007 period show very little improvement in average Dissolved Oxygen (DO) and BOD levels. On BOD a "pass" grade of less than 7 mg/L (Class C) was not achieved at any of the five testing stations monitored. Of greater concern perhaps was the deterioration in pollution levels at some stations. Achieving a Class C in BOD is a more distant prospect than a decade before. DO levels show similarly disappointing trends.

PHOTO 8.5
Polluted *estero*, Guadalupe

Source: Photo taken by the author

PHOTO 8.6
Stagnant *estero*, Makati

Source: Photo taken by the author

Something external to the original ambit of the project is the condition of the city's *esteros* (see Photos 8.5 and 8.6). Here even more alarming data over time emerges. Of six *esteros* monitored from 1999–2006, BOD levels ranged from 30 mg/L to 85 mg/L — some twelve times the Class C cut-off point. Any substantial change then to the health of the Pasig River system will require a concerted effort to turn around the condition of some twenty-nine minor and major tributaries and *esteros*. While several initiatives have been proposed, cleaning of *esteros* requires considerable LGU commitment and coordination as well as alternative sites for those households affected. While one official noted that "the idea is to start with the river", he did concede that without addressing the wider catchments of the Pasig efforts would be "a waste of time". Yet there are few political and financial options to clean *esteros* up without creating a significant and potentially violent stand-off.

Civil Society and the Rehabilitation of the Pasig: Contrasting Views

Swyngedouw and Heynen[56] have argued that

> there is no such thing as an unsustainable city in general. Rather, there are a series of urban and environmental processes that negatively affect some groups while benefiting others. … [urban] environmental transformations are not independent from class, gender, ethnicity or other power struggles and, in fact, often tend to be explained by these social struggles.

Though many officials are keen to frame the rehabilitation of the Pasig River as an environmental project it is impossible to separate the social and political context from its objectives and operations. Indeed, the Achilles' heel of the rehabilitation of the Pasig, in the past and now, has been the inability to find a way through the *mêlée* of state/civil society conflict which has, at times, threatened to consume any progress that is made.

Those associated with the project have found communities somewhat frustrating and difficult to deal with. Over time others have lost patience and largely abandoned dialogue. Much of this resistance and reticence to participate in the project appeared to be unanticipated by project stakeholders. A widely held perception was that the project would be supported by all, but instead opposition NGOs "and other so-called representatives seemed to spring up overnight". Many of these are seen by those coordinating the project as opportunist, extorting money from communities in the guise of representing the project, or rallying opposition for the benefit of largely peripheral political agendas. Community leaders of affected communities and a number of NGOs tell a different story however, and one which largely portrays the project as a threat to the rights of the poor to decent shelter, access to employment and adequate representation in decisions which affect their lives.

There are few actual examples of formalized relationships and partnerships which have developed around the project and between communities, government, the private sector and donors. This has been a missed opportunity and stands in contrast to initiatives dealing with similar environment/housing/livelihood dynamics in other Southeast Asian cities.[57] What environmental consciousness and community mobilization that has occurred (for example the distribution of materials to schools, public concerts, writing contests, symposiums and parades) has tended towards maintaining project directions and legitimizing actions, rather than developing communication channels, building consensus and exploring alternatives in a strategic and reflexive way. Less attention has been given to the Pandora's Box of complaints raised from communities which see environmental issues as part and parcel of traditional battles over livelihoods, housing rights and tenure security. Hence direct experiences with communities have been described as "frustrating" due to "talking about different things, on different levels", rather than on the environment which managers see the project's sole focus. The conflict between communities,

NGOs and government has also created tensions for the ADB itself, leaving some staff feeling that for the great part they have been left in an invidious position between government and community conflicts.

Affected communities have clearly sought to shift a relatively narrow agenda of sustainability toward a broader debate on needs. While it is acknowledged that environmental issues are important for the poor, the project has been criticized (in most cases successfully) as opposed to people's basic needs. Resistance, however, has not been uniform in either objectives or goals. While a number of NGOs have sought at one time or another to engage the PRRC and ADB, there are also NGOs and communities which have over time taken a position of outright opposition and hostility to the project. A broad criticism though, has been that efforts to clean up the Pasig River have failed to be inclusive of community needs and voices. One example of this is the belated move towards allowing communities to develop their own "People's Plans" for consideration part way through the project, and in response to community demands to offer alternatives to eviction. However, while several communities developed "People's Plans", few elements have been incorporated into project design, to the anger of many. One NGO head claimed that efforts to develop alternative community-based environmental programmes "were never acknowledged" and "People's Plans" were not treated seriously, leading to the conclusion that "parks are more important than people in the Philippines". Another NGO, which progressively withdrew from the project over time, cited that there was no uniformity with the rules of easement, and that the project had failed to move beyond an elitist view of the river; "A river should have a community but this has never been acknowledged, but this was part of our People's Plan."

For many communities, awareness of the PRRC and the Pasig River's rehabilitation is essentially at the level of the impact on them, but this community-based perspective has rarely been acknowledged. Community leaders have continually questioned who the project is for, whose environment it is, and who will be able to enjoy the benefits of its cleaning — given that they will be relocated 50 kilometres away in the process. In the words of one community leader, "Whose vision is being represented and where the hell did it come from? Who is the 'we' in the Master Plan? It is not the vision of the people along the river. There is no clear plan for the people affected."

This, and other disappointments and conflicts, has lead to a significant stand-off between riverside communities and a project focused on environmental issues. Government blames the people while affected communities blame government, and industry. They feel that there is a government bias towards industry; "it's their friends after all". In addition, transparency is seen as lacking with regard to easements. One community organizer quipped that Malacañang (the official riverside residence of the president) itself was in violation of the ten-metre easement rule but appeared to have fallen off the project's map.

What is evident is that the urban poor have become increasingly defensive as the project has evolved. In response they want the focus to be on helping them become more sustainable communities alongside the river, and believe that this is possible through greater tenure security and livelihood options. Such perspectives are also common in moves elsewhere in the developing world to explore community-based solutions to environmental problems.[58] Resistance has become embedded as promised upgrading projects and urban renewal areas (URAs) have not eventuated on any meaningful scale (by 2008 four in-city URAs had been established, totalling just 4.9 hectares).

In contrast, those associated with the project argue that its significance transcends environmental achievements. River rehabilitation and a greening of the physical environment is also part of (re-) legitimizing the role of government and institutions. Water quality may not change for the better, at least in the short term, but the project must continue "to establish the credibility of the government and the project itself". In essence government agencies see rehabilitation of the Pasig as a medium through which to re-assert power over urban space.[59]

CONCLUSION: REVIVING AN AGENDA

The Pasig River Rehabilitation Project has suffered from being a project with deep ambitions but shallow roots. While one ADB staff member claimed that "we are on the cusp of achieving a number of objectives", many PRRC officials and community leaders interviewed portrayed a project in terminal predicament. Even the ADB was reportedly tempted to cancel the loan at one stage, such was the frustration over progress and levels of conflict. This clear divergence of views is not surprising, given the historical lack of consensus over change in the Philippines, but it also reflects the serious absence of project partnership and communication and the failure to build consensus.

Many of these challenges are beyond the scope of what can be achieved through river rehabilitation. Nevertheless they are no less important. The potentially significant achievements of addressing the chronic pollution of the Pasig River remain locked within the highly confrontational and politicized atmosphere which pervades state/ society relations in which political space is vigorously contested. The environment remains subordinate to other issues and conflicts. Problems with coordination; the difficult relationship between LGUs and NGOs; a lack of consultation; frustration at the lack of progress on the "parks"; difficult institutional and political relationships, all reflect a failure to develop constituencies of change and much needed community support in urban planning and development. Indeed the rehabilitation of the Pasig River is notable, even unique, for the absence of partnership with communities. Instead it has become mired in a bureaucratic and organizational system which was never likely to gain traction or achieve significant goals by itself.

In contrast affected communities have attempted, though also struggled, to shift attention to tenure, security and livelihoods. Even NGOs that were initially behind the project found that people were rarely motivated by environmental problems, in spite of the clear impact of polluted environments on their health, and the health of their children. This is a significant finding. Partly this is a result of the historical lack of attention given to environmental programmes and the roles communities can play in gaining empowerment through environmental transformation and assuming responsibility for the environment (particularly in urban settings). Environmental action has often come from the "outside" in the form of grand ambitions. Yet, as Roy[60] has suggested, communities are more likely to be concerned and motivated by the everyday "politics of shit", that is in finding shared solutions to the lack of adequate sanitation and other fundamental services and rights at the level of the community. The failure to connect these everyday needs and experiences with the wider ambition of government and international donors to create a world-class river system fundamentally explains the position in which parties find themselves today.

Environmental initiatives such as efforts to "save" the Pasig have traditionally failed because they have not found a balance between environmental and social needs and priorities. There is, to a varying degree, a continuation of intolerance to alternative voices in current initiatives. Though linear parks have created more accessible entry points to the river, as has a relaunched ferry service, the poor have rarely benefited from such change. As one resident remarked: "Is this project to clean the river — or help make better communities? If it is the latter then I will support it."

Community empowerment in dealing with environmental pollution has proved to be critically important more often than not — including in urban settings. No country has the capacity or resources to develop mega-projects to deal with environmental issues in isolation of the actions of its communities. As an example, the cost of upgrading the Pasig River to Class C has been estimated at US$10 billion. Instead what is needed is a shift from an environmental discourse and vision based upon global desires to one inclusive of social justice and sustainability.[61] Ness and Low[62] also make the point that cities which are able to turn environmental conditions around demonstrate "the capacity to *recognize* problems, *understand* them by discovering their causes and consequences, and then *act* on that understanding".

The following key lessons may then be identified:

* Beyond participation, ownership is crucial to environmental management programmes. Local institutions and populations need to be involved in the design and implementation process. Communities need to have a stake in both process and outcome;
* Communication, shared knowledge/capacity and transparency are important in building awareness and changing attitudes. Ultimately change requires significant investment in information, education and advocacy, including from communities themselves;
* Effective and sustained change is normative and strategic. Programmes need to be participatory, creative, and develop both leadership and co-responsibility among key stakeholders.

In a recent study of water provision UNHABITAT have reaffirmed such lessons, that "the barriers to improved provision are not so much technical or financial but institutional and political".[63] However the emphasis on participation and strengthening of local communities to hold (especially) local government to account has been minimal. Yet in the absence of local democratic space and resulting checks and balances there exists an undue dependence upon political institutions. While clearly critical actors in efforts to transform the palpably sick Pasig River, government has continued to see those bordering the city's rivers and *esteros* as a threat rather than as a resource or as partners in change. Thus, projects to clean waterways have been characterized by mutual mistrust if not outright hostility, rather than offering an opportunity for new paths out of the malaise. Such a position does not necessarily mean an over-reliance on community solutions. Communities, much like the state and private sector, cannot bring about sustainable cities in isolation. There simply cannot be successful environmental outcomes if the respective roles and responsibilities of states, communities and the private sector are not recognized, legitimized and exist in balance.

Acknowledgements

Initial research for this chapter was conducted while I was a visiting research fellow at ISEAS in 2004. I thank ISEAS for its support. I also wish to acknowledge those who so freely gave their time for interviews in Manila between 2004 and 2006. This research is dedicated to Ate Poning and her family.

Notes

1. Asian Development Bank (ADB), *Emerging Asia: Changes and Challenges* (Manila: Asian Development Bank, 1997); Asian Development Bank (ADB), *Asian Environmental Outlook 2001* (Manila: Asian Development Bank, 2001).
2. United Nations Environment Programme (UNEP), *First ASEAN State of the Environment Report* (Jakarta: ASEAN Secretariat, 1997), p. 116.
3. L. Gezon and S. Paulson, eds., "Place, Power, Difference: Multiscale Research at the Dawn of the Twenty-first Century", in *Political Ecology across Spaces, Scales, and Social Groups* (Piscataway, NJ: Rutgers University Press, 2005), p. 8.
4. G. McGranahan, et al., *The Citizens at Risk: From Urban Sanitation to Sustainable Cities* (Sterling, VA: Earthscan, 2001), p. 5.
5. T. Forsyth, *Critical Political Ecology: The Politics of Environmental Science* (London: Routledge, 2003), p. 20.

6. P. Robbins, *Political Ecology: A Critical Introduction* (London: Blackwell, 2004), p. 11.

7. M. Carley, "Top-down and Bottom-up: The Challenge of Cities in the New Century", in *Just Sustainabilites: Development in an Unequal World*, edited by J. Agyeman, R.D. Bullard, and B. Evans (London: Earthscan, 2001), p. 14.

8. A.A. Escobin and N.D. Briones Jr, "Institutional Partnerships in the Rehabilitation of Biñan River, Laguna, Philippines", *Journal of Environmental Science and Management* 4, nos. 1–2 (2001): 29–41; R.G. Mercado, "Environment and Natural Resources Management: Lessons from Programme Innovations of Selected Philippine Cities", in *Model Cities: Urban Best Practices* Volume 2, edited by Ooi Giok Ling (Singapore: Urban Management Authority and the Institute of Policy Studies, 2001); S. Boonyabancha, "Baan Mankong: Going to Scale with 'Slum' and Squatter Upgrading in Thailand", *Environment and Urbanization* 17, no. 1 (2005): 21–46.

9. A.S. Rola and C.O. Tabren, "Saving a River: Why do Local Governments Matter?" *Journal of Environmental Science and Management* 4, nos. 1–2 (2001): 57–67.

10. Xavier Huetz de Lemps, "Waters in Nineteenth Century Manila", *Philippine Studies* 49 (4th Quarter 2001): 488–517.

11. J.U. Nierras, "Tropical Urban Ecosystem Study: Case Study of Metropolitan Manila", in *Tropical Urban Ecosytem Studies Volume 4: Environmental Profiles of Selected Cities in Southeast Asia*, edited by S. Sham and M. Ahmad Badri (Malaysia: National MAB Committee, 1988), p. 105.

12. V.R. Villavicencio, "Philippines", in *Environmental Management in Southeast Asia*, edited by Chia Lin Sien (Singapore: Singapore University Press, 1987), p. 93.

13. Nierras, *Tropical Urban Ecosystem Study*, p. 108.

14. Ibid., p. 91.

15. Villavicencio, *Philippines*, p. 94.

16. Cited in ibid., p. 90.

17. T. Ohmachi and E.R. Roman, eds., *Metro Manila: In Search of a Sustainable Future* (Quezon City: Japan Society for the Promotion of Science and University of the Philippines Press, 2002), p. 5.

18. World Bank, *Philippine Environment Monitor: Water Quality* (Manila: World Bank, 2003), pp. 21–23.

19. See G. McGranahan, "Urban Transitions and the Spatial Displacement of Environmental Burdens", in *Scaling Urban Environmental Challenges: From Local to Global and Back*, edited by P.J. Marcotulio and G. McGranahan (London: Earthscan, 2007), pp. 18–44.

20. The 1991 Local Government Code transferred from national government agencies to LGUs the principal responsibility for the delivery of basic services and the operation of facilities in following areas: agricultural extension and outreach, social forestry, environmental management and pollution control, primary health care, hospital care, social welfare services, water supply, communal irrigation, land use planning and repair and maintenance of local infrastructure facilities. See R. Manasan, "Devolution of Environmental and Natural Resource Management in the Philippines: Analytical and Policy Issues", *Philippine Journal of Development* 29, no. 1 (2002): 35.

21. Ibid., p. 41.

22. Ibid., pp. 41–42.

23. Ibid., p. 42.

24. Chua Y.T. and S.S. Coronel, eds., *The PCIJ Guide to Government* (Metro Manila: Philippine Center for Investigative Journalism, 2003), p. 267.

25. Ibid., pp. 256–57.

26. Ibid., p. 258.

27. McGranahan, et al., *The Citizens at Risk*, p. 87.

28. E. Gagalac-Regis, M. labra-Espina, and M.Y. Yacat, *The Pasig River: Caring for a Dying Ecosystem* (Metro Manila: Pasig River Rehabilitation Commission, 2001).

29. K. Constantino-David, "Unsustainable Development: The Philippine Experience", *Development in Practice* 11, no. 2–3 (2001): 234.

30. H. Katayama, "Weak State and Strong Society: Politics of the Clean Air Act", in *Metro Manila: In Search of a Sustainable Future*, edited by T. Ohmachi and E.R. Roman (Quezon City: Japan Society for the Promotion of Science and University of the Philippines Press, 2002), p. 23. This figure is almost exactly double the estimate of solid waste generated in 1982, of 2,650 tonnes/day, with a similar collection rate

of 69 per cent. See Ir R.D. Charifa, "Tropical Urban Ecosystems: Case of Metro Manila, Philippines", in *Tropical Urban Ecosytem Studies Volume 4: Environmental Profiles of Selected Cities in Southeast Asia*, edited by S. Sham and M. Ahmad Badri (Malaysia: Malaysian National MAB Committee, 1988), p. 105.

31. T.G. Hingco, "Waste Disposal Problems in Metro Manila and the Response of the Urban Poor", in *Urban Growth and Development in Asia Volume II: Living in the Cities*, edited by G.P. Chapman, A.K. Dutt, and R.W. Bradnock (Aldershot: Ashgate, 1999), p. 275.

32. World Bank, *Philippine Environment Monitor: Environmental Health* (Country Office Manila, 2007).

33. McGranahan, et al., *The Citizens at Risk*, p. 107.

34. Hingco, *Waste Disposal Problem in Metro Manila*, p. 279.

35. World Bank, *Philippine Environment Monitor*, 2007, pp. 11–24.

36. I. Ishikawa, T. Nakanishi, and Xin Qian, "Basic Viewpoints for the Rehabilitation of Water Environment", *Metro Manila: In Search of a Sustainable Future*, edited by T. Ohmachi and E.R. Roman (Quezon City: Japan Society for the Promotion of Science and University of the Philippines Press, 2002), p. 250.

37. Hingco, *Waste Disposal Problem in Metro Manila*, p. 276.

38. Ibid., p. 275.

39. Greenpeace Southeast Asia, "Industrial Pollution in Pasig River" (Greenpeace Southeast Asia Backgrounder, 2001).

40. Hingco, *Waste Disposal Problem in Metro Manila*, p. 269.

41. Ibid., p. 271.

42. Charifa, *Tropical Urban Ecosystems Study*, pp. 116–17.

43. Nierras, *Tropical Urban Ecosystem Study*, p. 102.

44. Ibid.

45. Hingco, *Waste Disposal Problem in Metro Manila*, p. 278.

46. Villavicencio, *Philippines*, pp. 86–87.

47. Constantino-David, *Unsustainable Development*, p. 236.

48. Ibid., p. 236.

49. Since implementation, the project now complements the Philippines Medium Term Development Plan (MTDP 2004–10); the Comprehensive and Integrated Infrastructure Program (2007–10); and the Pasig River Dredging Project (2008–11).

50. DENR (Department of Environment and Natural Resources), "Pasig River Rehabilitation Commission" <http://www.prrc.com.ph> (accessed 9 September 2008).

51. M.P. Oderon, "A Glimpse of the Vitality that is Pasig River", *The River Post* 3, no. 2 (July–December 2001).

52. One community leader I spoke with estimated that in Pasig City alone there were 38,000 people living along waterways. The number of those living in settlements within the Pasig River catchment may be as high as 4.4 million.

53. D. Storey, "Housing the Urban Poor in Metro Manila", *Philippine Studies* 46 (Third Quarter 1998): 267–92.

54. E. Berner, *Defending a Place in the City: Localities and the Struggle for Urban Land in Metro Manila* (Quezon City: Ateneo de Manila Press, 1997).

55. D. Murphy and T. Anana, *Pasig River Rehabilitation Program* (Habitat International Coalition/Urban Poor Associates, 2004); UPA (Urban Poor Associates) *Urban Poor Associates New Digest* <http://jlagman17. blogspot.com> (accessed 19 August 2008).

56. Swyngedouw and Heynen, "Urban Political Ecology, Justice and the Politics of Scale", *Antipode* 35, no. 5 (2003): 901.

57. S. Boonyabancha, *Baan Mankong*.

58. J. Du Plessis, "The Growing Problem of Forced Evictions and the Crucial Importance of Community-based, Locally Appropriate Alternatives", *Environment and Urbanization* 17, no. 1 (2005): 123–34.

59. A. Loftus and F. Lumsden, "Reworking Hegemony in the Urban Waterscape", *Transactions of the Institute of British Geographers* 33 (2008): 110.

60. A. Roy, "Urban Informality: Toward an Epistemology of Planning", *Journal of the American Planning Association* 71, no. 2 (2007): 147–58.

61. G. Shatkin, "Planning to Forget: Informal Settlements as 'Forgotten Places' in Globalising Metro Manila", *Urban Studies* 41, no. 12 (2004): 2469–84.

62. G.D. Ness and M.M. Low, eds., *Five Cities: Modelling Asian Urban Population-Environment Dynamics* (Oxford: Oxford University Press, 2000), p. 44.

63. UNHABITAT, *Water and Sanitation in the World's Cities: Local Action for Global Goals* (London: Earthscan, 2003), p. xvii.

References

Asian Development Bank (ADB). *Asian Environmental Outlook 2001*. Manila: Asian Development Bank, 2001.

———. *Emerging Asia: Changes and Challenges*. Manila: Asian Development Bank, 1997.

Berner, E. *Defending a Place in the City: Localities and the Struggle for Urban Land in Metro Manila*. Quezon City: Ateneo de Manila Press, 1997.

Boonyabancha, S. "Baan Mankong: Going to Scale with 'Slum' and Squatter Upgrading in Thailand". *Environment and Urbanization* 17, no. 1 (2005): 21–46.

Carley, M. "Top-down and Bottom-up: The Challenge of Cities in the New Century". In *Just Sustainabilites: Development in an Unequal World*, edited by J. Agyeman, R.D. Bullard and B. Evans. London: Earthscan, 2001.

Charifa, Ir R.D. "Tropical Urban Ecosystems: Case of Metro Manila, Philippines". In *Tropical Urban Ecosytem Studies Volume 4: Environmental Profiles of Selected Cities in Southeast Asia*, edited by S. Sham and M. Ahmad Badri. Malaysia: Malaysian National MAB Committee, 1988.

Chua, Y.T. and S.S. Coronel, eds. *The PCIJ Guide to Government*. Metro Manila, Philippine: Center for Investigative Journalism, 2003.

Constantino-David, K. "Unsustainable Development: The Philippine Experience". *Development in Practice* 11, nos. 2-3 (2001): 234.

DENR (Department of Environment and Natural Resources). "Pasig River Rehabilitation Commission". <http://www.prrc.com.ph> (accessed 9 September 2008).

Du Plessis, J. "The Growing Problem of Forced Evictions and the Crucial Importance of Community-based, Locally Appropriate Alternatives". *Environment and Urbanization* 17, no. 1 (2005): 123–34.

Escobin, A.A. and N.D. Briones Jr. "Institutional Partnerships in the Rehabilitation of Biñan River, Laguna, Philippines". *Journal of Environmental Science and Management* 4, nos. 1-2 (2001): 29–41.

Forsyth, T. *Critical Political Ecology: The Politics of Environmental Science*. London: Routledge, 2003.

Gagalac-Regis, E., M. labra-Espina, and M.Y. Yacat. *The Pasig River: Caring for a Dying Ecosystem*. Metro Manila: Pasig River Rehabilitation Commission, 2001.

Gezon, L. and S. Paulson. "Place, Power, Difference: Multiscale Research at the Dawn of the Twenty-first century". In *Political Ecology across Spaces, Scales, and Social Groups*, edited by S. Paulson and L.L. Gezon. Piscataway, NJ: Rutgers University Press, 2005.

Greenpeace Southeast Asia. "Industrial Pollution in Pasig River". Greenpeace Southeast Asia Backgrounder (2001).

Hingco, T.G. "Waste Disposal Problems in Metro Manila and the Response of the Urban Poor". In *Urban Growth and Development in Asia Volume II: Living in the Cities*, edited by G.P. Chapman, A.K. Dutt and R.W. Bradnock. Aldershot: Ashgate, 1999.

Huetz de Lemps, Xavier. "Waters in Nineteenth Century Manila". *Philippine Studies* 49 (4th Quarter 2001): 488-517.

Ishikawa, I., T. Nakanishi, and Xin Qian. "Basic Viewpoints for the Rehabilitation of Water Environment". *Metro Manila: In Search of a Sustainable Future*, edited by T. Ohmachi and E.R. Roman. Quezon City: Japan Society for the Promotion of Science and University of the Philippines Press, 2002.

Katayama, H. "Weak State and Strong Society: Politics of the Clean Air Act". In *Metro Manila: In Search of a Sustainable Future*, edited by T. Ohmachi and E.R. Roman. Quezon City: Japan Society for the Promotion of Science and University of the Philippines Press, 2002.

Loftus, A. and F. Lumsden. "Reworking Hegemony in the Urban Waterscape". *Transactions of the Institute of British Geographers* 33 (2008): 110.

Manasan, R. "Devolution of Environmental and Natural Resource Management in the Philippines: Analytical and Policy Issues". *Philippine Journal of Development* 29, no. 1 (2002): 35.

McGranahan, G. "Urban Transitions and the Spatial Displacement of Environmental Burdens". In *Scaling Urban Environmental Challenges: From Local to Global and Back*, edited by P.J. Marcotulio and G. McGranahan. London: Earthscan, 2007.

———. et al. *The Citizens at Risk: From Urban Sanitation to Sustainable Cities*. Sterling, VA: Earthscan, 2001.

Mercado, R.G. "Environment and Natural Resources Management: Lessons from Programme Innovations of Selected Philippine Cities". In *Model Cities: Urban Best Practices* Volume 2, edited by Ooi Giok

Ling. Singapore: Urban Management Authority and the Institute of Policy Studies, 2001.

Murphy, D. and T. Anana. *Pasig River Rehabilitation Program*. Habitat International Coalition/Urban Poor Associates, 2004.

Ness, G.D. and M.M. Low, eds. *Five Cities: Modelling Asian Urban Population-Environment Dynamics*. Oxford: Oxford University Press, 2000.

Nierras, J.U. "Tropical Urban Ecosystem Study: Case Study of Metropolitan Manila". In *Tropical Urban Ecosytem Studies Volume 4: Environmental Profiles of Selected Cities in Southeast Asia*, edited by S. Sham and M. Ahmad Badri. Malaysia: National MAB Committee, 1988.

Oderon, M.P. "A Glimpse of the Vitality that is Pasig River". *The River Post* 3, no. 2 (July–December 2001).

Ohmachi, T. and E.R. Roman, eds. *Metro Manila: In Search of a Sustainable Future*. Quezon City: Japan Society for the Promotion of Science and University of the Philippines Press, 2002.

Robbins, P. *Political Ecology: A Critical Introduction*. London: Blackwell, 2004.

Rola, A.S. and C.O. Tabren. "Saving a River: Why do Local Governments Matter?". *Journal of Environmental Science and Management* 4, nos. 1–2 (2001): 57–67.

Roy, A. "Urban Informality: Toward an Epistemology of Planning". *Journal of the American Planning Association* 71, no. 2 (2007): 147–58.

Shatkin, G. "Planning to Forget: Informal Settlements as 'Forgotten Places' in Globalising Metro Manila". *Urban Studies* 41, no. 12 (2004): 2469–84.

Storey, D. "Housing the Urban Poor in Metro Manila". *Philippine Studies* 46 (Third Quarter 1998): 267–92.

Swyngedouw and Heynen. "Urban Political Ecology, Justice and the Politics of Scale". *Antipode* 35, no. 5 (2003): 901.

UNHABITAT. *Water and Sanitation in the World's Cities: Local Action for Global Goals*. London: Earthscan, 2003.

United Nations Environment Programme (UNEP). *First ASEAN State of the Environment Report*. Jakarta: ASEAN Secretariat, 1997.

Urban Poor Associates (UPA). *Urban Poor Associates New Digest*. <http://jlagman17.blogspot.com> (accessed 19 August 2008).

Villavicencio, V.R. "Philippines". In *Environmental Management in Southeast Asia*, edited by Chia Lin Sien. Singapore: Singapore University Press, 1987.

World Bank. *Philippine Environment Monitor: Environmental Health*. Country Office Manila, 2007.

_____. *Philippine Environment Monitor: Water Quality*. Manila: World Bank, 2003.

9

THE PRIVATIZATION OF WATER SERVICES IN METRO MANILA:
Lessons from a Mixed Outcome

Lorraine Carlos Salazar

INTRODUCTION

Among developing countries, the Philippines has been in the forefront of privatizing its urban water systems. The Metro Manila Water and Sewerage System (MWSS) was privatized in 1997 as a concession covering water and sanitation services. The concession was split into two, covering a twenty-five-year period, and awarded on the basis of an international bidding procedure that was recognised as open and transparent, and declared the biggest water privatization in the world during the time. The contract was divided with the hope that doing so would facilitate the work of the regulator in introducing benchmarking and quasi-competition.

This chapter examines the experience of water privatization in the Philippines, focusing on the case of Metro Manila where water and sewerage services were privatized in 1997. A new and all Filipino partnership of DM Consunji Holdings Incorporated and Metro Pacific Investments Corporation (DMCI-MPIC) took over the management of Maynilad Water Services in 2007.[2] However, the outcome of this takeover is still uncertain and as such, will not be discussed in this chapter.

Most countries that have privatized water provision have experienced a series of problems and, in some cases, have been classified as failures. However, the experience of privatization in Manila, with one well-performing and one unsuccessful concessionaire, offers valuable insights into what enables successful water privatization.

To this end, this chapter examines the issue of water privatization in five parts. The first section presents the arguments for and against privatization and identifies the proponents of each alternative. The second section looks at water provision before privatization in Metro Manila. The third section considers the privatization process, while the fourth looks into the outcomes of privatization thus far. The conclusion sums up the evidence and formulates lessons that can be drawn from the Metro Manila experience.

PROS AND CONS OF WATER PRIVATIZATION

In 2002, the UN Committee on Economic, Social and Cultural Rights released a General Comment on the Right to Water, declaring that access to sufficient, safe, physically accessible, and affordable water for personal and domestic use is a basic human right. The General Comment provided a detailed blueprint by which states and international actions could apply this principle to laws and policies. States were obliged to use available resources effectively in a concrete and targeted manner to ensure that all have access to water. At present, at least 1.2 billion people have no such access and an additional 2 billion have no access to sanitation services. The UN has set the target of reducing this proportion by half by 2015 as part of the Millennium Development Goals.[1]

Traditionally, water supply and sanitation systems (WSS) were considered a public utility. Water, being an essential public and merit good, was considered a politically sensitive commodity that exhibited network and natural monopoly characteristics. Today, this thinking is slowly changing.

In the past decade, rethinking on how water services can be best provided has been underway, led by France, the United Kingdom, and the United States. These approaches have, in turn, been popularized by the World Bank and other major international financial institutions among developing countries. The increase in private sector participation in the delivery of urban water supply and sanitation was brought about by the perception that governments were less able to manage the sector efficiently and do not have as much access to funds needed to undertake investments as compared to the private sector.[3]

As the World Bank makes it part of its lending conditionality to introduce private sector participation in water provision, the involvement of the private sector in urban WSS has been on the rise.[4] Between 1990 and 1997, the cumulative new private sector capital expenditure on WSS in developing countries has risen to US$25 billion compared to US$297 million during 1984–1990. By 1997, a total of ninety-seven projects were implemented in thirty-five developing countries ranging from management contracts to leases, concessions, divestitures, and build-operate-own-transfer (BOOT) agreements. This increase has been driven by the need for increased capital investment in WSS in cities of developing countries, which have been experiencing growing urban populations and a reduction in assistance from aid agencies to rehabilitate and expand their water systems.[5]

Yet, government failure does not automatically justify private sector involvement. Turning a state monopoly into a private monopoly may exacerbate rather than improve the situation, as the monopolist takes advantage of its privileged position in the market at the expense of the users. Thus, setting up a capable and effective regulatory system after the introduction of private participation is crucial.

On another level, the assumption that water is a natural monopoly has been put under question. While the water supply chain exhibits economies of scale, its various stages can actually be vertically unbundled, allowing the entry of various providers at some of the stages (from raw water supply, water treatment, water distribution, wastewater collection, and wastewater treatment). In addition, metering, operations and maintenance, and billing aspects of service provision could be parcelled out from the core WSS sector. In the same way, firms can be given contracts to undertake significant investments in specific infrastructural areas. In sum, it is now increasingly recognized, based on the work of Baumol, Panzar, and Willig (1982) that as long as a market is contestable or if there is potential for firm entry, a single provider may not necessarily behave monopolistically as long as there is potential competition for the market. Thus, bidding procedures and contract design should be carefully prepared and are important aspects of any privatization exercise.

There are six possible methods of private sector participation (PSP) in water:[6]

1. Service contracts — the simplest forms of PSP involving short-term contracts to provide limited services such as installing meters, meter service readings, repairing leaks, and mailing bill statements. Service contracts entail carrying out specific duties and do not require any overall private sector responsibility for system operation.

2. Management contracts — are short-term contracts, typically five years, where a private firm becomes responsible for operations and management. They do not usually require any private investment. The company does not assume commercial risk or have any direct legal relationship with the consumer. The national or local government maintains financial responsibility for the system and the capacity to plan and finance system expansion.

3. Leases — are contracts allowing a private operator to rent facilities from the public authority for a specified period of time. The public authority retains ownership and responsibility for system finance and expansion. Meanwhile the private concessionaire is responsible for financing working capital and accepts some commercial risk in the day-to-day operation of the system. The contractor has a direct interest in maximizing bill collection because its profits are dependent on revenue generated less operating costs and rental fees.

4. BOT/BOOT/BOO contracts — are mechanisms that allow a private contractor to build, own, operate, and transfer a specific capital investment. The investment is normally substantive and the contract period is long enough to allow for the recovery of capital expenditure. Generally, the public authority guarantees a certain level of demand, such as volume of water provided. The contractor accepts the risk if this demand is not met.

5. Concessions — are long-term contracts, usually for twenty-five years, which require a private company to invest in the system. The concessionaire is responsible for the system's operations, maintenance, and expansion. The concessionaire receives payment directly from the consumer and accepts the risk that costs may fall below revenues. The contract period is usually long enough to allow the contractor to recover investment costs. Penalties may be imposed upon the contractor if specific targets are not met. The assets themselves, however, remain as public sector property.

6. Divestiture — may be partial (allowing for shared government and private responsibility for service provision, through a separate corporate entity) or full (by transferring assets to the private sector through sale of assets or shares, or management buyouts). Generally, a corporate agreement will stipulate private and public responsibilities, including representation on board of directors and division of profits.

International financial institutions led by WB, IMF, and the regional development banks are calling for privatization of urban water services and actively promote its adoption as policy by linking loans and aids to the privatization of water supply systems. Yet, civil society activists worldwide who argue that water is a public commons that must not be privatized oppose such a move. They point out that water is a critical social good whose delivery should not be placed in the hands of firms pursuing the profit motive as this leads to discrimination in the provision of service towards those who can afford to pay, to the detriment of those who cannot.

Thus, there is an ongoing debate with regard to how to better provide water services worldwide, arising from differing assumptions. With this debate as background, the next section examines the case of privatizing water provision in Metro Manila.

PRE-PRIVATIZATION WATER PROVISION IN METRO MANILA

Background

The Philippines has an abundant annual rainfall of about 2,400 millimetres (mm). Of this amount, between 1,000–2,000 mm are accumulated as run-off at 421 principal river basins, 61 lakes, and countless small streams. Moreover, the country also has groundwater reservoirs covering a total area of approximately 50,000 square kilometres (sq km) and reliable surface water supply aggregate of 833 million cubic metres (mcm) per day.[7]

Clearly, water supply in the Philippines is plentiful. As in many developing countries, the problem lies not in the lack of water resources but in how water is distributed and managed, and is shaped by factors like population growth, economic progress, location, time, and climate. People lack access to safe water because the infrastructure and regulatory capacity to protect water sources and distribute water are not in place.

In a 1990 Census of Population and Housing, it was found that only 16 per cent of the total population living in urban centres and 54 per cent in rural areas have access to water supplies from wells, springs, streams, lakes, rainwater or vendors. The survey also revealed that 47 per cent of the total population in urban centres outside Metro Manila were not served by piped water supply.[8]

The Case of Metropolitan Manila

Metropolitan Manila, the Philippines' foremost urban centre, covers a total land area of 636 sq km. It has one of the oldest water systems in Asia, constructed in 1878 with 15 million litres per day capacity when the city had a population of only 300,000. This capacity has gradually been increased over the years through the construction of dams and pumping facilities.

In 1971, then President Marcos created the Metropolitan Waterworks and Sewerage System (MWSS) as an autonomous government owned and controlled corporation to operate and maintain water and sewerage services in the metropolitan area, including the province of Rizal, and parts of Cavite, totalling a land area of 200,000 hectares.

Starting the 1980s, industrialization and increasing population growth has put much pressure in the capacity of the MWSS to distribute water and provide sewerage services. Its network deteriorated and required rehabilitation and expansion to meet the increasing demands of the metropolis. Yet, the government had too many competing demands on its limited resources to act on this.

By 1997, MWSS was providing the area an estimated 3200 million litres of water daily to a population that has ballooned to 11 million. MWSS was only able to serve 65 per cent of the population, with at most sixteen hours of water supply per day. The remaining 35 per cent relied on private deep wells or had no water connection. The majority of these were composed of the city's poorest residents and often had to pay ten times as much for water.

Cholera epidemics often occurred and these were blamed on old, contaminated pipes.

While 976 million cubic metres of tap water were delivered in 1995, only 426 million were actually paid for. This meant that 56 per cent of water was unaccounted for, also known as non-revenue water (NRW). Water loss due to leaks, open hydrants, and illegal connections were widespread throughout the city.[9] The MWSS tried to make up for this waste by charging higher prices, but its revenues were not enough to invest in improving and expanding the infrastructure. See Table 9.1.

With regards to sewerage, the MWSS provided sewer connections to a miniscule 8 per cent of the population. The majority of uncollected wastewater went into septic tanks and was eventually discharged into the municipal waterways and drainage systems, which led to the ocean. Of the sewage collected, 99 per cent was

TABLE 9.1
Pre-Privatized MWSS Operational Highlights, 1997

Population in the service area	11 million
Population served	
1. water supply	7.5 million
2. sewerage	0.78 million
Total number of connections	815,000
Average daily water production	3,000 million litres
No. of treatment plants	3
Total length of pipeline	12,000 km
Average daily water availability	16 hours
Average daily non-revenue water	56 per cent
Water loses (May 1996), per capita daily	133 litres
Consumption billing efficiency	42.87 per cent

Source: Raj Chotrani, "Lessons from Philippine Water Privatization", *Asian Water*, July 1999, at <http://www.mwss.gov.ph/news/default.asp?action=article&ID=66> (accessed 1 August 2005).

dumped, without treatment, into Manila Bay. Thus, pollution due to biochemical oxygen demand was estimated at 980 tonnes a day.[10]

By the 1990s, the level of quality of water service was described as one of the worst in Asia. From 1993 to 1995, MWSS' net income fell by 62 per cent due to rising costs and interest payments. The MWSS needed around P7 billion (US$253 million) for a major pipe replacement and rehabilitation which the government could not afford because of budgetary limitations. Financing could only come only from international institutions but creditors such as the World Bank and the Asian Development Bank, which accounted for US$249 million of the MWSS' US$307 million long-term loans as of 1995, were not keen to lend to the government. Instead, they encouraged private sector takeover of the MWSS.[11]

Thus, the MWSS was a quintessential example of an inefficient and costly state enterprise that was unable to deliver the public service it was tasked to provide. It was saddled with corruption and red tape, was overstaffed, and unable to improve its network because of the government's limited budgetary allocation.

STEPS TOWARDS PRIVATIZATION

In December 1994, then President Fidel Ramos convened a National Water Summit to respond to an imminent "water crisis". Ramos was convinced that the solution to Manila's water problems was to involve the private sector in the operation and management of the MWSS. In June 1995, he successfully prodded Congress to pass Republic Act 8041, also known as the "National Water Crisis Act". The passage of the act signalled the determination of the executive to solve the metropolis' water problem. The law provided for the reorganization of the MWSS and granted the president the power to privatize it.[12]

In 1996, the government hired the International Finance Corporation (IFC) as technical and financial adviser to manage the privatization process. The MWSS privatization was patterned after the Buenos Aires experience, where, just as in Manila, a deteriorating system dating from the turn of the century had to be reformed. The IFC drafted the concession agreement and designed the bidding process for selecting two private utility operators. The auction was scheduled for January 1997. The government decided to adopt a concessional model as the mode of entry. The MWSS would retain ownership of fixed assets but would transfer operational and investment responsibility to winning bidders. Operation and maintenance of common infrastructure would then become the shared responsibility of the operators. In order to ensure competition, Metro Manila was divided into two franchise areas — the East and West Zones — two geographically separate but vertically integrated areas.[13] The two areas were auctioned off to two twenty-five-year concessions through competitive bidding and the winners chosen by virtue of the lowest price bid. The concessionaires were to gain rights to water from the Angat Dam, which supplies 97 per cent of Metro Manila's water needs.

An estimated US$7 billion was expected to be invested by the concessionaires within the twenty-five-year period to improve the quality of the system. The World Bank considered the privatization of the MWSS as the "world's largest privatization exercise" when it was undertaken in 1997.[14] Privatization was anticipated to lead to capital investment and operational efficiencies that would expand water and sewerage coverage and to relieve the government of the financial burden in improving urban water facilities.

The winners were made responsible for handling water treatment, distribution, tariff collection, facility improvement, and overall management. After twenty-five years, the private sector was expected to have earned from its investments, cleaned up the system, put all MWSS' financial obligations in order and laid down an efficient water supply for the metropolis. The MWSS became a residual office, though it retained ownership of the water facilities. A regulatory office was created to regulate the concessionaires and set water rates.

The concessionaires were required to pay fees totalling P30 billion (US$1.2 billion at 1997 exchange rates) over the twenty-five-year concession period. This amount included debt servicing for MWSS' existing foreign debt obligations while the remaining aspect of the fee was for the rental of MWSS facilities. The government expected to earn US$4 billion in revenues, with the concessionaires paying a commencement fee of US$5 million and an annual fee of US$1.8 million each. In addition, an estimated US$3 billion in income taxes were expected to be collected over the entire concession period.[15] The government's earnings would cover the debt service requirements of the MWSS, which was reduced to a regulatory agency. The companies were expected to not make a profit for the first twelve to fifteen years of their contracts, largely because they would be required to make large capital investments and, for the first ten years, would be prohibited from raising prices relative to inflation. Overall, however, they were guaranteed dividends of at least 12 per cent.

The MWSS-Regulatory Office

The MWSS Regulatory Office (RO), created under the Concession Agreement, was tasked to protect consumer interest, conduct tariff rate determinations, and monitor the concessionaries performance relative to their service obligations. It was allocated an operating budget of P200 million (US$8 million in 1997), obtained from the concession fees. A panel of five members all appointed by and reporting to the MWSS board managed the RO.

Service Obligations

The concessionaires were expected to achieve the following goals:[16]

* Make water coverage universal by 2006;
* Increase sewerage coverage to 83 per cent by 2021;

TABLE 9.2
Service Targets (in per cent coverage)

Service	YEAR					
	1996	2001	2006	2011	2016	2021
Water service	67	87	98	98	98	98
Sanitation	0	39	40	36	33	29
Sewerage	8	7	15	26	38	54

Source: Mark Dumol, *The Manila Water Concession: A Key Government Official's Diary of the World's Largest Water Privatisation* (Washington, D.C.: The World Bank, 2000), p. 121.

- Reduce non-revenue water (NRW) to less than 35 per cent by 2021; and
- Make water available twenty-four hours a day at pressure adequate for a three-storey building by 2001.

Rate-Setting Procedures

The concession agreement enumerated three ways of adjusting tariffs. These are through: 1) consumer price index (CPI) adjustment, to be used every year, 2) extraordinary price adjustment (EPA), to be used to counter "unforeseen events" and 3) rate re-basing adjustment, to be used every five years.

Any tariff adjustment determined by the regulatory office that would exceed the 12 per cent Rate of Return on Base (RORB) provided by law would be treated as an expiration payment in favour of the concessionaire at the end of the twenty-five-year concession period. This mechanism was to ensure that concessionaires get a "guaranteed rate of return" for their investment.[17]

Dispute Settlement Mechanism

An arbitration panel of three members was established outside the MWSS to address and resolve disputes between the regulator and the respective concessionaires. In the event of minor disputes, the arbitration panel members would be appointed by the regulator, the respective concessionaire, and the chairman agreed to by the two parties. If a major dispute arises, the president of Paris-based International Chamber of Commerce (ICC) would appoint the chairman.

Minimal Opposition to Privatization

Given the inefficient service of the MWSS, there was no public clamour opposing its privatization, especially because the new price of service was either 50 or 75 per cent lower than the 1997 MWSS rate. The main opposition to privatization came from its employees who were afraid of getting displaced. The overstaffed government utility had 8,000 employees for only 779,380 connections, or a ratio of over 10 per 1,000.

After being reduced to a regulatory authority, the MWSS would only retain about 100 to 200 employees. The MWSS offered the rest a voluntary early retirement incentive package. The new concessionaires hired employees who chose not to retire on a six-month contractual basis, during which their performance was reviewed. Those whose performances were deemed unsatisfactory were laid off. The concessionaires agreed to recognize the current labour union and offered generous severance packages to those who were dismissed or who chose to resign. Those accepting a regular job with the concessionaires were allowed to own a combined total of 6 per cent of the companies' stock.[18]

The Bidding Participants

When the privatization of MWSS was announced, about fifty local and foreign companies expressed interest in participating in the process. However, with the government setting strict criteria, only four joint-venture consortia were prequalified to bid. The requirements for bidding were:

- The interested party be composed of a "local sponsor" and an "international operator";
- The "international operator" show proven experience and expertise in the provision of water supply and sanitation services; and
- The joint venture be at least 60 per cent Filipino owned.

The four prequalified groups were:
- International Water (United Utilities of the United Kingdom and Bechtel of the United States) and the Ayala Corporation;
- Lyonnaise des Eaux (France) and Benpres Holdings;
- Compagnie Generale des Eaux (France) and Aboitiz Equity Ventures; and
- Anglian Water International (UK) and Metro Pacific Corporation.[19]

A competitive bidding procedure was adopted wherein the bidders were asked to propose rate bids for the two concession areas. The bids were coefficients representing discounts against the existing average tariff of MWSS, estimated at P8.78 per cubic metre in January 1997. The other condition was that no single bidder would be allowed to win both concessions, to prevent turning water services from a public monopoly into a private monopoly.

The bidding process itself was transparent and fair, with four well-known and established local business families in tandem with internationally-established water operators. As it turned out, Manila Water Co, led by the Ayala Corporation, underbid all competitors in both zones by an astounding 50 per cent or more. The corporation was thus given the East Zone to operate and manage at a price of P2.32 per cubic metre of water. Yet, in line with the bidding rules, the government awarded the West Zone to Maynilad Water Services Incorporated of Benpres and Lyonnaise des Eaux, which quoted a price of P4.97 per cubic metre — twice as high as Manila Water's asking price of P2.51 for that area.

TABLE 9.3
Bidders Tariff for the Concessions

Bidder	West Zone		East Zone	
	Existing Tariff (P/cu metre)	Bid Tariff (P/cu metre)	Existing Tariff (P/cu metre)	Bid Tariff (P/cu metre)
Maynilad Water Services Inc. (Benpres Holdings and Lyonnaise des Eaux)	8.78	4.97	8.78	6.13
Manila Water Company, Inc (Ayala Corp. and Intern'l Water)	8.78	2.51	8.78	2.32
Aboitiz equity Ventures and Compagnia Generale de Eaux	8.78	4.99	8.78	5.52
Metro Pacific and Anglian Water Int'l	8.78	5.87	8.78	5.66

Source: Mark Dumol, *The Manila Water Concession: A Key Government Official's Diary of the World's Largest Water Privatisation* (Washington, D.C.: The World Bank, 2000), p. 131.

Thus, at the start of privatization, the price of water in the East of the metropolis was about half that of the price in the West. Such a discrepancy was deemed acceptable since both prices were considerably lower than the previous MWSS tariff.

The Concessionaires

Given the enormous amount of investment and financial expertise expected, only huge Philippine conglomerates, in tandem with foreign joint venture partners, prequalified to join in the privatization exercise. Benpres and Ayala Corporation are owned by two of the richest families in the country with extensive interests in various economic sectors.

Manila Water Company

The East Zone Concession was awarded to the Manila Water Company, a joint venture between the Ayala Corporation, United Utilities of the United Kingdom, and Bechtel of the United States. The East Zone included the major cities of Manila, Quezon, Pasay, Caloocan and Muntinlupa and covered around 6.3 million residents and about 63 per cent of the water supply coverage.[20]

The Ayala family controlled 58 per cent of the Ayala Corporation. The other substantial shareholders of the Ayala Corporation were Mitsubishi Corporation of Japan (with 19.1 per cent of the shares), Shoemart Incorporated (with 4.4 per cent), and the public (with 18.5 per cent).[21]

The Ayala family is one of four Filipino families consistently listed in *Forbes Magazine*'s list of world billionaires.[22] It is one of the oldest and richest business families in the country, tracing its ancestry from Spaniards who settled in the Philippines in the seventeenth century.[23] The family's main holding company, the Ayala Corporation, has grown from a business house founded in 1834 by Domingo Roxas and Antonio de Ayala to one of the largest and most widely diversified conglomerates in the Philippines.

The Ayalas are particularly well known for developing residential and business real estate, transforming the 930-hectare Hacienda Makati into what is now Makati City, the central business district of the Philippines. Aside from its investment in Manila Water, the Ayala Corporation's diverse business involvement includes telecommunications (Globe Telecoms), real estate and hotels (Ayala Land), financial services (Bank of the Philippine Islands, the country's number one bank), electronics and information technology (Integrated Microelectronics Inc., and iAyala Company, Inc.), automotive distribution (Honda Cars and Isuzu Automotive Dealership Inc.), and international operations (Ayala International Pte Ltd with investments in real estate and property in Japan, Hong Kong, Singapore, Australia, and Malaysia).[24]

Maynilad Water Services Incorporated

The second concessionaire was a joint venture between Bepres Holdings of the Lopez family and Ondeo, a subsidiary of the French multinational Suez Lyonnaise des Eaux. Suez's roots lies in the building of the Suez Canal in the nineteenth century. It is presently one of the world's biggest companies involved in, among other things, water provision. It is in *Fortune's* top 100 companies, employing around 173,000 worldwide and serving 125 million water costumers.[25]

The Lopez family is one of the Philippines' most recognizable business families. Like the Ayalas, the Lopezes have a long record of business involvement in the country, dating back to the early nineteenth century. Unlike the Ayalas, however, the Lopezes have also been involved in politics. According to the Lopez family's own account of their history, the family's involvement in Philippine business and politics started in the early 1800s in Jaro, Iloilo, where Basilio Lopez was a local trader and a *gobernadorcillo* (municipal judge or governor). The Lopezes pride themselves in the family's leap to prominence through its involvement in sugar growing and its consequent move to Metro Manila and eventual diversification to the urban economy via involvement in power generation (Meralco) and mass media (ABS-CBN, the *Manila Chronicle*).

Alfred McCoy traces what he calls the "spectacular postwar climb of the Lopez brothers, Eugenio and Fernando, based on their masterful manipulation of the state's regulatory and financial powers".[26] He describes the Lopezes as "the most successful rent seekers, prospering largely because they were skilled in extracting special privileges from the state apparatus ... relying on state licenses that restricted access to the market".

When President Marcos declared martial law in 1972, he targeted the Lopezes as one of the supposed oligarchs dominating the economy. Even though Fernando Lopez was Marcos' vice-president, he shut down the ABS-CBN radio and television network and the *Manila Chronicle*, both owned by the Lopez family. In addition, Eugenio Lopez was forced to sell his shares in Meralco, the country's biggest electricity distributor, to a group led by well-known Marcos cronies. Only after Marcos was deposed in 1986 did the Lopezes regain control of their former companies.[27]

After February 1986, the Lopezes worked towards restoring their vast family business, as well as entering new sectors that were being made available by the liberalization of the economy. Benpres Holdings was incorporated in 1993 as the family's flagship company as the Lopezes diversified into new business ventures.[28] The Lopez family was one of the biggest beneficiaries of economic liberalization as it won contracts to manage privatized services (water and tollways), bolstered its control over its original businesses (media and power generation), and gained access to the liberalized telecommunications sector.

Benpres serves as the Lopez family's holding company in its diverse investments in various businesses such as broadcasting (ABS-CBN, the country's number one television and radio network), cable (Sky Cable), telecommunications (Bayantel), power generation and distribution (First Philippine Holding Company, Meralco, Philec, First Gas Holdings Corporation, First Philippine Industrial Park, First Philippine Pipeline Incorporated, and First Generation Holdings Corporation), water (Maynilad Water Services Inc.), banking (PCIBank, which was disposed of in 1999), infrastructure and toll development (First Philippine Infrastructure Development Corporation), property development (Rockwell Land Corporation), information technology (e-Lopez and Bayantrade), and healthcare delivery (the Medical City).

OUTCOMES OF PRIVATIZATION

The concessionaires took over the operation of water and sewerage services to Metro Manila from 1 August 1997. Up to the day of the turnover, the process of privatization was deemed a success due to the open and transparent manner in which it was conducted. However, the turnover proved untimely as it coincided with the July 1997 Asian financial crisis.

At the onset, both companies faced enormous problems and challenges unforeseen when the privatization exercise was being undertaken. First, the financial crisis led to a massive devaluation of the peso, falling from P26 to P52 to the U.S. dollar. With the devaluation, the value of the loans in peso terms taken over by the concessionaires almost doubled overnight, leading to higher operating costs. In addition, banks became reluctant to provide financing for expansion. Secondly, the El Nino phenomenon brought about a drought that led to lower water supply and poorer water quality. These two unexpected events dealt a double blow to both consortia.

Due to the financial crisis, both concessionaires asked for a foreign currency differential adjustment (FCDA) and tariff increases even before the scheduled rate review. The Regulatory Office approved their request, resulting in two tariff increases since 1997. First, in October 2001, tariffs in Maynilad areas rose from P6.58 per cubic metre to P15.46, and in Manila Water areas, rates increased from P2.95 to P6.75. Secondly, in January 2003, rates jumped a further 81 per cent in the East Zone to P12.21 and 36 per cent in the West Zone, to P21.11. This means that they have become 5.4 and 7.3 times higher than the original tariff in 1997.[29]

Civil society groups protested the regulatory process of approving water rate increases claiming that the burden of the crisis was being passed wholly to the consumers, without letting the concessionaires shoulder some of the commercial risks of operating a business. In August 2002, Bantay Tubig (Water Guards), a coalition of civil society groups was established to represent consumer interests in the regulation of water.[30]

Nevertheless, much has changed since the two private water companies won the concessions to take over Manila's waterworks. Although there is dispute as to the exact figures, the two companies have connected about two million people to the network within the first five years. Water loss, the decade-old problem of the MWSS, however remained high in the West Zone while it was slowly reduced in the East Zone.

The Failed Case of Maynilad[31]

In December 2002, debt-ridden and unable to raise capital from the financial market, Maynilad Water of the Lopezes and France's Suez, decided to pull out of its twenty-five-year contract by March 2003 — essentially abandoning a concession serving 6.5 million people in the western part of Metro Manila. Maynilad's move was a response to its failure to convince the Regulatory Office to grant it a further rate increase. Maynilad blamed the government for its failure to deliver water services to its consumers and sought the return of US$303 million it claims it invested in the privatized water utility.

A contentious legal arbitration ensued, which reached the Paris-based International Chamber of Commerce (ICC) arbitration panel. Before a decision was handed down, the Arroyo government reached a deal with Maynilad's owners in 2004. The deal involved a debt-equity conversion that would give government 60 per cent majority control over Maynilad. In exchange, the government would forego about P8 billion pesos that Maynilad owes MWSS, converting this to equity in the company and further absorbing some additional P10 billion of the company's debt. The government would have majority stake in the company, reducing to a minority the Benpres-Ondeo Group. Civil society groups have complained that the deal was a bailout of an influential family which should be allowed to fail rather than saddling taxpayers with the burden of its debts, inefficiencies and mismanagement.[32]

As of 2005, audited financial statements indicate Manila Water is slowly making a profit. Maynilad Water, however, claims that it was hit hard by the Asian financial crisis. Because of the financial crisis, Maynilad had cut spending for expansion and maintenance, had fallen behind in payments to its contractors as well as its concession fees, and was unable to access the financial market to finance its expansion.[33]

Maynilad Water blames its losses on the heavy debt burden assumed by the company upon privatization in 1997. Of the two concessionaires, Maynilad shouldered 90 per cent of the foreign debt of the old MWSS, while Manila Water took over the remaining 10 per cent. It seems that Maynilad agreed to this lopsided division because the loan was spent in improving MWSS's infrastructure located in the West Zone.[34]

Yet, blaming the government for this unbalanced sharing of debt was being dishonest. At the start, Maynilad was agreeable to shoulder this risk in order to gain control of the MWSS' water distribution assets. Yet, it immediately changed its tune in the aftermath of the financial crisis.

Analysts further argue that the financial crisis was just part of the story. Inefficiency and possible mismanagement also played a role in Maynilad's problems. In 1997, when it took over the concession, water losses were estimated at around 56 per cent. Maynilad's NRW rose to 60 per cent in 1998 and 68 per cent in 2002.

In addition, compared to Manila Water, Maynilad's operating expenses were much higher. MWSS consultants found that Maynilad's total operating cost per cubic metre of water sold was 10.45 pesos, while that of Manila Water was 4.45 pesos in 2001. In addition, Maynilad's spending patterns revealed operational inefficiency and weak management controls. For instance, its staff numbers were 29 per cent higher than originally considered in its bid. Reportedly, although Maynilad cut the number of supervisors, professional and technical staff, and rank and file employees by 378, it nonetheless hired an additional 46 new top managers. The company also had huge expenses for contracted services such as management and technical fees paid to Ondeo and a Benpres Holdings affiliate. These expenses grew at a faster rate than revenues in the first six years of the water concession.

The MWSS consultants also noted that Maynilad Water abolished its engineering department. Yet, it contracted out the job to two external parties, including a joint venture of the major shareholders. The MWSS consultants wondered if the spin-off resulted in any savings for Maynilad, considering that more than half of the abolished engineering unit staff were redeployed within the company. Finally, it was found that Maynilad purchased 80 per cent more computers per employee than Manila Water. The consultants noted that Maynilad bought the computers from IBM France, another company affiliated with Suez.[35]

The More Promising Case of Manila Water

Given Manila Water's extremely low bid in 1997, it would have been the one expected to run into greater risk of financial problems. Yet, in contrast to Maynilad's failure, the performance of Manila Water was a success.

First of all, from 1997 to 2000, Manila Water improved its water provision. The company increased its billed volume of water by 70 per cent from 440 million litres per day (mld) to over 700 mld. The company also expanded the area receiving twenty-four-hour water supply from an estimated 15–20 per cent to over 60 per cent. Thirdly, the company broadened its customer base from 65 per cent to 88 per cent of the population in the East Zone. Manila Water claims that these performance improvements were achieved through the enhancement of customer focus, fiscal discipline and cost-effectiveness, re-orientation of employees on the value of quality service, business focus and accountability for performance, and reduction of non-revenue water (NRW) from 63 per cent to 58 per cent.[36]

Secondly, the company started improving sewerage and sanitation services for the East Zone by installing low-cost package sewerage treatment plants in several communities. In July 2005, Manila Water secured a Y6.59 billion loan (US$64 million) from the World Bank, through the Land Bank of the Philippines, to improve the sewerage coverage of Metro Manila from the current 10 per cent to 30 per cent in the next five years. This project is expected to bring Manila at par with other SEA megacities in terms of environmental compliance and quality of life.[37]

Thirdly, Manila Water improved customer service by setting up a call centre and strengthened its branch offices network to systematize customer service and relationships. It also launched "Tubig para sa Barangay" [Water for the Urban Poor] to enable poor communities to avail of water via legitimate connections. Since 1997, 35,000 households have benefited from this project as it minimized illegal connections and leaks and improved the quality of life of the urban poor.[38]

Fourthly, Manila Water absorbed 2,165 employees from MWSS in August 1997. This went down to 1,641 in December 1997 and to 1,577 in December 1998. As of 2000, the company has 1,540 employees, with a manpower productivity ratio of 3.7 employees per 1,000 connections. This is a massive improvement from the ratio of 8.5 prior to privatization. Currently, 95 per cent of Manila Water's staff are former MWSS employees.

In July 2005, Manila Water announced its interest in buying 30 per cent stake in Maynilad, as the latter's ownership reverted to government.[39] Manila Water is also bidding to take over the water services in Cebu. Its success has also allowed the company to venture internationally. Manila Water is currently involved in an ongoing management contract for the operation of a US$200 million water and wastewater facility in Tirupur, India. In addition, it has teamed up with Larsen and Toubro Ltd, India's largest engineering and construction firm, and the Mahindra Group, one of India's leading conglomerates, to bid for the Delhi water privatization in October 2005.[40]

CONCLUSION

Water privatization in Metro Manila had mixed outcomes. The privatization of the East Zone under Manila Water was a success while that of the West Zone under Maynilad was a failure.

About half of the two million people added to the water network belonged to poor households, who would not have been connected if the MWSS remained in charge. Despite the failure of the West Zone and its return to the government, a million poor people given direct water connection in five years is already a notable achievement.

New service connections, which averaged only 17,040 a year from 1991 to 1995, tripled to 53,921 a year after privatization. Of course, it was not altruism that drove the concessionaires to focus greater attention on the poor. Rather, it was a two-pronged business strategy, which not only provided water services to previously unconnected poor households but at the same time reduced non-revenue water, resulting in higher revenue collection. Previously, much of MWSS' water losses were due to illegal water connections in slum areas. Thus, providing water access to the urban poor not only benefited the households themselves but also improved the company's bottomline.

As the above discussion has shown, the careful design of the Manila Water privatization resulted to its being an open, transparent, and successful process. Discounting the unpredictable developments like the El Nino drought and the 1997 financial crisis, the biggest challenge after privatization was with regards to regulation. In particular, while a regulatory body was created, this did not necessarily translate into regulatory capacity, credibility, and independence.

According to the findings of the Asian Development Bank, there is no universal model in establishing a regulatory body or building a regulatory framework.[41] Regulation is a constantly changing and evolving process. Concession contracts should not be treated as static documents and that renegotiation, when necessary, should be undertaken. In the process of doing so, information should be made available, not merely to the concessionaires but also to the consuming public.

In the Philippines, the creation of the Regulatory Office was an attempt to respond quickly to the need for a regulatory mechanism so that the privatization process would not be derailed. Consequently, many of the regulatory provisions in the concession contract were not thought out.[42]

Evidently, there is a need to think through carefully the post-privatization regulatory framework, and not merely the privatization process itself. More importantly, establishing a regulatory body with political independence, credibility, and capacity is essential. Such a body should be composed of members appointed for a fixed period of time and only removed for abuse of authority or illegal acts. Furthermore, transparency in the regulatory decision making process as well as access to legal recourse whenever necessary are key ingredients of a post-privatization regulatory framework.

Despite the problems and challenges, the privatization of the Manila water system led to concrete, beneficial results. Even people who are critical of the failure of Maynilad acknowledge the general improvement in infrastructure and level of service in the metropolitan area, in contrast to the former situation under the MWSS. Privatization may not be the panacea that applies to all the problems of urban water and sewerage systems among developing countries worldwide, but in the case of the Philippines, it certainly brought about concrete gains though with some painful losses, as one turned out as a success case while another needed state bailout.

Notes

1. See <http://www.righttowater.org.uk/code/Policy_1.asp>.
2. "Maynilad on the Mend: Rebidding Process Infuses New Life to a Struggling Concessionaire" (Manila: Asian Development Bank, May 2008).
3. Such a shift in thinking had already occurred in telecommunications, electricity, and now, in water. See Nick Johnstone, Libby Wood, and Robert Hearne, "The Regulation of Private Sector Participation in Urban Water Supply and Sanitation: Realising Social and Environmental Objectives in Developing Countries", *Environmental Economic Programme Discussion Paper DP 99–01* (September 1999): 1.
4. See "Promoting Privatisation" at <www.publicintegrity.org/water/printer-friendly.aspx?aid=45> (accessed 1 August 2005).
5. Johnstone, Wood, and Hearne, p. 2. It has to be pointed out, however, that there are numerous examples of efficiently managed public water systems in developing countries such as the examples of Ecuador, Chile, Zimbabwe and Botswana. These successes have been attributed to the provision of a certain degree of autonomy to the service provider as well as the introduction of effective incentives to the provider and its staff members. See also Estache, 1994; Ingram and Kessides, 1994; and Nickson, 1997.
6. Johnstone, Wood, and Hearne, pp. 3–4. Concessions have been the most popular form of PSP in terms of both number and size of investment,

while BOTs are second most popular. Regionally, investments have been concentrated in Latin America and East Asia. Sub-Saharan Africa accounts for less than 1 per cent of total investment. See also Judith Rees, "Regulation and Private Participation in the Water and Sanitation Sector", *Global Water Partnership Technical Advisory Committee Background Paper no. 1* (July 1998): 15–21.

7. Lazaro, MacLeod, and Vigilar, "Privatisation: Philippine Water Industry Comes of Age", at <http://www.mwss.gov.ph/news/default.asp?action=article&ID=67> (accessed 1 August 2005).

8. Ibid.

9. Alexander Orwin, "The Privatisation of Water and Wastewater Utilities: An International Survey", August 1999 at <http://www.environmentprobe.org/enviroprobe/pubs/ev542.html#Asia> (accessed 1 August 2005).

10. Ibid.

11. Roel Landingan, "Loaves, Fishes and Dirty Water: Manila's Privatized Water Can't Handle the Pressure", in <http://www.publicintegrity.org/water/printer-friendly.aspx?aid=51> (accessed 1 August 2005).

12. According to a top government official involved in MWSS's privatization, the process of privatizing the MWSS was influenced by the model undertaken in resolving the Philippine power crisis in 1993, which demonstrated the effectiveness of private sector participation in infrastructure. See Mark Dumol, *The Manila Water Concession: A Key Government Official's Diary of the World's Largest Water Privatisation* (Washington, D.C.: The World Bank, 2000).

13. This follows after the model of Paris water privatization where the city was divided into two areas, via the River Seine. In the case of the Philippines, the Pasig River demarcates the two zones.

14. See Dumol, 2000.

15. See Lazaro, MacLeod, and Vigilar.

16. Dumol, 2000. See also Orwin, 1999.

17. Arthur McIntosh, *Asian Water Supplies: Reaching the Urban Poor* (Manila: Asian Development Bank, 2003), pp. 169–71.

18. Orwin, 1999.

19. Dumol, 2000, p. 84.

20. Lazaro, MacLeod, and Vigilar.

21. See <http://www.ayala-group.com> (accessed 15 February 2003).
22. *Forbes Magazine,* 20 August 2001.
23. See <http://www.ayala-group.com/about/history.asp> (accessed 15 February 2003).
24. See <http://www.ayala-group.com/businterests/realestates.asp> (accessed 15 February 2003).
25. <www.publicintegrity.org/water/printer-friendly.aspx?aid=47> (accessed 1 August 2005).
26. Alfred McCoy, ed., "Rent Seeking Families and the State", in *An Anarchy of Families: State and Family in the Philippines* (Wisconsin: University of Wisconsin Center for Southeast Asian Studies, 1993), p. 435.
27. See Oscar Lopez, "An Open Letter to Juan Ponce Enrile, 2 October 2002" at <http://www.benpres-holdings.com/press-10202.html> (accessed 20 February 2003). The Aquino government returned control of ABS-CBN, Meralco, and PCIBank to the Lopez family.
28. See Benpres Profile at <http://www.benpres-holdings.com/h-heritage2.html> (accessed 20 February 2003).
29. Violeta Q. Perez-Corral, "The Failed Water Privatisation in Manila", at <http://www.jacses.org/en/sdap/water/report04.html> (accessed 5 August 2005). See also McIntosh, 2003, p. 175.
30. See <www.ipd.ph/Bantay%20Tubig/web-content/factsheet/crisis_origin.html> (accessed 1 August 2005).
31. For further details, see Jude Esguerra, "The Corporate Muddle of Manila's Water Concessions: New Rules, New Roles: Does PSP Benefit the Poor?", paper written for Water Aid and Tearfund, 2003.
32. See <http://www.ipd.ph/Bantaypercent20Tubig/web-content/factsheet/gma_deal.html> (accessed 1 August 2005).
33. Landingin, 2003.
34. Ibid.
35. Ibid.
36. See <http://www.manilawater.com/au_manila03.cfm> (accessed 1 August 2005).
37. *Philippine Star,* 25 July 2005.
38. McIntosh, 2003, p. 171.
39. *Business World,* 27 July 2005.

40. *Philippine Star*, 25 July 2005. The Delhi water supply and sewerage privatization project is part of a US$100 million World Bank loan to the Indian government. It is a six-year management contract for the operation and development of water and sewerage system to improve water services to approximately 1.4 million people. Manila Water has already prequalified for the bid.
41. Asian Development Bank, *Regulatory Systems and Networking: Water Utilities And Regulatory Bodies: Proceedings of the Regional Forum, Manila 26–28 March 2000* (Manila: Asian Development Bank, 2001), p. 38
42. Ibid., p. 171.

References

Adam, Christopher, William Cavendish, and Percy Mistry. *Adjusting Privatisation: Case Studies from Developing Countries*. London: James Currey Ltd., 1992.

Arriens, Wouter Lincklaen, Jeremy Bird, Jeremy Berkoff, and Paul Mosley. *Towards Effective Water Policy in the Asian and Pacific Region, Volume 1*. Manila: Asian Development Bank, 1996.

Asian Development Bank. *Regulatory Systems and Networking: Water Utilities And Regulatory Bodies: Proceedings of the Regional Forum, Manila 26–28 March 2001*. Manila: Asian Development Bank, 2001.

———. *Water for All: The Water Policy of the Asian Development Bank*. Manila: Asian Development Bank, 2001.

Baumol, William, John Panzar, and Robert Willig. *Contestable Markets and the Theory of Industry Structure*. New York: Harcourt Brace Jovanovich, 1982.

Cajudo, Cynthia. "The Privatisation of a Local Water District: A Case Study". In *East and Southeast Asian Network for Better Local Governments: New Public Management: Public Private Partnership*. Manila: Konrad-Adenauer Foundation, 2000.

Chotrani, Raj. "Lessons from Philippine Water Privatisation". *Asian Water* (July 1999) at <http://www.mwss.gov.ph/news/default.asp?action=article&ID=66> (accessed 15 August 2005).

David, Cristina. "Private Sector Participation in Water Supply and Sanitation: Realising Social and Environmental Objectives in Manila".

In *Private Firms and Public Water: Realising Social and Environmental Objectives in Developing Countries*, edited by Nick Johnstone and Libby Wood. Cheltenham, UK: Edward Elgar, 2001.

Dumol, Mark. *The Manila Water Concession: A Key Government Official's Diary of the World's Largest Water Privatisation*. Washington, D.C.: The World Bank, 2000.

Esguerra, Jude. "The Corporate Muddle of Manila's Water Concessions: New Rules, New Roles: Does PSP Benefit the Poor?". Paper written for Water Aid and Tearfund, 2003.

Hall, David. "Financing Water for the World: An Alternative to Guaranteed Profits". Paper commissioned by Public Services International to be presented at the Third World Water Forum, Kyoto, Japan, March 2003. <www.psiru.org>.

———. "Privatisation, Multinationals, and Corruption". *Development in Practice* 9, no. 5 (November 1999): 539–56.

Johnstone, Nick, Libby Wood, and Robert Hearne. "The Regulation of Private Sector Participation in Urban Water Supply and Sanitation: Realising Social and Environmental Objectives in Developing Countries". *Environmental Economic Programme Discussion Paper DP 99–01*, September 1999.

Kikeri, Sunita, John Nellis, and Mary Shirley. *Privatisation: The Lessons of Experience*. Washington, D.C.: The World Bank, 1992.

Landingan, Roel. "Loaves, Fishes and Dirty Water: Manila's Privatized Water Can't Handle the Pressure". <http://www.publicintegrity. org/water/printer-friendly.aspx?aid=51> (accessed 1 August 2005).

Lazaro, A., S. Macleod, and G. Vigilar. "Privatisation: Philippine Water Industry Comes of Age". <http://www.mwss.gov.ph/news/default. asp?action=article&ID=67> (accessed 1 August 2005).

"Maynilad on the Mend: Rebidding Process Infuses New Life to a Struggling Concessionaire". Manila: Asian Development Bank, May 2008.

McIntosh, Arthur. *Asian Water Supplies: Reaching the Urban Poor*. Manila: Asian Development Bank, 2003.

Mumssen, Yogita and Brian Williamson. "Comparative Analysis of Regulation". In *Reinventing Water and WasteWater Systems: Global Lessons for Improving Water Management*, edited by Paul Seidenstat, David Haarmeyer, and Simon Hakim. Canada: John Wiley and Sons, 2002.

Rees, Judith. "Regulation and Private Participation in the Water and Sanitation Sector". Global Water Partnership Technical Advisory Committee Background Paper no. 1, July 1998.

United Nations Economic and Social Commission for Asia and the Pacific. *Sustainable Development of Water Resources in Asia and the Pacific: An Overview*. New York: United Nations, 1997.

_____. *Urban Water Resources Management*. Water Resources Series no. 72. New York: United Nations, 1993.

_____. *Water Resources Development in Asia and the Pacific: Some Issues and Concerns*. Water Resources Series no. 62. New York: United Nations, 1987.

10

SINGAPORE'S EXPERIENCE IN WATER RESOURCE MANAGEMENT

Wong Kai Yeng

Singapore today is regarded by others to have done well in its sustainable water management strategy, both in securing sufficient water supplies to meet its needs and in managing water demand through public education and ownership. Singapore's application of technology to produce NEWater, a high-grade reclaimed water, to supplement its conventional water sources, has attracted much interest from water utilities companies worldwide. Our extensive water conservation efforts and community-driven programmes have successfully reduced the island's per capita domestic consumption to one of the lowest in the tropical region.

Singapore water companies and the Public Utilities Board (PUB) have also been making their mark in the lucrative global environment and water industry business. Singapore water company, Hyflux, has established recycling and desalination plants in China and the Middle East. Sembcorp Industries also has collaborations with the Chinese government to set up and run an industrial water recycling facility in China's Jiangsu province. Singapore also hosted the inaugural Singapore International Water Week from 23 to 27 June 2008 and more than 8,500 representatives from governments, utility providers, businesses, and academia were at the meeting. Besides launching the water fund, over S$367 million (US$250 million) of deals were signed at this meeting. The second which was held from 22 to 26 June 2009 attracted over 10,000 attendees. About $2.8 billion deals were inked at this event. The latest Singapore International Water Week held in 2011 attracted 13,500 delegates with MOUs reaching S$2.9 billion.

NEWater has also won the "Environmental Contribution of the Year" title in the Global Water Awards 2008. Singapore is also one of the first countries in the world outside the Middle East which has demonstrated that membrane-based desalination can be carried out at an affordable cost.

Yet, despite all these, Singapore consistently continues to be ranked poorly in international studies conducted on water availability. For example, in the United Nations World Water Development Report, Singapore was ranked 158th out of 193 countries in terms of water availability.[1] While this apparent dichotomy is puzzling, it highlights a general lack of awareness and information on how Singapore has been able to overcome the odds and build up a sustainable water management strategy, even though it is not blessed with natural water sources.

Indeed, sustainable water management requires nations not only to ensure adequacy in water supply, but also necessitates the management of water demand. This is aptly captured in Singapore's PUB corporate tagline "Water For All: Conserve, Value, Enjoy".

Singapore's achievements thus far do not come without its fair share of pain and knocks. However, through far-sighted long-term planning backed by strong political will, Singapore has successfully managed to build up a robust, diversified and sustainable water supply system to support our economic and social growth.

Singapore's ability to create a sustainable water supply despite its lack of natural resource has been hailed as an international success story. This chapter charts the various measures that Singapore has adopted to achieve this milestone — from the expansion and clean-up of local sources to new technologies, and demand management tools. It also shows how the local water authority, PUB, through its management of the entire water loop, has ensured that even used water and stormwater collection is optimized for potable water supply.

BUILDING UP A RELIABLE SUPPLY OF POTABLE WATER

Barely forty years ago, no one would be able to imagine that Singapore would be where it is today. Indeed, during the early post-independence years in the 1960s, Singapore was faced with many challenges.

One of these challenges was to build up a reliable supply of clean potable water to keep pace with population expansion and industrial development. This, however, was not an easy task. Firstly, there was insufficient proper infrastructure for collection and storage of rainwater, and the treatment and distribution of potable water. This was compounded by poor public health conditions brought about by the lack of proper sanitation facilities. This contaminated and polluted the water courses and rivers and made the treatment of water for potable use very costly and difficult.

Recognizing the extent of the problem, the government embarked on projects to construct new reservoirs to secure new supplies of water in addition to the existing MacRitchie, Pierce, and Seletar Reservoirs. The first major projects were completed in the mid 1960s to enable the supply of water from Johor.

In 1975, two other major schemes were completed. A dam was constructed at the upper reaches of the old Peirce Reservoir (later renamed Lower Peirce Reservoir); and Kranji and Pandan Reservoir were created. By 1981, four other rivers — Murai, Poyan, Sarimbun and Tengeh — were dammed and converted into reservoirs. 1986 heralded the completion of the major projects, with the formation of Lower Seletar Reservoir, Bedok Reservoir, and Bedok Waterworks. The unique feature of the Bedok project was its pumped inflow stormwater collection stations to tap the storm run-offs.

CLEANING UP OF THE SINGAPORE RIVER

Besides the expansion of our water supply, pollution control strategies and measures were adopted and enforced. This proved to be a major turning point as these tough pollution control measures allowed Singapore today to harness the rivers and watercourses to augment its water supply needs.

In 1977, then Prime Minister Mr Lee Kuan Yew launched a ten-year programme to clean up the Singapore River. This was to be an important milestone in Singapore's water story. At that time,

FIGURE 10.1
Extent of Clean-up

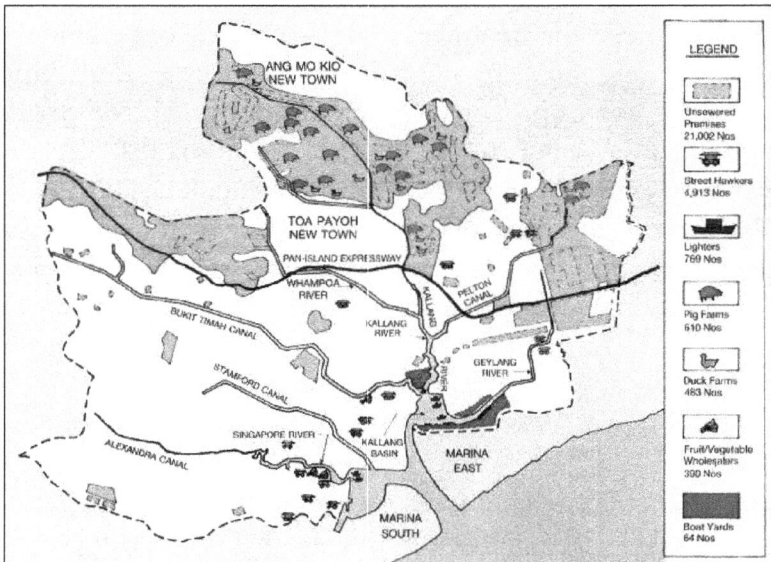

Source: Public Utilities Board, Singapore.

the Singapore River and its surrounding areas were heavily polluted due to the presence of commercial activities taking place along the river banks, industries and farms located along the upstream rivers, and extensive street hawking with no proper sanitary and sewerage facilities. Figure 10.1 shows the extent of the clean-up.

It was a massive clean-up operation involving many different government agencies. Table 10.1 shows the involvement of

TABLE 10.1
Some of the Ministries and Statutory Boards Involved in the Clean-up

Ministries/Statutory Boards	Areas of Responsibility
Housing & Development Board	• Redevelopment of squatter colonies over eight years • Clearance and resettlement of pockets of squatters within three years
Primary Production Department	Phasing out or resiting of pig and duck farming in five years
Urban Redevelopment Authority	Redevelopment of run-down urban areas over eight years
Port of Singapore Authority	• Enforcement and resiting of riverine activities • Continuing enforcement against dumping of refuse and discharge of wastewater from boats into rivers • Enforcement against derelict boats
Ministry of Environment • Sewerage Department • Hawkers Department	• Enforcement against unsewered premises in sewered areas in five years • Extension of sewers over eight to ten years • Resiting of all street hawkers

the major agencies in the clean-up. Pollutive activities located along the riverbanks were either phased out or relocated to new premises with proper pollution control facilities. The river beds were dredged and the muddy banks were transformed into nice sandy beaches. Riverside walkways were tiled and landscaping and turfing along the river banks were carried out. At the same time, massive resettlement of squatters was carried out and more than 26,000 families were moved into proper public housing with sanitary facilities.

The river cleaning up exercise did more than just physically cleaning up the Singapore River. It was significant from a water resource viewpoint as it built on to the separation of the stormwater and sewerage collection systems, and allowed rainwater to be collected and stored in the reservoirs without having it polluted with sewage and rubbish from homes and industries.

Equally important, it inculcated a mindset change in Singaporeans towards keeping Singapore's rivers and waterways, drains and canals clean. After years of having a river in the city centre that is dirty, polluted and dirty, the sight of a clean river free of offensive smell and able to support marine aquatic life created a sense of pride among Singaporeans.

Because of this, PUB was then able to move from collecting rainwater from natural catchment areas to also collecting rainwater from drains and canals in housing estates and urban areas. This facilitated the development of more water catchment areas, including those in urban new towns in Singapore.

WATER SUPPLY MANAGEMENT

Singapore's overall approach in ensuring adequacy of water supplies is based upon three strategies: (1) diversification of sources; (2) leveraging on R&D and technology; and (3) management of the water loop.[2]

While the development of new water catchment areas remains a priority, there is a limit to the amount of rainwater that can be collected through this means especially given Singapore's small land mass. Singapore therefore invested heavily in R&D and technology to explore new non-conventional sources of water supplies, namely, desalination and NEWater.

Desalination

As early as the mid-1980s, the possibility of desalination to expand Singapore's water stocks and diversify our sources of water supply was explored. However, for reasons of cost and the ready availability of water from local sources and from Johor, seawater desalination was put on hold.

With technological advancement and breakthroughs in membrane technology in the 1990s bringing costs down, plans to desalt seawater were subsequently revived in the late 1990s. Private companies were invited to build a new desalination plant in Tuas on a "design-build-own-operate" basis and to sell the desalinated water to PUB for distribution through the water supply system.

The tender for the desalination plant was eventually awarded in January 2003 for the supply of 30 million gallons per day (mgd) of desalinated water to PUB for twenty years. Commencement of the supply of water from the desalination plant to the potable water grid began in September 2005. The PUB announced an open tender for Singapore's second desalination plant in 2010. This plant will be one of Singapore's largest water supply infrastructure project with a planned output of about 70 mgd and is scheduled to start operation by 2013. In the future, the desalination programme will produce around 30 per cent of Singapore's water requirements.

NEWater

NEWater is a shining example of Singapore's use of technology to increase its water sources. Using a three-step process of microfiltration, reverse osmosis and ultra-violet (UV) radiation, used water is treated to high-quality recycled water called NEWater for direct non-potable use in industries and the commercial sector. A small portion of NEWater is also injected back into the reservoirs for indirect potable use. However, the main objective of NEWater is really to replace potable water for non-potable use in industries and the commercial sector.

Currently, five NEWater plants supplying a total of 102 mgd are in operation. The fifth plant is located at the Changi Water Reclamation Plant and was officially opened on 3 May 2010. Initially, the plant will produce 15 mgd but is scheduled to increase to 50 mgd eventually. Together with desalinated water, NEWater can supply over 50 per cent of Singapore's total water demand by the year 2012. By 2060, the PUB plans to triple the present NEWater capacity so that it alone can meet 50 per cent of future water demand.

NEWater and desalinated water, together with Singapore's local water sources and imported water from Johor, forms what is known as its "Four Taps" — four diversified, independent sources of water supply to meet Singapore's needs.

New Technologies

Besides NEWater and desalination, PUB continues to invest heavily in R&D and to be on the look-out for new technology improvements in the areas of water and used water treatment. This has resulted in the test-bedding of several new projects such as the Membrane Bioreactor (MBR) and the Variable Salinity Plant (VSP). If successful, these projects will eventually be scaled up to augment the existing processes and enhance the reliability of water supplies.

Increasing our Water Catchment Areas — Marina Reservoir

With the technology breakthroughs especially in membrane technology, it is now possible to convert previously untapped regions in Singapore into water catchment areas. One such example is the Marina Basin, right in the middle of the city centre.

Construction is completed to dam up the mouth of the Marina Channel with a barrage. This project is a unique three-in-one initiative aimed at achieving three objectives: (1) to create a new reservoir to augment our water supply, (2) to act as a tidal barrier for flood control and (3) the new body of freshwater at constant level will be a major lifestyle attraction of the city centre.

Eventually, the entire Marina Basin will be converted into a freshwater reservoir, Singapore's fifteenth reservoir. Dubbed "the reservoir in the city", it will be the first reservoir in Singapore to be created within a city. Together with other ongoing water schemes, this project will increase the island's water catchment areas from half to two-thirds of Singapore.

There are pockets of low-lying areas in the city such as Chinatown, Boat Quay, Jalan Besar and Geylang. These areas are below or slightly above high tides and are therefore prone to flooding whenever heavy rain coincides with high tides. The proposed barrage will act as a tidal barrier to keep out high tides, with floodgates and pumps to release excess stormwater during heavy rains.

As the water in the Marina Basin will be unaffected by tides, its water level will be kept constant and Singaporeans can therefore enjoy a variety of water sports all year round. Citizens and visitors alike will then be able to indulge in recreational activities such as canoeing, kayaking, sailing, water skiing and wind surfing, in addition to the water taxis and pleasure cruises that ply the area today.

Used Water Management — Deep Tunnel Sewerage System (DTSS)

The use of technology extends beyond potable water supply to also other areas such as used water treatment. The Deep Tunnel Sewerage System (DTSS) is one such example. The DTSS involves the construction of a 48-kilometre long tunnel to divert used water to a centralized treatment plant at the southeastern end of Singapore. This will then free up the land occupied by the existing water reclamation plants and pumping stations for other economic use. The project[3] is currently underway and was completed in 2008.

The DTSS project is an integral piece of the strategy to manage the entire water loop as it allows the collection and channeling of used water into water reclamation plants for treatment and subsequently to NEWater plants for production into NEWater. This will maximize every drop of used water collected for re-use and reduce the demand on fresh potable water.

Stormwater Management

The physical separation of stormwater collection from used water collection theoretically allows every drop of rainwater to be collected and stored in Singapore's reservoirs. However, tropical rainfalls are often characterized by high intensity over a short duration. In cases where this coincides with high tides, it often results in flooding in low lying areas in parts of Singapore.

PUB's strategy in stormwater management is to reduce the flood prone areas while at the same time collect as much of the rainfall as possible in the reservoirs through the drains and canals.

WATER DEMAND MANAGEMENT — 3P ENGAGEMENT

With two-thirds of Singapore set to become water catchment areas by 2009, almost every Singaporean will eventually work, live or play in water catchment areas. It is therefore critical to engage the 3P (people, public, private) sector and make sure everyone plays his or her part by not littering or polluting the catchment so that the water sources remain clean and the water quality remains of high standard.

This new emphasis on engaging 3P partners is embodied in the "Conserve, Value, Enjoy" part of PUB's tagline. It calls on PUB's 3P partners to conserve water, to keep the water catchments and waterways clean, and to build a relationship with water. This tagline recognizes that the government's effort alone is insufficient, and that it requires the collective effort of every Singaporean to realize the vision of having a sustainable supply of clean water for all.

One key strategy in the 3P engagement approach is in the area of water demand management. This stems from the recognition that water sustainability needs to be managed not only from the supply angle, but equally important from the demand perspective. To this end, PUB has embarked on community-driven public education programmes, such as the Water Efficient Homes Programme, and the Water Efficient Buildings Programme to encourage house owners and building owners to adopt water conservation measures.

At the same time, the industrial and commercial sectors are encouraged to switch from potable water to NEWater for their process and air-conditioned cooling uses to reduce potable water consumption in the non-domestic sector.

Results have been encouraging and the domestic per capita domestic consumption level decreased to 155 litres per day in 2009. The aim is to lower this further to 147 litres per day by 2020.

PUB has also recently opened up its reservoirs for recreational activities such as kayaking that the public can participate in. This is to encourage Singaporeans to participate in water activities in the reservoirs so that they experience first-hand the cleanliness of the water sources and the importance of keeping them clean. Over time, it is hoped that through such interactions, Singaporeans will develop a sense of shared ownership of the water resources and this will translate into positive behaviour such as good water conservation habits, not littering or polluting the water catchments, etc.

CONCLUSION

The search for new sources of water for Singapore is never-ending. Being a water-scarce city state, the availability of water for life, work and play will always be of vital national importance. At the same time, while efforts in curbing water demand has been effective, there is a need to continue to push on to encourage greater ownership by Singaporeans and the 3P sectors towards valuing Singapore's precious water resources.

More needs to be done, and more will be done. Together with its 3P partners, PUB is confident of a secured and sustainable supply of water for all Singaporeans for generations to come.

Notes

1. See Table 4.3 of *United Nations World Water Development Report 2: Water, A Shared Responsibility* (United States: UNESCO-WWAP, 2006).
2. The water loop is a process cycle that traces a drop of water as it passes through the various phases of rainfall precipitation, collection, storage, treatment, re-use and discharge.
3. This comprises of the construction of the North Tunnel, Spur Tunnel, the Changi Reclamation Plant and the effluent outfall.

Reference

United Nations World Water Development Report 2: Water, A Shared Responsibility. United States: UNESCO-WWAP, 2006.

11

THAILAND'S WATER SECTOR:
Overview and Implications

Sukontha Aekaraj

INTRODUCTION

Both the availability and use of water are changing. Water availability can be understood within the context of the dynamics of the water cycle. These resources are renewable (except for some groundwater), but only within clear limits, as in most cases water flows through catchments or river basin that are more or less self-contained. Water resources are also variable, over both space and time, with huge differences in availability in different parts of the world and wide variations in seasonal and precipitation in many places. This variability of water availability is one of the most essential characteristics of water resource management.

The precipitation that falls on land surface is the predominant source of water required for human consumption, agriculture and food production, industrial waste disposal processes and for support of natural and semi-natural ecosystems. Thailand's primary source of water is run-off diverted by humans for use in irrigated agriculture, in industry and in homes (rural and urban); for consumption of various kinds; and for waste disposal. It is the water of evapo-transpiration that mainly supports forests, rain-fed cultivated and grazing land, and a variety of ecosystems.

It has been estimated that more than 2 billion people are affected by water shortages in over forty countries: 1.1 billion do not have sufficient drinking water and 2.4 billion have no provision for sanitation. At present many developing countries have difficulty in supplying the minimum annual per capita water requirement of 1,700 cubic metres of drinking water necessary for active and healthy life for their people.[1]

Because of population growth, the average annual per capita availability of renewable water resources is projected to fall from 6,600 cubic metres to 4,800 cubic metres (m^3) in 2025. Given the uneven distribution of these resources, some 3 billion women and men will live in countries — wholly or partly arid or semi-arid — that have less than 1,700 cubic metres per capita, the quantity below which people start to suffer from water stress. Also by 2025, an estimated 4 billion people, or more than half the world population, will live in countries where more than 40 per cent of renewable resources are withdrawn for human uses — another indicator of high water stress under most conditions. A withdrawal over 40 per cent of renewable water means that water replenished yearly into the system cannot be met or recharged.

Southeast Asia's stock of water resources varies across the different countries.[2] This can be reflected in many parameters: Water per capita data is an example. Thailand has 3,264 cubic metres per year while Lao PDR's is 34,435 cubic metres per year (m^3/yr). A vast diversity in water characteristics provides each country with its own module or appropriate strategies for water management. Although these countries may not have a physical scarcity of water, it is important to note that seasonal scarcity does occur. Climate change and extreme events such as more frequent landslides and flash floods in many part of the region also point to the need to better manage water resources in order to buffer seasonal fluctuations in supplies.

As water by itself is considered to be both a natural resource and an input to activities, its role differs according to different sectoral needs. This make the scheme of water management a less than simple task. Water can be associated with domestic consumption, agriculture, industry, electricity, environment, etc. If water resources are not managed properly, adverse impacts will be imposed on the various sectors, and usually the poor is the worst hit.

Such a trend makes for competing uses of water unavoidable; in Southeast Asian countries this situation has become a reality where the need for water in various activities have to be traded off. By the end of the twentieth century the total population of the region exceeded 550 million. This is expected to rise by around 50 per cent, or by an additional 250 million, by 2025. By that year, per capita water will drop from 10,000 to 6,700 cubic metres.

The impacts from climate change and extreme events comprising flood and drought are not clear for Southeast Asian countries. Floods and drought conditions of varying intensity have been experienced at one time or another. The frequency of floods and drought appears to be increasing in recent years, and there is now heightened expectations from the public for the authorities to address such problems, given that large populations live and make their livelihoods in low-lying areas.

Most of the causal factors of floods and droughts are known but some are still not fully understood. These include climatic change and the occurrence of El Nino and La Nina that seem to come in regular intervals causing widespread damage such as floods, droughts and their consequent effects such as forest fires, and higher incidence of water related and respiratory diseases. In some areas, land use changes resulting from shifting cultivation and forest clearing are markedly changing run-off patterns and increasing flood and landslide hazards.

In many places, water quality has deteriorated dramatically, particularly in regions with intensive agriculture and large urban/ industrial areas. Pollution from bacteria, human waste, high concentration of nutrients, sedimentation and rising salinity are ever-growing problems throughout the world. Groundwater, the preferred source of drinking water for most people in the world, is also being polluted, particularly through industrial activities in urban areas and agricultural chemicals and fertilizers in rural areas.

Although several ASEAN countries have water quality monitoring and classification initiatives, statistically sound monitoring designs, long-term data storage facilities with accessible data, standardized reporting systems for water quality seem to be lacking or do not exist.[3]

It is not clear that whether or how water monitoring and reporting is linked to water resource policy, planning and decision-making frameworks. The water quality focus in ASEAN is on user groups, most notably potable water, water for recreational use, commercial fisheries and irrigation. The protection of water resources from an ecologically sustainable perspective receives little if any explicit water quality attention. Water resources for ecosystem services are generally viewed as a competing trade-off in the spectrum of water uses, in competition with water for drinking and irrigating crops, dilution of waste, self-purification, and the provision of food.

This chapter looks into Thailand's water sector and its related sectors, particularly by changes in water uses including population growth, agricultural demand, energy requirement, urbanization, economic growth and industry. All these factors affecting water uses in Thailand are presented in order to understand the overall aspects of water resources and its management.

THAILAND'S WATER RESOURCES

Thailand, a tropical land in the centre of Indochina peninsula, is bordered on the north by Lao People's Democratic Republic (Lao PDR), on the east by Lao PDR and Cambodia, on the south by the Gulf of Thailand and Malaysia, and on the west by Myanmar and the Andaman Sea. The total land area of the country is about 512,000 square kilometres (km²). As of 2010, the estimated population is about 66.5 million with a growth rate of 0.7 per cent.[4] The urban population was estimated at about 11 million with high concentration in the capital and the regional centres.

The country is still considered an agricultural-based country with a total agricultural area of about 265,200 km². In 2005, 47.4 per cent of the population engaged in agriculture; however, agricultural production accounts for only about 9.3 per cent of total GDP.[5]

Due to rapid economic development in the past decade, water demand has continued to grow. Two out of the four regions, namely the northeast and the central regions, have been experiencing frequent droughts, while flooding also occurs more frequently due to deforestation. The water resources development budget has been increasing and represents a large portion of the national development budget. However, there are currently constraints for large water resources development projects and also protests against such developments, the reason being that of the need to provide areas for human settlement.

The agricultural sector remains the main user of available water and accounts for 71 per cent of total water demand, while industrial use accounts for only 2 per cent, with domestic use accounting for 5 per cent, and the remaining 22 per cent for conserving environmental functions. However, the trend will change with reductions from the agricultural sector and increases from both the industrial and domestic water sectors.

In 2000, statistical survey revealed that 97 per cent of urban population access to safe drinking water from many sources, which are piped water systems, rain water jars, bottle water and protected wells. For the rural population, about 91 per cent have access to such drinking water sources.

SURFACE WATER RESOURCES

Thailand can be divided hydrologically into twenty-five river basins.[6] The average annual rainfall for all over the country is about 1,700 millimetres (mm). The total volume of water from the rainfall in all river basins in Thailand is estimated at 800,000 million cubic metres (mcm), of which 75 per cent or around 600,000 mcm is lost through evaporation, evapo-transpiration and infiltration, and the remaining 25 per cent of 200,000 mcm constitutes the run-off that flows in rivers and streams. As the population of Thailand is around 65.7 million, the availability of water resources is 3,264 cubic metres per person each year, which is statistically considered to be highly adequate. As mentioned earlier, the minimum annual per capita water requirement of 1,700 cubic metres of drinking water is necessary for active and healthy life for populations.

GROUNDWATER RESOURCES

Groundwater is an important source of water supply in Thailand. Public water supplies for one-fifth of the nation's 220 towns and cities and for half of the 700 municipalities are derived from groundwater. It is estimated that around 75 per cent of domestic water is obtained from groundwater sources. Groundwater system in Thailand is mainly recharged by rainfall of about 38,000 mcm and seepage from the rivers. Some amount of rainfall percolated through the ground settles in the 101,240 square kilometres of unconsolidated strata which can absorb and retain about 10 per cent of annual precipitation.

It was estimated from hydrological balance studies on Thailand that about 12.5 to 18 per cent of rainfall would infiltrate soils, and about 9 per cent of rainfall would reach aquifers. However, this estimate is valid only for the basins under favourable geologic conditions such as those in the Northern Highlands, the Upper

Central Plain, and along the Gulf Coastal Plain. For the other basins, such as those in the Lower Central Plain, including Bangkok and in the Khorat Plateau, it was estimated that only 5–6 per cent of rainfall reaches the aquifer. In addition, groundwater storage in the southern part of Thailand are beach-sand aquifers, located for 300 kilometres along east coast of Gulf of Thailand, which is mainly used for domestic consumption.

More than 200,000 groundwater well projects were undertaken by both government and private sectors amounting to a total capacity of about 7.55 million m^3/day (2,700 million m^3/year). It is estimated that 75 per cent of domestic water is obtained from groundwater sources which can serve approximately 35 million people in villages and urban areas.

WATER PROVISION AND WATER DEMAND

The average annual rainfall of the whole country is about 1,700 mm, ranging from 1,200 mm annually in the north and central plain, and up to 2,000–2,700 mm in the western, southern and eastern parts of the country. About 29 per cent of the surface run-off, approximately 70,770 mcm annually, is kept in various sizes of about 650 large and medium scale together with 60,000 small-scale water resources development projects all over the kingdom, covering about 31 million rai (4.96 million hectares) irrigable areas.

Although the water resources development programme has been implemented continuously for more than eighty years, rapid rural development, industrialization, tourism development and population growth has drastically raised the water demand for domestic use, agriculture and other purposes. Inefficient use of water by the various sectors and deteriorating water quality due to the excessive use of fertilizer and pesticides, urban sewage and industrial wastes have also created more serious problems to the availability and adequacy of water resources. In 2000, water demand for irrigable areas and other uses for the whole country was estimated to be 88,700 mcm/year and expected to be 109,350 mcm/year by 2006. Hence, the nation is facing serious supply constraints for further growth due to various problems in the water resources development scheme.

WATER RESOURCES MANAGEMENT IN THAILAND

Thailand's past three decades of sustainable and rapid economic development has stimulated an explosive expansion of demand for water services for domestic and industrial water supply, irrigation, and power. The government has devoted significant resources to meeting these demands, and an approach toward water management in Thailand has emerged with an emphasis on an expansion of access to services, electricity, irrigation and water supply for domestic purposes.

This approach was successful in giving millions of Thai access to potable drinking water, water to produce cheap and abundant food, and to generate hydroelectricity. However, as water has become increasingly scarce, this approach alone is no longer appropriate. The government now faces a different and more complex set of challenges, comprising both supply- and demand-side questions:

- Is the resource base, including both water and watersheds, being managed in a sustainable manner?
- How can a balance be achieved between use and conservation?
- Are there opportunities for a more effective management of existing sources of supply?
- Who will water be allocated to and how will it be allocated?
- Is participation really needed in water management?
- Who will provide and deliver services and who will pay for them?

CHALLENGES IN WATER RESOURCES MANAGEMENT

To Meet the Need of the People: Water Supply or Water for Consumption

The water-related UN Millennium Development Goals (MDGs) on environmental sustainability aimed to stop the unsustainable exploitation of natural resources and to halve the proportion of people who are unable to reach or afford safe drinking water. The World Summit on Sustainable Development in Johannesburg in 2002 set targets which included halving by 2015 the proportion of people without access to safe drinking water and basic sanitation, developing by 2005 integrated water resources management, and significantly improving the lives of at least 100 million slum dwellers by 2020.

For Thailand, the national water policy and a government policy set the goal to increase access of villages to pipe water supplies from 76 per cent to 100 per cent by 2009. It is Thailand's greatest challenge to meet this basic need in the water sector. These challenges can be met owing to the close collaboration that has existed between villagers and government agencies, with many village water supply systems now being managed successfully by the local communities. However, water quality in the system of some villages' water supply may not be up to acceptable standards but solutions have been developed and because Thais are generally health conscious, they tend to avoid drinking unsafe water, replacing it with bottled water that is more hygienic.

Rural Areas

Before 1997, the responsibility of providing water supply to rural areas was undertaken by several central agencies. The responsibilities included the setting of policy and plans, allocating budgets, determining technology models, and providing service delivery. However, as there were various agencies working together, this resulted in a redundancy and lack effective collaboration. In 1997, the new constitution gave communities the right to manage local natural resources including water. Since 1999 as a result of the decentralization policy, Local Government Units (LGUs) have been given the authority of managing local water resources and with budget directly allocated to such bodies.

The responsibilities given to these LGUs included the construction and management of local infrastructure such as road, water source, and local markets for water, etc. However, investment in constructing and managing water sources has been hampered due to many factors. A study of the National Economic and Social Development Board in 2003 mentioned that the readiness of LGUs was a main constraint.[7] All LGUs were relatively new organizations and their managerial capacities especially of the sub-district levels were quite limited in almost every area such as budget planning, personnel and their vision. On the technical side, the design and supervision of the construction of water sources was something that most of the LGU's officials were under-qualified to undertake.

The Department of Water Resources (DWR) was set up in 2003 according to public sector reform by the amalgamation of many water-related agencies, thus giving a mandate for the department to act as a policy body in water resources and also implement small-scale construction. Since 2003, the DWR has set standards and guidelines for the rural waterworks system and also its costing to serve as a reference point for LGUs. The DWR has also provided training for water user groups and LGUs to manage their own waterworks system.

However, since early 2004, the DWR has been assigned to construct the system and then be responsible in implementing the government's goal of increasing village water supplies from the present 76 per cent to 100 per cent by 2009. The budget has also been increased for the DWR since 2004 for this purpose. In this regard,

DWR has been temporarily assigned to help LGUs to expedite the provision of tap water to the rural communities.

Urban Areas

The Metropolitan Waterworks Authority (MWA) is responsible for providing raw water, production, and distribution of piped water in the area of Bangkok and its vicinity. The Provincial Waterworks Authority (PWA), on the other hand, is responsible for the survey and procurement of raw water for production, and distribution of piped water throughout urban areas of the country with the exception of Bangkok and its vicinity. Municipalities carry out surveys, design and construct waterworks systems to their respective areas in addition to those functions performed by PWA.

Quality control of water supplies in urban areas is ascertained using physical, chemical, and biological analysis, and is performed regularly on raw and piped water in accordance with national and the World Health Organization (WHO) standards. As of 2000, the number of piped water samples that meet the physio-chemical, and bacteriological standards in urban areas in Bangkok and its vicinity were 99.7 per cent and 100 per cent respectively. While in municipalities (jurisdiction of the PWAs), standards were 67.8 per cent and 86.6 per cent respectively.

Involving the Private Sector in the Piped Water System

The MWA and PWA have been moving towards corporatization through a committee for establishing a company which comprises agencies concerned with water and water supply, and other financial agencies. The process has been carefully considered, and the committee has been responsible for designing a regulatory body for creating and implementing an appropriate legal and economic regulatory framework.

The PWA established the Eastern Water Resources Development and Management Public Company Limited or East Water, to develop and manage the main pipelines of water distribution in the eastern seaboard areas, in order to serve water demand in this industrial area which is the backbone of Thai industries. Demand for pipe water in the area can be divided into two sectors, domestic consumption and industry, and from the projection between 2003 and 2023, demand will increase from 145.7 mcm to 334 mcm. Considering present capacity of water source of 178.8 mcm, this means that ensuring an adequate provision of future water supplies in this area will be critical.

Another example of a public-private partnership in water supply can be is the Phathum Thani Water Supply Project of PWA. It granted a concession to the Thames Water Company to produce clean water and distribute such supplies to water users in the project area. Moreover, PWA also granted a concession to a private sector to supply water in the Phuket province. The Universal Utilities Company Limited of East Water is the investor and provider of tap water production and distribution in many areas through the long-term concessions from PWA and the municipality mainly in the eastern seaboard and adjacent areas.

Concessions has been given by the DWR to 105 small private entrepreneurs to expand tap water in areas where there is no access by the MWAs and PWAs. In this case, DWR acts as a regulator to supervise these concessionaires. For example, when a land development project starts, it has to ask for a concessionaire in operating its own pipe water supply.

Water and Agriculture

Thailand is an agricultural exporting nation where most of its rural poor, the most susceptible group, are involved in agricultural production. Thailand remains firmly committed to sustainable agricultural production by providing half of its budget on agriculture to irrigation. To address efficient mobilization and use of water for food production, the national water policy has called for a nationwide distribution of water for subsistence irrigation up to the limits of the capacity of the river basins. The Royal Irrigation Department, which is the responsible agency follows this policy by allocating a budget for water resources management based on opportunity and constraints of each river basin in its strategic and action plan.

In the dry season, for a country of tropical monsoons like Thailand, water from controlled sources such as reservoirs has to be distributed according to priorities and needs. The first priority of allocation, which comprises the bulk, goes to households for consumption and then to other purposes like agriculture. The system of water allocation also takes into account the distribution of water for maintaining the ecosystem and preventing sea intrusion.

Water allocation for agriculture is conducted on two levels: Allocation from the main storage area to secondary or sometimes tertiary canals, including operations and management (O&M) is undertaken by government agencies; the allocation at the on-farm level is undertaken by farmers and water user groups/organizations. Thailand has been promoting an increasing responsibility of water allocation activities to water user groups/organizations to manage and allocate water in its secondary canals.

At present, irrigated water used in agriculture is approximately of 70 per cent of the total water storage capacity of all reservoirs and structures. Agriculture in rain-fed areas utilizes water more economically, for example water stored in paddy fields at higher elevation of a basin will flow to paddy fields at a lower elevation. Though there are no drainage canals in the rain-fed areas, a certain amount of water is discharged downstream in the basin, and then repeatedly used.

Water and Electricity

In Thailand, hydropower accounts for only 5 per cent of the total electricity generated. Due to an expansion of economic activities the need for electricity has been increasing every year. Thailand has been planning to increase supply to cover the growing demand and is now under several contracts with its neighbouring countries to purchase electricity in order to partly help to stabilise an economic expansion in the north, northeast, and eastern regions. Countries which sell hydroelectricity depend on water to provide hydropower.

Many hydropower projects in Indochina are privately owned, for example the Nam Theun 2 (please see <www.namtheun2.com>). Considering that oil prices have been very high recently and still on the rise, more attention may now be placed on hydropower as a source to provide future electricity supplies. Opportunities will be present in planning for irrigation, flood control, town water, *et cetera* in the downstream. However considering huge and sometimes negative impacts of dam construction on human settlements and the environment, the matter should be given further consideration and deliberation.

Water Quality and Investment in Wastewater Treatment

Water pollution from land-based activities is largely associated with the process of increasing urbanization, industrialization, and agricultural activities. The major sources of pollution have been domestic sewage, industrial wastes, and agricultural wastes. The main pollutants that pose problems to water quality are organic wastes, bacteria, nutrient, heavy metals, pesticides, and other chemical substances.

For major rivers of the country, the observed water quality problems take the form of dissolved oxygen depletion, loss of aquatic life and fish, high ammonia nitrogen content, high coliform bacteria, and the eutrophication phenomena. Generally speaking, these problems are more serious during the summer low-flow periods when there is minimal dilution capability available. Once water quality problems have been identified, it is necessary to develop targets for restoration in order to undertake the planning exercise on a basin-wide basis.

Thailand has developed masterplans for water quality management for all twenty-five river basins. Plans for water quality management and the construction of wastewater treatment facilities in municipalities is prioritized and recommended as well as the control of wastewater from industrial and agricultural sources. Water quality modelling and the geographic information system (GIS) have also been continually developed and used as tools to help decision-makers in water quality management.

Water pollution control practices in Thailand take the following form:

- Pollution load assessment: This is to identify present and expected pollution loads from land-based sources disposed into the various receiving water waterways. Priority for treatment facilities would also be set up.
- Wastewater treatment and disposal: This is to identify appropriate and cost effective technologies for each location. Fees of waste discharges are also studied and applied to many sites in the near future.
- Cleaner production and technology: This is to support private sectors to use cleaner production and technology for reducing environmental impacts.
- Monitoring and enforcement: This is to meet a requirement of proper assessment and improvement of water quality. Standards has been used as a tool for enforcement.
- Cooperation with related agencies and local communities.

In trying to achieve cleaner water, there has been an attempt to apply the polluter-pays-principle (PPP). The main objectives of PPP are to control water pollution. So far, four municipalities have been applying the PPP and a few are leaning towards the idea of adopting this measure. The user fee is calculated using four principles: 1) different fees for different users to reflect the cost of plant construction, operations and personnel; 2) fee is substantial for continued effective operation; 3) fee is affordable to all users; 4) wastewater treatment operation is simple and manageable by a local authority.

Challenges faced in this area include:

1. Public opposition both to the construction of plants and user charges, lack of understanding is a major obstacle which makes it difficult to select the construction site.
2. Lack of data aggregation to correctly calculate user fee.
3. Funding is insufficient, all the construction sites rely on limited government budgets.
4. Political interference makes it difficult for regulations to be enforced, polluters may refuse to pay and politicians are too afraid to loose votes by going against voters.

Time and considerable effort are needed to overcome these challenges. Policy in this area should be clear and practicable and the involved institutions should be furnished with a wide range of capacity-building.

Watershed Management and Conservation

Upstream watershed management in Thailand has been introduced since 1965. Several projects related to a conservation of the areas have been implemented. This includes a participatory approach in forest protection, reforestation, and rehabilitation of water sources in high-elevated areas, and land use planning. For example, one of the projects in the north of Thailand serves as a very good case in point. The project site located in Chiang Mai of the Ping River Basin aimed to rehabilitate upper forested areas by developing irrigation water.[8] The forest in the upper part has been rehabilitated to benefit both economic activities as well as environmental conservation. In the reservoir, fishery and other agricultural projects in surrounding areas have also been studied and developed. The project has provided a model for farmers for replication elsewhere. At the same time, the government agencies have developed projects that would serve the purpose of sustainable development.

River Basin Management

As mentioned earlier, Thailand is divided hydrologically into twenty-five major river basins. Integrated water resources management or IWRM has applied to Thailand since 1998. In 1999, the first two pilot river basins were formulated with River Basin Committees (RBCs) and the integrated plans of water resources management in the river basin context were introduced. These two river basins were the Ping in the north and the Pasak in central Thailand. With experiences derived from such pilot projects, Thailand has now established twenty-nine RBCs to manage the twenty-five river basins in the whole country.

Capacity-building is one of the most important factors that have to be continuously implemented. In Thailand, capacity-building has been achieved by networking of people of all levels and, whenever possible, all existing groups of stakeholders including local administrative bodies, water user groups, and civil societies.

The experiences in the river basin management in Thailand can be summarized as follows:

- Truly, IWRM is a process that can be implemented at a river basin level.
- Inter-disciplinary knowledge has to be applied in practising river basin management especially when the need is focused on breaking the administrative boundaries of river basins in order to derive a genuine integrated management and

coordination is really needed for the people who are involved in the mechanism.

• It is important to link the mechanism from the lowest appropriate levels to the national level. In order for decision-making to come from all stakeholders, IWRM has to make sure that stakeholders become part of the decision-making process, that a balance is kept, and that the implementation stage is carefully monitored. Assessment plays an important role in this case.

The roles of all groups should be clearly identified, but this can be time-consuming. There is also a need for a group of key players to act as a catalyst for changes and such players should be influential enough to induce the government support the road map and/or the action programme. One of some critical factors is consistency in pursuing the IWRM objectives and patience in doing so.

WATER GOVERNANCE AND ITS IMPLICATIONS FOR IWRM: THAILAND'S EXPERIENCE

Drawing from the guidelines set in the Eighth National Plan (1996–2001), the development and management of both surface and groundwater resources should be a systematic river basin approach with regard to economic and social factors and environmental impacts. The processes of IWRM were properly introduced and practised in Thailand since 1997–98 at both the national and basin level.

Since there has been no comprehensive act on water resources, and, moreover, the existing regulations being used by various government agencies are different, it is essential to create a new water resources act for common practice by all agencies concerned. At present, the process of drafting water resources act is ongoing. It emphasizes stakeholder consultation in collecting issues for formulation of the draft.

The integrated plan on water resource development, water allocation, water conservation, flood mitigation and water quality will be formulated for all twenty-five river basins. And an integrated budgetary system for water resource management that includes the requirement from each river basin is in preparation. It is planned that uniform measures and analytical methods will be set up to assess data and establish a data network system for possible information exchange and dissemination. And the system of assessment in water resources will be introduced at the national as well as basin level.

INSTITUTIONS

National Framework

In the past, there were many government agencies and private parties involved in the development and exploitation of the river basin surface and groundwater resources, but cooperation and coordination between them have been weak. Even when there has been cooperation between operating agencies leading to a plan for the equitable allocation of water, it has often been challenged by various parties and interest groups. The result has often been a compromise, very time consuming and ineffective. In view of the lack of coordination, the government decided to establish a central agency in water resources management in order to formulate plans, coordinate plan implementation, and carry out other works concerning the management of water resources.

The National Water Resources Committee (NWRC) was established in 1989 with the intention to serve as an apex body for setting policies and plans for national water resource development. The Office of National Water Resources Committee (ONWRC) was established officially in 1996. In 2002, after a bureaucratic restructuring of Thailand, the Department of Water Resources under the Ministry of Natural Resources and Environment was established in order to work at a national level for the management of water resources.

Establishment of River Basin Organization

The NWRC has worked to strengthen the mechanism of IWRM in Thailand since 1997. In 1999, the first two RBCs were established in the Ping and Pasak river basins as a pilot project. This recognized the need for decentralization as an important step in water resources management. Each RBC consists of qualified persons drawn from the public and private sectors. The RBC sets policies on water resources planning, development, and projects, operation of facilities, and water allocation, and it also oversees all water-related activities in the river basin including the resolution of water conflicts between various users.

Lessons and experiences from the pilot project have been thoroughly studied and the RBCs have now been expanded to the other twenty-three river basins. Presently, the RBCs are established in all twenty-five river basins in the country. The RBCs comprise of representatives from related government agencies, local administrative bodies, water user groups, NGOs, and experts in related fields and they have staff of the Regional Office of the Department of Water Resources (DWR) works as the secretariat in each of the RBC. Most of the RBCs are chaired by the governors of the provinces, where the river basins are largely located, but during 2003–07 there was one RBC that was chaired by a representative of the civil society in the Bang Pakong Basin.

While the national level agency is in charge of policy matters and supervision of water management as a whole, the RBC is responsible for the actual management of the river basins and it also implements some of associated projects and activities. The national agency provides technical, research information, and financial support to the RBCs. The RBC is also responsible for developing basin-specific programmes in close consultation with basin stakeholders in order to incorporate their particular needs and concerns.

Problems Encountered

1. The traditional way of separating planning and budget allocation in government sectors prevent integrated thinking and actions.
2. The present administrative boundaries in Thailand makes it difficult to effectively formulate and implement an integrated plan, and actions.
3. Transferring decision-making to RBCs has not been easy; there was a need for considerable compromise between government officials and civil societies, as well as capacity-building for all groups to be familiar with inter-disciplinary knowledge.
4. Even at the RBCs level, one cannot assure an involvement that ensures equitability, transparency, and sustainability. Except where participatory can be done at the smallest units or really at the grass-roots level, which is again a difficult task and is time consuming, working against the very grain of the government to be speedy and effective.

CASE STUDY OF THE RIVER BASIN IN THAILAND

The Bang Pakong River Basin[9]

The Bang Pakong River Basin comprises a catchment area of 18,500 square kilometres which discharges into the Gulf of Thailand. Tidal influence is pronounced, with brackish water reaching 120 kilometres upstream during the dry season when freshwater run-off is minimal. The basin contains a mixture of land uses ranging from wet and dry season rice, annual and perennial crops, rubber plantations, tropical forests, wetlands, and settled areas comprising villages with home gardens and mixed orchards. The irrigated area within the basin is estimated at 388,000 hectares. The basin's fishery resources are valuable and include both freshwater and marine catch as well as pond-raised fish, oysters, mussels and prawns.

Given its proximity to the Bangkok metropolitan area and the eastern seaboard, the basin has been the target of considerable economic investment. Government has emphasised supply management and engineering solutions for the region's water needs. A diversion dam constructed 70 kilometres from the Gulf of Thailand was completed in 2000 to supply water for municipal and irrigation users. The dam was briefly operating before severe environmental problems forced a suspension of operations. Downstream of the dam, tidal fluctuations have caused overbank flood which has damaged properties and eroded river banks. Upstream, the operation of dam gates has prevented the tidal flushing of the river waters laden with sewage, agricultural drainage and effluent from pig farms and aquaculture ponds. Consequently there has been a worsening of water quality. The dam operation has reduced tidal flows reaching upstream fishery enterprises that require brackish water. Furthermore, the dam gates, when closed, has presented a barrier to the migration of fish.

The diversion dam's troubled operation has shed light on the need for better basin planning, which takes into account competing resource uses as well as the need for real participation among the various stakeholders groups of the basin in making their own decisions.

Towards Better Water Resources Management

Many steps have been taken to promote water resources management in the basin. In July 2001 a Bang Pakong River Basin Committee was established which included forty-four members from the various stakeholders groups.[10] While these efforts point in the right direction, additional support would be required to promote meaningful stakeholder participation to increase cross-sectoral involvement. In particular, the concerns of local government administration and non-governmental actors must be brought to bear in water allocation procedures and basin-wide decision-making.

The Bang Pakong possesses a special character. In one of its upstream tributaries, dry season water shortages are a common occurrence while downstream, before the construction of the dam, populations near the Gulf of Thailand had learnt to take advantage of the brackish water regime such as shrimp farm in their economic activities. Generally, poor water quality in the river basin has been a threat in some areas, especially for downstream people. At the estuary of the Bang Pakong River itself, the major problem is low dissolved oxygen and high organic matter content which is mostly caused by effluents from livestock and fisheries like pig and prawn farms.

The Bang Pakong is a part of the eastern coast confronting the Gulf of Thailand and contains an important estuarine ecosystem with remarkable biological diversity. Fish species in the river are rich and diverse. Its estuary used to be covered with mangrove forest. Since 1975 it had gradually decreased however there has been a slight recovery since 1996.

Water accounting calculations in the Bang Pakong show that gross inflow in the wet season is greater than the quantities of depleted water, but is less than depleted water in the dry season. Water shortages seem to be a serious problem in the near future, and this will be aggravated by the pollution of water sources. Therefore, a wide range of measures for water resources management is needed, ranging from improving water quality, decreasing non intended water use and increasing the efficient use of water to modifying crop schedules or cropping patterns.

The Department of Water Resources (DWR) has developed a series of important tools for water management in the context of the Bang Pakong River Basin. As mentioned earlier, a local water management body, the River Basin Committee (RBC), has been created to contribute to the implementation of the decentralization policy. The formulation of an integrated plan for water resources management is also underway. The process of formulating a plan now incorporates elements of people's participation, something different from past planning exercises. However, DWR intends to go beyond these initial steps, realizing the importance of involving people more naturally and independently, on their own initiative and their own enthusiasm. For this purpose, the Bang Pakong has been selected for a River Basin Dialogue initiative, especially when civil societies have shown an eagerness in managing their own resources and when they reflected it in voting their representative to be a chair of the RBC.

The Bang Pakong Dialogue

The Bang Pakong Dialogue aimed at developing and using a consultation platform for solving problems and addressing issues of concern. At the same time, linkages with and supportive actions for the Bang Pakong River Basin Committee (BP-RBC) will be established in order to increase the competency of the BP-RBC. In doing so, stakeholders identification is an important step.

In 2003 the Bang Pakong Dialogue was introduced with an initial support of the Regional Office for Asia and Pacific of Food and Agricultural Organization (FAO), the United National Environment Programme (UNEP), and the Secretariat of the Global Dialogue on Water, Food and Environment. During 2004 to 2006, it was implemented as a collaborative work between DWR, Kasetsart University, and International Water Management Institute (IWMI) under a financial support from the Asian Development Bank (ADB) Water Fund.

This collaboration aimed to implement the work with the BP-RBC and other civil society's partners in understanding water allocation components, developing its model, involving people stakeholders, and identifying small water related projects to be implemented by the civil societies themselves, especially in mitigating water pollution and other related issues.

LESSONS LEARNED FROM THE
BANG PAKONG DIALOGUE

What has been done?

The dialogue created a network of people who will share their experiences among themselves and to facilitate their working together on water related issues focusing on water allocation, with a support from the DWR. The selection of stakeholders was a crucial step of the initial stage after the introductory forum, because these people form a catalytic group for stimulating and incorporating water resources management into their communities' activities and expanding the dialogue to other communities through networking. Small group discussions were held to provide some recommendations on strategies for drawing people's attention on water resources management. It was agreed that the selection of the key stakeholders from the four provinces would be made on the basis that they already actively support environmental work in their communities or they are already involved in some kind of networking in different areas. It was also agreed that the meeting should be conducted in a very informal manner without a rigid agenda.

Thirty-two stakeholders, eight per province, were thus selected to attend the meeting which was held in a very cosy and friendly environment. In the meeting, the facilitator asked the participants to convey their attitudes and opinions on water resources in an open manner. Apart from the problems and requirements of the basin, it emerged that an important topic that most participants wanted to discuss was a basin network on water resources. Many practical ideas for networking were floated at the meeting. An example of an unsustainable network was discussed and many recommendations to avoid such kind of experiences were made. A good network has to be open, with clear and distinct goals, addressing mutual interests, but should not be tied to strict regulations in order to allow flexibility. The network should generate its own revenue, which would lead towards self-sufficiency in managerial capability and long-term sustainability. Information should be shared in the network. What should be avoided is a network established by a government agency with money allocated for set-up and limited support. This type of network becomes inactive shortly after its creation and ultimately disappears.

Other issues raised in the meeting varied from capacity-building for local government units and others, awareness raising and dissemination of information in order to promote transparency. Many activities were recommended, in particular, aiming at improving water quality. This denotes their familiarity with activities of pollution control which have been introduced to them by government agencies for nearly ten years, and which they commonly practise, and the severity of the water pollution problem for them. Many of the recommended activities can be considered as land-based activities, which are also related with water and thus integrated by natural processes. For example, some participants recommended an expansion of chemical-free agriculture, which is water-friendly and has been successfully implemented in some areas of the Sra Kaew province in the upstream reaches of the basin.

What should be done next?

Further analysis is needed on grouping the problems, requirements, and stakeholders by using the outputs from this forum and meeting, and other secondary sources. However, existing studies should be analysed not only for the purpose of being a source of information for identifying problems, requirements, and stake-holders but also for their dissemination to the people in the basin. The dissemination of knowledge is one of the requirements identified in the meeting.

Considering IWRM, water resources management of the basin should embrace all aspects of water management and other related issues: Water allocation, prevention/alleviation of problems occurring from freshwater and brackish water uses and water shortages, efficient uses of water, controlling and managing polluted water including land-based activities, upstream watershed management, and coastal zone management, etc. These things can be managed at a unifying scale at the basin/sub-basins strata and within specific areas. Some matters for further investigation will be further identified during the project time.

Stakeholders concerned are various and include, to name a few, natural leaders of the communities, members of local government units, members of the communities, and members of the RBCs. Different groups of problems and requirements will be identified and dialogues will be held separately for different categories of the stakeholders involved. After the grouping of problems, requirements, and stakeholders, thematic consultations will be organized in order to include number of people at the level of the smallest possible units or grass-root level into the process. After a series of such consultations, one or two basin-wide forums should be organized to seek consensus on common issues that will gradually emerge from the thematic consultations.

The group of thirty-two participants of the meeting that has already been held will be the dialogue's resources persons, and networking between them in the field of water management will be promoted, through such means as keeping them in regular contact, training to be coordinators for water resources management of the basin, and budget permitting, for study tours to other river basins. Local research will be promoted and a decision support system or tool for the evaluation of water allocation scenarios at basin level will be developed in close cooperation with them. It is hoped that, with all these activities, the dialogue will be an effective tool for conflict prevention.

The dialogue will help the BP-RBC in identifying problems, requirements, and stakeholders as seen by the people in the basin. It will help the BP-RBC in working out its duty in water resource management. The dialogue will be a good platform for consensus-building and this agenda will be raised in the BP-RBC meetings for further consideration and endorsement. It is therefore essential that the BP-RBC should be kept continuously informed of the dialogue's work.

RECOMMENDATIONS

The purpose of this chapter was to synthesize related sectors in water and to analyse how each sector could work with one another. However, due to limited timeframe and available resources, the chapter has given recommendations on the management of two important sectors, which now encounter an urgency in policy and plan development and implementation, these being water for consumption and water for industry.

It is recognized that in order to meet the target of increasing rural water supply to cover 100 per cent of households in the year 2009, there may be difficulties faced in terms of government budget constraints and personnel. Therefore, a complementary strategy should be considered, that is, promotion of small-scale entrepreneur and even villagers to be a concessionaires in building and operating rural water supply.

With the MWR and PWR moving towards a privatization model for larger-scale water supply management projects of a corporatized or liberalized nature, the introduction of competition or commercial incentives by deregulation, re-regulation, and restructuring (that is, unbundling) of utility companies is crucial. Competition is a means to provide incentives for greater investments. While technological advances have extended the potential for competition, regulation is necessary to ensure that competition actually emerges.

In the industrial zone where many big industries concentrate in the eastern seaboard, planning has been formulated ahead for the provision of water. In the meantime, when the area experiences low precipitation and water in the reservoirs has been overused, the problem of water shortages occur. Apart from the solutions that are tackled by the government, the private sector or the industries themselves should prepare for future water shortages by applying water-saving technology or even desalination of seawater.

Finally, when water is increasingly scarce, equitable water allocation between sectors should be thoroughly identified and systematic methods should be established.

Notes

1. See *United Nations World Water Development Report: Water for People, Water for Life* (United States: UNESCO-WWAP, 2003); and *United Nations World Water Development Report 2: Water, a Shared Responsibility* (United States: UNESCO-WWAP, 2006).
2. *State of Water Resources Management in ASEAN* (Jakarta: ASEAN Secretariat, October 2005).
3. Ibid., p. 1.
4. See Basic ASEAN Indicators at <http://www.aseansec.org/19226. htm>.
5. See ASEAN Statistical Pocketbook 2006 at <http://www.aseansec. org/22109.htm>.
6. This section draws from Country Profiles, "Thailand", International Commission on Irrigation and Drainage (ICID) <www.icid.org/ country.htm>.
7. Office of the National Economic and Social Development Board, Office of the Prime Minister, "Study on Management and Utilization of Small Scale Water Development Projects", Bangkok, July 2003.
8. See the study on the Chao Phraya River Basin (Thailand) at <http: //www.unesco.org/water/wwap/case_studies/chao_phraya/index. shtml>. The full report can be found at *United Nations World Water Development Report: Water for People, Water for Life* (United States: UNESCO-WWAP, 2003).
9. See Department of Water Resources, Ministry of Natural Resources and Environment, "Study of Bang Pakong Dialogue Programme", Bangkok, February 2003; and Department of Water Resources, Ministry of Natural Resources and Environment, "Study of Water Resources

Master Plan of the Bang Pakong River Basin", Bangkok, March 2003).

10. Ibid.

References

ASEAN Statistical Pocketbook 2006 <http://www.aseansec.org/19188.htm>.

Bank of Thailand <http://www.bot.or.th/homepage/index/index_e.asp>.

Country Profiles. "Thailand". International Commission on Irrigation and Drainage (ICID) <http://www.icid.org/country.html>.

Department of Mineral Resources, Ministry of Industry. "Study on Master Plan and Initial Design of Groundwater Recharge". Bangkok, 2000.

Department of Water Resources, Ministry of Natural Resources and Environment. "Study of Water Resources Master Plan of the Bang Pakong River Basin". Bangkok, March 2003.

―――. "Study of Bang Pakong Dialogue Programme". Bangkok, February 2003.

Office of the National Economic and Social Development Board, Office of the Prime Minister. "Study on Management and Utilization of Small Scale Water Development Projects". Bangkok, July 2003.

Office of the National and Social Development Board and United Nations Country Team in Thailand. "Thailand Millennium Development Goals Report 2004". Available online at <http://www.undp.or.th/mdgr.htm>.

Office of the National Water Resources Committee, Office of the Prime Minister and the World Bank. "Study on the Chao Phraya Basin Organization Establishment Project". Bangkok, October 2000.

Royal Forestry Department, Ministry of Agriculture and Cooperative. "A Document on Upper Watershed Management". Bangkok, 1998.

Royal Irrigation Department, Ministry of Agriculture and Cooperative. "His Majesty the King and Water Resources Development Work". Bangkok, November 1987.

Secretariat of the Prime Minister, Office of the Prime Minister. "King Bhumibol: Strength of the Land". Bangkok, 2000.

State of Water Resources Management in ASEAN. Jakarta: ASEAN Secretariat, October 2005.

Taesombut, V., et al. "Regional Study on the Development of Effective Water Management Institutions: A Case Study of the Bang Pakong River Basin Thailand". Thailand Research Fund, 2002.

Tingsanchali T. "Assessment of Water Resources and Water Demand by User Sectors in Thailand". Bangkok: UNESCAP, 1991 and other studies derived from Royal Irrigation Department and Department of Water Resources.

UN Millennium Development Goals <http://www.un.org/millennium goals/>.

United Nations World Water Development Report: Water for People Water for Life. United States: UNESCO-WWAP, 2003.

United Nations World Water Development Report 2: Water, a Shared Responsibility. United States: UNESCO-WWAP, 2006.

World Summit on Sustainable Development <http://www.un.org/esa/ sustdev/adissues/water/water.htm>.

12

WATER RESOURCES AND ISSUES CONCERNING SUSTAINABLE WATERSHED MANAGEMENT PRACTICES IN VIETNAM

Le Dinh Thanh

BACKGROUND

It is very clear that for the world, water is a critical resource that will become increasingly scarce in the coming decades. Of the earth's freshwater, about two-thirds is polar ice and most of the remainder is groundwater of depths about 200 to 600 metres, but most groundwater is saline below this depth. Freshwater in rivers and lakes, as estimated by UNESCO (1978), is about 93,120 cubic kilometres (km^3), about 0.266 per cent of total freshwater in the world. Compared to total water supplies in the world (freshwater and non-freshwater), rivers and lakes only constitute about 0.0072 per cent of the total. That is why water is now a very critical and important resource for human development.[1]

In Southeast Asia, the average water availability per capita is about 4,900 cubic metres (m^3), but the water resources vary with space and time. For example Laos has the highest water per capita (about 35,000 m³), while Singapore has the lowest (about 155 m³), with Vietnam (an inland country) estimated at about 3,870 m³.[2] For most rivers in the region, water flows during the flood season occupies about 70 to 80 per cent of the total water supply during the year. For Southeast Asia, the Mekong River is the largest, with a total watershed area of 795,000 square kilometres (km²). The length of the main river is 4,400 kilometres (km), and average discharge is 15,000 cubic metres per second (m³/s). The Mekong River Basin flows across six countries: China (165,000 km²), Myanmar (24,000 km²), Thailand (184,000 km²), Laos (202,000 km²), Cambodia (155,000 km²), and Vietnam (65,000 km²). See Figure 12.1. Total annual water volume of the Mekong River is about 508 billion

FIGURE 12.1
Mekong River Basin

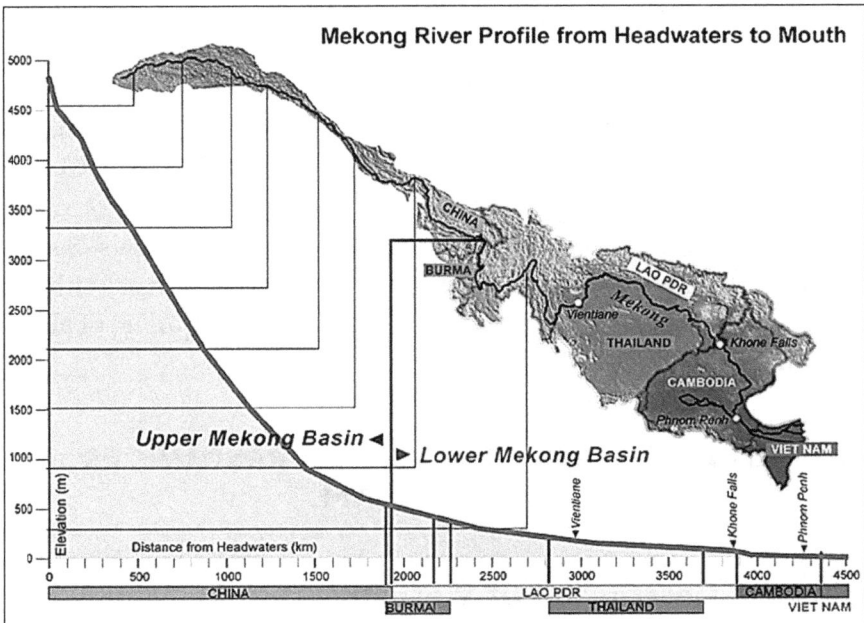

Source: Water Utilization Programme, Mekong River Commission, *Overview of Hydrology of the Mekong Basin,* 2005.

cubic metres (bcm). More than 75 per cent of this occurs during the flood season. In recent years, water resources in the various countries in Southeast Asia have increasingly been under pressure to meet requirements of the various sectors including agriculture, industry, and domestic uses. Therefore, water management in watersheds has become a very important task for sustainable development and for meeting these diverse needs.

One issue of watershed management and conservation is the impact on the environment, especially water quality in the rivers. In recent years, water pollution has been occurring in some rivers due to activities from industry, agriculture, domestic and others sectors.

In Vietnam, there is a dense network of rivers with many international rivers that originate in catchments outside the country, for example, the Red River in the north, the Mekong River in the south, and the Ma River in North Central Vietnam. In general, about two-thirds of the water resources of the country originate from outside its political boundaries; this makes Vietnam susceptible to water resource decisions made in the upstream countries. As an estimate, the total annual run-off of rivers in Vietnam is about 830 bcm, but this mainly occurs during the rainy season (or flood season). For the six to seven months of dry season, there is a shortage of water where run-off is only 15–30 per cent of the total water flows. Beside of the surface water, Vietnam has groundwater resources with the total potential exploitable reserves of the country's aquifers of about 60 bcm per year.

RIVER BASINS AND WATER RESOURCES IN VIETNAM

Physical Description of Vietnam

Forming the eastern seaboard of the Indochinese peninsula, Vietnam is a country with total land area of approximately 333,000 square kilometres, of which mountainous area occupy about 70 per cent of the total land area, with many mountainous ranges along northern and western borders. The country is over 1,600 km long, and 200–400 km wide in the north and south. At its narrowest point in the central region, it is only 50 km wide. Vietnam shares its border with China in the north, Laos and Cambodia in the west; and in the south and east of Vietnam lies the East Sea belonging to the Pacific Ocean with a total coastal line length of about 3,260 km.

The average annual rainfall of Vietnam is about 1,900–2,000 mm, but differs across the country. Around 70 to 75 per cent of this occurs during the rainy season from May to October, when the southwest monsoon brings warm, moist air across the Indochinese peninsula.[3] This incidentally also causes the floods in rivers. At the same time, the northern and central parts of the country are subject to typhoons. In general of about four to six typhoons occur along the coastal areas each year.[4]

Vietnam has 2,360 rivers with length of at least 10 kilometres, and about 300 lakes and lagoons distributed throughout the country. In Vietnam, there are more than one hundred estuaries along 3,260 km of coastal line, in which some large estuaries such as Red River in the north and Mekong River in the south have deltas with 1 million hectare of rich land. Most rivers of the country flow to the sea along Vietnam's coastal line (except the Bang Giang–Ky Cung, Se San and Sre Pok), and they play a very important role with regard to the environment and ecology of the coastal zones.

The rivers in Vietnam have different features depending on the topographical and climatic conditions such as the Red, Ma, and Ca river basins in the north, or the Dong Nai, and Mekong rivers in the south with three parts of the basin: Upper, middle and lower river; but almost all the river basins of Central Vietnam have only two parts: An upper and a lower river basin, because the topography in this region is very narrow and steep. Most of Vietnam's rivers originate from the upper countries. The river basins of the country can be divided into two groups:

(i) A transboundary/international river basin, such as basins of the Red River in the north, Ma and Ca Rivers in the central part, or Mekong river in the south of Vietnam; and

(ii) A national river basin (total basin area located in Vietnam), such as Thai Binh River in the north, or Ba River and Dong Nai River in the south. The major river basins in Vietnam are indicated in Figure 12.2.

It can be said that Vietnam's water resources are relatively abundant, as it receives an average rainfall of 1,944 mm per year. Of this amount, about 1,003 mm is lost by evaporation, leaving only 941 mm. This provides about 310 bcm of surface water for Vietnam each year. Vietnam is a country well endowed with a huge source of freshwater coming from neighbouring countries through the various river systems. The amount of freshwater provided by rivers is around 520 bcm, about 1.7 times more than water from within the country. But some transboundary rivers such as the Ky Cung River in Lang Son province and Bang Giang River in Cao Bang flow into China. Tributaries of the Mekong River such as Nam Rom (Lai Chau province), Sekong (Thua Thien Hue province), SeBang Hien (Quang Tri province), Se San (Kon Tum, Gia Lai province), Sre Pok (Dak Lak, Dak Nong province) flow to Laos and Cambodia, but their waters later return to Vietnam through the Mekong River Delta.[5]

In summary, Vietnam has an average annual surface water of about 830 bcm, in which the total surface water from within the country constitutes about 310 bcm, while external sources flowing into Vietnam makes up about 520 bcm or 63 per cent of the total (mainly of Red and Mekong rivers). Water is retained in rivers, lakes, canals, reservoirs and lagoons for human uses and development of the ecosystem. From Table 12.1, it can be seen that the biggest surface water resource is the Mekong River, and the second is the Red River. The distribution of surface water resources per region in Vietnam is shown in Figure 12.3a.

FIGURE 12.2
The Major River Basins in Inland Vietnam

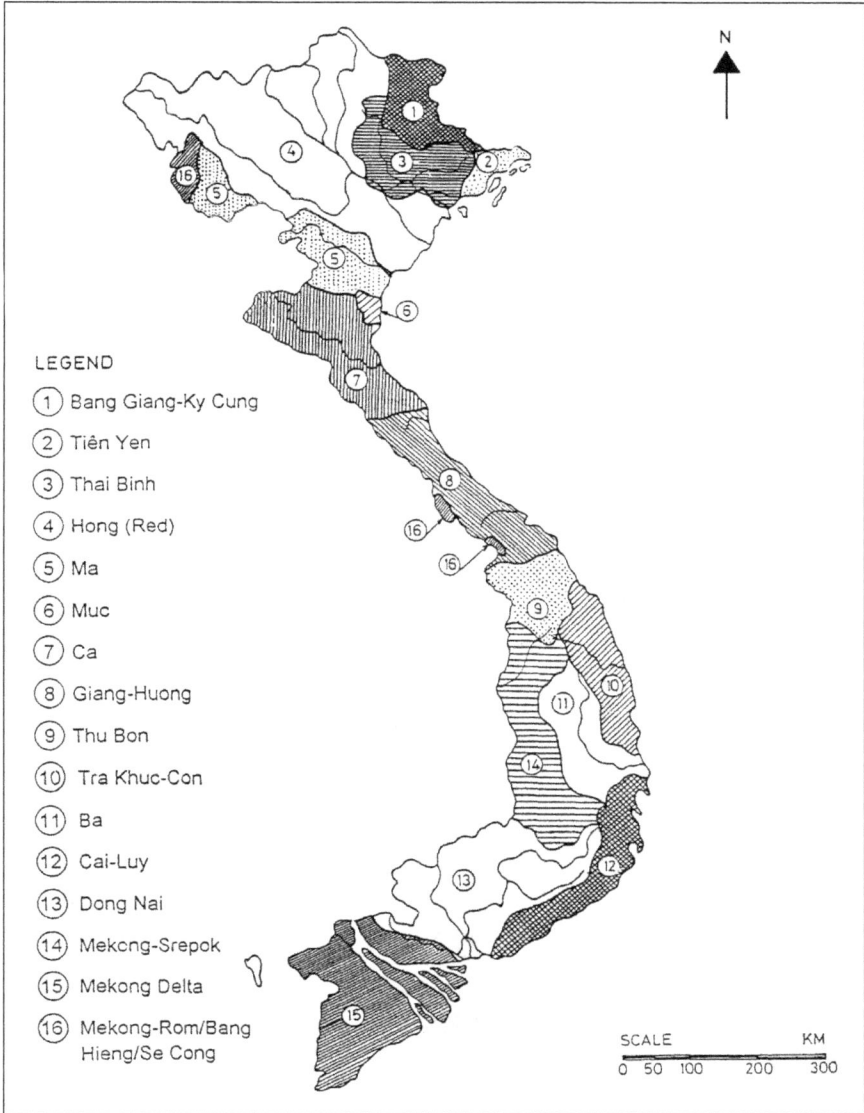

LEGEND
1. Bang Giang-Ky Cung
2. Tiên Yen
3. Thai Binh
4. Hong (Red)
5. Ma
6. Muc
7. Ca
8. Giang-Huong
9. Thu Bon
10. Tra Khuc-Con
11. Ba
12. Cai-Luy
13. Dong Nai
14. Mekong-Srepok
15. Mekong Delta
16. Mekong-Rom/Bang Hieng/Se Cong

Source: Le Dinh Thanh, *Extreme Rainfall and Flood in Vietnam*, Workshop on Hydrological Extremes and Climate in Tropical Areas and their Control, Bressia University, Italia, 2003.

TABLE 12.1

Ten Biggest River Basins of Vietnam

N	River basin	Drainage area (km²) Total	Drainage area (km²) in Vietnam	Mean rainfall (mm)	Mean runoff (10⁹ m³)
1	Mekong	795,000	72,000	1,500	475.0
2	Red	155,000	72,700	1,650	121.0
3	Ma	28,400	17,700	1,400	16.6
4	Ca	27,200	17,730	1,700	21.9
5	SrePok	17,300	17,300	2,000	14.5
6	Dong Nai	14,900	14,900	2,400	17.3
7	Bang Giang–KyCung	13,000	12,400	1,400	7.9
8	Thu Bon	10,000	10,000	2,800	15.8
9	Ba	7,510	7,510	2,400	8.5
10	Giang–Huong	7,000	7,000	2,600	11.1

Source: Le Dinh Thanh, *Extreme Rainfall and Flood in Vietnam*, Workshop on Hydrological Extremes and Climate in Tropical Areas and their Control, Bressia University, Italia, 2003.

FIGURE 12.3(a)

River Run-off per Region (bcm)

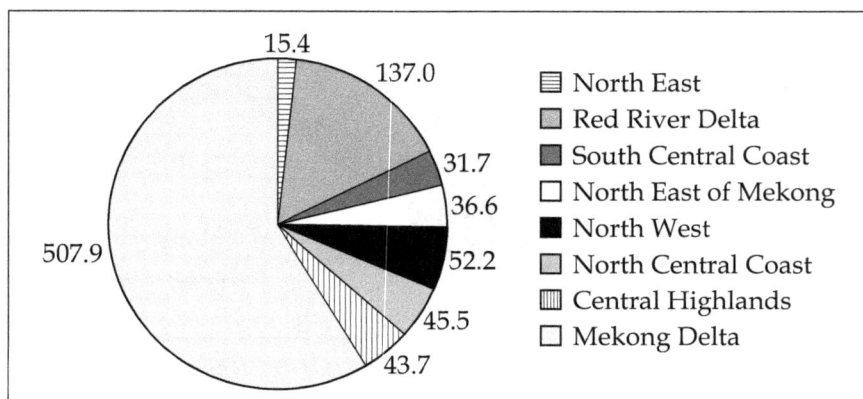

Source: The World Bank, DANIDA, MONRE, *Vietnam Environment Monitor 2003*.

The total potential exploitation of groundwater from the aquifers of the country has been estimated to be around 60 bcm per year, this mainly located in the northeast region and Mekong Delta where the Red River and Mekong River is situated, and the limited resources of groundwater in the north central region of Vietnam where there are the short and steep rivers of the country (see Figure 12.3b). But less than 5 per cent of the total reserves are exploited for Vietnam as a whole, as over-exploitation of groundwater may result in falling water tables and the intrusion of salinity, especially in the deltas. Most waters of estuaries and coastal areas are affected by salinity and tide from the sea, and the long coastline of 3,260 km makes the country extremely vulnerable to natural disasters such as typhoons or sea-level rise with the global climate changes.

In Vietnam, data on water quality is very poor compared to data on water quantity. From the available data on water quality of rivers, it can be said that the quality of water in the upstream

FIGURE 12.3(b)
Exploitable Groundwater (bcm)

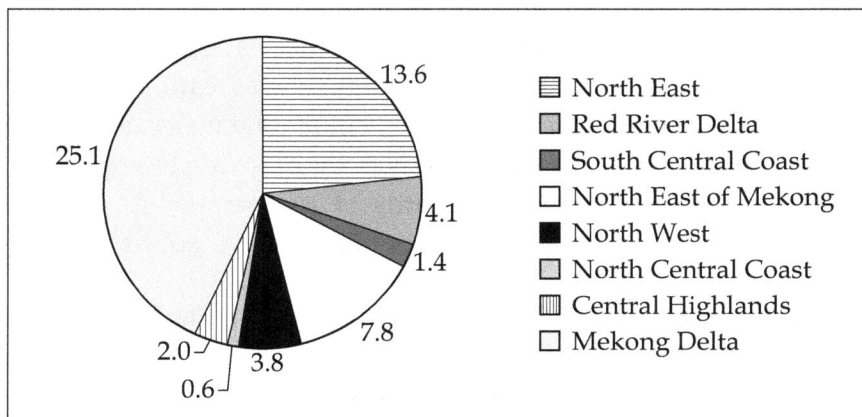

Pie chart values: 13.6, 4.1, 1.4, 7.8, 3.8, 0.6, 2.0, 25.1

Legend:
- North East
- Red River Delta
- South Central Coast
- North East of Mekong
- North West
- North Central Coast
- Central Highlands
- Mekong Delta

Source: The World Bank, DANIDA, MONRE, *Vietnam Environment Monitor 2003*.

areas of most rivers has remained good, while downstream waters are often polluted mainly by activities from urban areas and industries.

WATER UTILIZATION IN VIETNAM

In Vietnam, the uses of water can be divided into two groups:

(i) Consumption uses such as irrigation, industrial uses, domestic uses; and
(ii) Non-consumption uses such as navigation, hydropower, and others.

For the first group, the major activity for which large quantities of water is used is irrigation for agricultural activities, followed by industrial activities, aquaculture, services, and domestic consumers. Total irrigation demand in 2004 was 62.2 bcm (84 per cent of total water demand of the country),[6] and, on average, the total irrigated area increases by 3.4 per cent per year. Currently, irrigation systems of the country can supply water for only 7.4 billion hectares (or about 80 per cent of total cultivated land). The government plans to irrigate an area of 12 million hectares by 2010, which means that water demand for irrigation will be about 88.8 bcm.

The amount of water for domestic use is small compared to consumption by irrigation. In 1990, it was estimated to be 1.341 bcm. Presently, it is about 2 per cent of total water demand of the country, but it will reach 3.088 bcm by 2010 due to population growth and higher living standards of the people. At present, about 60 per cent of Vietnam's population have access to clean water.

Recent studies indicate that in the coming decades, water consumption will increase rapidly. Compared to consumption in 2000, the total water consumption of all sectors will increase by 14 per cent by 2010, 25 per cent by 2020, and 38 per cent by 2030.

This means by 2030, the total water consumption of the country will increase to 90 bcm/year, or approximately 29 per cent of the water resources formed within Vietnam.

In the non-consumptive water sectors, hydropower has a large potential and is important for development of the country as it is considered as a clean source of energy. Vietnam has an estimated hydropower potential of about 14,000 to 17,000 megawatts (MW), in which nearly 3,600 MW have been developed and operated, and about 800 MW are under construction. The largest hydropower plant in Vietnam are the Hoa Binh (1,920 MW) on Da River, Thac Ba on Chay River (108 MW), Tri An on Dong Nai River (400 MW), and Yaly on Se San River (700 MW). By 2012, several large hydropower dams will be constructed such as the Huong Quang on Da River system (305 MW), Son La Upper Hoa Binh dam on Da River (2,050 MW), and Dong Nai 3, 4 on Dong Nai River (510 MW).

DIFFICULTIES AND COMPLEXITIES OF SUSTAINABLE MANAGEMENT OF WATER RESOURCES IN VIETNAM

Water plays a very important role in the development of a country, and also for the ecological systems of the river basins. Therefore, in the concept of sustainable development, it can be said that sustainable watershed management is very much related to water resource management of the watersheds.

Nearly 63 per cent of Total Surface Water Resources Originate outside Vietnam

As mentioned above, 520 bcm of 830 bcm of surface water of Vietnam comes from outside (mainly the Mekong and Red rivers). For example, the Mekong River in the south has more than 90 per cent of its total basin area outside Vietnam, and the Red River in the north has about 57.2 per cent of its basin area in China. Problems related to pollution may arise with the processes of industrialization, urbanization, rapid agricultural development and other activities in the upper countries. The high demands on water resources in their territories may change the hydrological regimes of the lower reaches of rivers affecting supplies to Vietnam. This is especially true for the Mekong River Delta which will face the risk of water shortage in future if the upper countries utilize a flow of about 1,200–1,500 m³/s during the dry season. Therefore, now the Mekong River Commission is carrying out some programmes concerning the implementation of the Mekong Agreement, such as the Water Utilization Programme (WUP), Basin Development Programme (BDP) and Environmental Programme (EP).

Water Resources Vary with Space and Time, and Increase Natural Disasters

The annual average rainfall of whole country is 1,944 mm. In some areas in Vietnam this reaches up to 3,500–5,000 mm (Bac Quang in Ha Giang province), and even 8,000 mm in Bach Ma (southern part of Thua Thien Hue province), but in some places, only less than 700 mm of rainfall is gathered, for example 700 mm in Phan Rang (Ninh Thuan province), or 400 mm in Phan Ri (Binh Thuan province). The variation of water resources can be seen in the northeastern parts of Vietnam with an area of 65,327 km² having only 0.236 million cubic metres (mcm)/km², but it is 12.792 mcm/km² in the 39,709 km² of Mekong River Delta, which works out to be about fifty-four times higher.

In a year, the rainfall in the four to five months of the rainy season provides about 80 per cent of water for the year, causing very severe floods, while during the dry season there is very little rainfall bar the hill regions of coastal Central Vietnam. In many rivers there is almost no flow, even in the basin of area of more than 500 km². There have been many historical floods, for example, the 1971 flood on the Red River Delta which caused the loss of millions of tonnes of paddy rice and affected 2.71 million people. From 1992 to 1999, floods in Central Vietnam killed 2,716 persons and resulted in monetary losses of more than VND 8,000 billion (US$0.46 billion). Between 1986 and 2002, there were thirty extremely heavy floods in a number of river basins in the country, especially the 1999 flood in the central part of Vietnam and the 2000 flood in the Mekong Delta. There were also serious droughts in the Central Highlands in 1997, 1998, 2003 and 2004–2005. For example, in 1998, 111,000 hectares of industrial and fruit tree areas were affected by the drought, causing destruction of over 19,300 hectares of crops. Around 770,000 people were affected by a shortage of drinking water. In Mekong Delta, the drought in 2003 was also serious for the region.

In relation to severe floods, the *Lao Dong* newspaper reported on 14 November 2003 ("Central Vietnam — the Floods Overlapped One Another") that:

> Ninh Thuan province — humans and properties lost; Khanh Hoa province — 28 houses collapsed due to whirlwinds; Phu Yen province — three people died and ships were carried away into the sea. Just as Binh Dinh and other south central provinces were recovering from a fierce flood, they were unprepared to "receive" a second flood as severe as the first. Reports by Provincial Flood and Typhoon Prevention and Control Boards (FTPCB) indicated that 13 persons died and were missing, and hundreds of houses completely collapsed at 16.00 hours on 13 November. Thus, the floods overlapped each other and caused death and grief. In Ninh Thuan, rain lasted for two days from 12 to 13 November, flooding 20,000 ha of crop and shrimp culture areas, causing an economic loss of VND 10 billion. The communes of An Hai, Phuoc Hai, Phuoc Son (Ninh Phuoc district), Xuan Hai (Ninh Hai district) and the two district Ninh Son and Bac Ai seem to be completely isolated. Inter-commune links and the Ninh Thuan–Lam Dong provincial road network have been isolated. As quickly reported by the provincial FTPCB, water levels in rivers exceeded the third alarm level by 0.12 m (0.22 m higher than the historic 1986 flood)

at 13.00 hours on the 13 November. In Phuoc Son commune, Ninh Phuoc district there were 70 households isolated on high lying mounds waiting for rescue forces. A railway section of 115 m running through Xuan Hai commune (Ninh Hai district) has been inundated by 1.0–1.5 m of water and the railway authority had to suspend its operations from 04.55 a.m. on the same day. In Ninh Thuan there were seven deaths and seven injuries, and Ninh Phuoc district is the most greatly affected where four people died. A power supply station in Phan Rang–Thap Cham provincial capital town was so inundated that it was unable to distribute electricity.

One of the biggest flood occurred on November 1999 by reason of a combination of cold atmosphere, tropical converge, and tropical low pressure from 1/XI to 6/XI/1999. The seven-day rainfall at many points on the Huong River Basin (Thua Thien Hue province) reached over 1,600 mm; in Hue it was 2,289.5 mm, in A Luoi it was 1,908.5 mm, and in Thuong Nhat it was 1,663.9 mm. From this extreme rainfall, on all tributaries of the Huong River, the floodwater levels exceeded alarming levels of about 0.5 to 1.0 m. The peak of the water level at Hue reached 5.91 m; it was higher by 2.81 m than the third alarm level.[7] Massive damages and losses were incurred in the economy, society and the environment. In Thua Thien Hue province, 472 persons have died, thousands of houses and schools were destroyed and damaged, and nearly 20 km of river banks were eroded. In the Mekong Delta, the flood on August to September 2000 rose to its highest water level at Tan Chau at 5.06 m and at Chau Doc at 4.90 m, the total water volume flowing to the Mekong Delta coming up 420 bcm, killing 448 people and inundating 2,751 schools (see Figure 12.4).

In relation to the Mekong Delta, the *Nhan Dan* newspaper on 22 April 2003, reported the following:

> Due to long lasting droughts Kien Giang province suffered a shortage of water for irrigation of 20,000 ha of crops and increase in salt intrusion from the West sea. In addition to the death of

FIGURE 12.4
Maximum Inundation Depth of 2000 Flood
in Mekong Delta

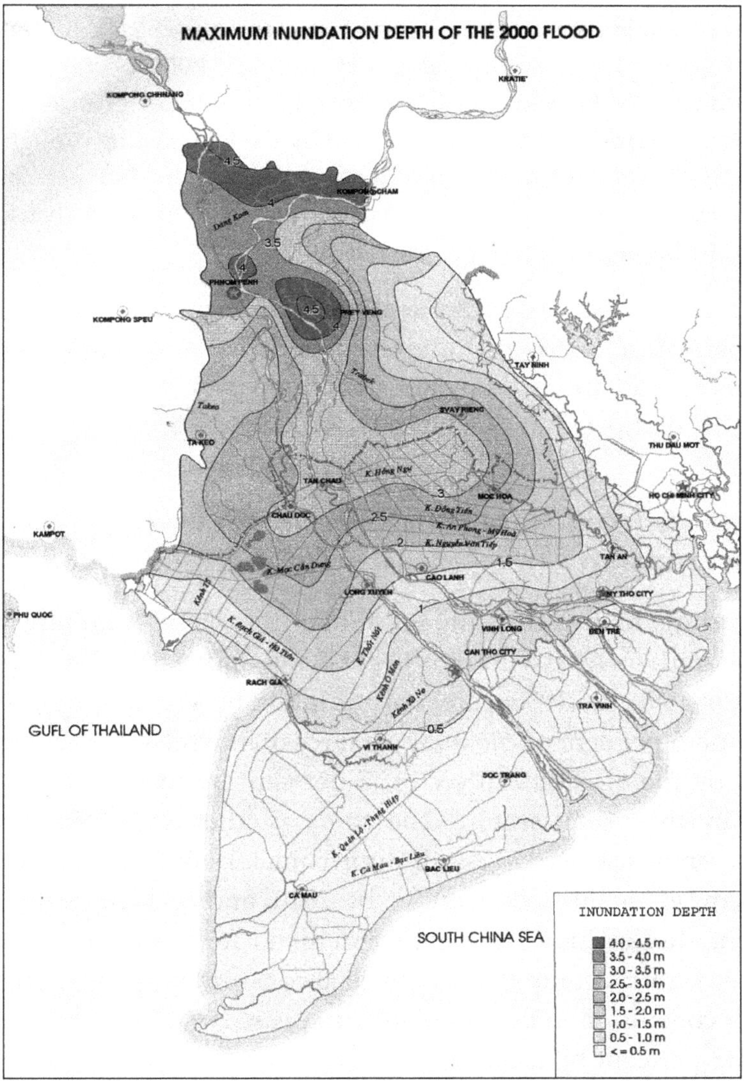

Source: Le Huy Ba and Nguyen Xuan Hien, *Assessment of Economic, Social and Environmental Impacts of the Floods of the Year 2000 in Mekong Delta*, Regional Training Workshop, Ho Chi Minh City, 2002.

sugarcane plants, 400 hectares of black pepper crops were seriously affected by the scarcity of water, leading to a decrease in the productivity by 40–50 per cent. It is predicted that areas of crops would be affected by the increased intensity of droughts and salt intrusion in days to come. In Soc Trang, there are 35,000 hectares of tiger prawn culture of which around 4,000 hectares are industrially farmed. But more than 4,000 hectares of extensive shrimp farming were badly affected by the long-lasting droughts and the salinity in the pondwater increased by 2–5 per cent (part per thousand). In My Xuyen, the most affected district, 3,200 hectares of shrimp were killed.

In November 2011, the death toll from weeks of flooding in Vietnam climbed to one hundred. Floods battered parts of central Vietnam, and more than half a million people have seen their livelihood affected in this latest event.

Conflicts from Rapid Increase in Water Consumption

According to the Institute of Water Resources Planning on a collaborative work with the World Bank and Asian Development Bank in 1996, the 1990 water consumption by Vietnam was 50 bcm (around 6 per cent of the total resources), in which 92 per cent was used by the agricultural sector, 5 per cent by industry and 4 per cent by the urban sector.[8] The study predicted that the volume of water in use would reach approximately 65 bcm/yr by 2000, 72 bcm/yr by 2010, 80 bcm/yr by 2020, and 87 bcm/yr by 2030. Recent studies indicate a higher demand for water consumption in the country, compared to the 2000 consumption level. The total water consumption is estimated to increase by 14 per cent by 2010, and 38 per cent by 2030.

The rapid increase in water consumption presents many difficulties for water management policy-makers in Vietnam, for example, the conflicts in using water resources between the different sectors or different parts of the basin, and conflicts between energy generation and flood control during the rainy season, and water supplies during the dry season and conflicts between water supply for aquaculture and environmental protection in the coastal areas.

POLLUTION OF SURFACE WATER IN MANY LOCATIONS

In general, the water quality of rivers, lakes, and reservoirs are presently good enough for user purposes (mainly upstream of most rivers and large lakes). But in the reaches and lakes where there are the industrial, urban zones, or tourism activities, the water resources there are polluted. In agriculture sector, using the fertilizers, pesticides and chemical matters has created pollution in canals, rivers and soils. Processing agricultural products after harvesting have also been creating pollution in water and soil because of the wastes generated.

Almost all the wastewater discharged from around seventy industrial parks and more than 1,000 hospitals nationwide is untreated. Rivers in urban areas, especially in major cities, are seriously polluted by untreated industrial wastewater. Groundwater is an important source for domestic, industrial and agricultural uses; most groundwater remains good, but there is evidence of pollution from poorly maintained septic tanks, industrial effluents and over-exploitation in some parts such as Hanoi, Ho Chi Minh City and along coastal zones. Water in the estuaries and irrigation systems are being polluted by wastewater and solid wastes from domestic and industrial activities because most large irrigation systems in Vietnam are located in the deltas or estuary regions with high population densities.[9]

In Vietnam, three river basins having serious problems in water quality and the environment:

(1) Nhue-Day River Basin, including Hanoi capital and some northern industrial parks; the area of this basin is more than

TABLE 12.2
Water Quality in Vietnam's Rivers

Region	River/site	Exceedance of Class A (Vietnam standard)
Red River Delta	Red River/Lao Cai	$1.5\text{--}2.0/NH_4$
	Red River/Dien and Hanoi	$3.8/BOD_5$
	Hong to Viet Tri	$2.0/NH_4$
	Cau River	$2.0/NH_4$
	Thuong River	$2.7/BOD_5$
North Central Coast	Hieu River	$2.0\text{--}3.0/BOD_5$
South Central	Huong River	$2.5/BOD_5$
	Han River	$1.0\text{--}2.0/BOD_5$
Southeast Coast	Sai Gon River	$2.0\text{--}4.0/BOD_5$

Source: The World Bank, DANIDA, MONRE, *Vietnam Environment Monitor 2003*.

8,000 km² (Hanoi city, and Hoa Binh, Ha Tay, Ha Nam, Nam Dinh and Ninh Binh provinces). About 3.5 million people live along the river, and the most urgent issue has been to reduce water pollution caused by industries, handicraft production and agricultural activities.

(2) Cau River Basin has an area of about 6,000 km², including the provinces of Bac Kan, Thai Nguyen, Vinh Phuc and Bac Ninh. Within the basin there are many industrial factories such as Song Cong and Thai Nguyen. Presently, the river is facing water shortages in the dry season, and heavy pollution in areas of rapid population growth, industrialization, urbanization, and agricultural development.

(3) Dong Nai-Saigon River Basin is 36,000 km² in South Vietnam. The economy on this basin is developing very rapidly. The basin accounts for 14.6 per cent of the land area of the country,

but its GDP makes up 40 per cent of national GDP. The basin has relatively large reserves of hydropower energy and some are being exploited (Tri An, Ham Thuan–Da Mi hydropower plants). But today, downstream of the river, there are many large centres of industrial zones, many of which are polluted in nature. In the dry season, there is a scarcity of drinking water and saltwater intrusion.

Pollution is rampant especially for the estuaries of coastal Central Vietnam where the water resources face many environmental problems (for example, droughts). In typical estuary parts of Da Nang city and Quang Nam, Khanh Hoa and Ninh Thuan provinces, the main problems are as follows:

- Shortage of freshwater during the dry season due to large variations in water distribution in rivers which has led to saltwater intrusion and increasing water pollution. In the downstream and estuary of the Thu Bon-Vu Gia, the tide and saltwater from the sea flows into the river through the Han Estuary (Da Nang) and Dai Estuary (Hoi An). For the Tra Khuc River, operation of the irrigation weir Thach Nham during the dry season reduces water flows to the estuary. This causes difficulties for the coastal environment, for example more water pollution, saltwater intrusion and lack of freshwater for demands. Up to now, in the upstream of Cai Nha Trang River, there has not been any significant hydraulic structure for irrigation but during the dry season, sea tides affect the estuary, especially the Cai Phan Rang River, which experiences very low rainfall, even though this river receives water from outside the catchment through the Da Nhim hydropower plant (on average about 16 m^3/s discharge), in the dry season. Due to the operation of the Nha Trinh–Lam Cam irrigation system, water flowing to this estuary is very minimal.
- Rapidly urbanization and industrization in all of the coastal and estuary regions of Central Vietnam in recent years has made

the water in several rivers very polluted. In the region of the estuary of Thu Bon-Vu Gia in Da Nang city, decades of sewage from industrial zones and domestic activities, for example, in the An Don, Lien Chieu and Hoa Khanh industrial zones, has created severe water pollution. Solid waste from Da Nang city amounts to nearly 200,000 tonnes per year (only about 70 per cent of this has been collected and treated) and this is another reason for water pollution. Quang Ngai town with a population of 150,000 people and some industrial factories located in downstream of Thach Nham irrigation system, is a main source of estuary and coastal pollution. The touristy Nha Trang city located in the estuary of the Cai Nha Trang river with hundreds of restaurants and shops along the river bank and beaches are a main reason for water pollution in the estuary. The downstream part and estuary of Cai Phan Rang River is the driest region of the country, especially during the dry season. In recent years, Phan Rang–Thap Cham town and many tourist and service zones along the beach have been developing very quickly, and has created pressures on the environment and water quality in the estuary and coast.

- During the dry season, water re-flows from irrigation and cultivation areas to the downstream and estuary of the rivers also create a lot of pollution. For example, along Cai Phan Rang River, there are many grape and onion fields which use many chemical fertilizers and pesticides, again increasing water pollution in its vicinity. Aquaculture and fishing activities in the estuary region also contribute to water pollution; for example, the fishing ports, and shrimp breeding on the sand fields of coastal zones, seafood processing, etc.

In the future, the quality of water resources in Vietnam will likely be more seriously affected if the rapid development of urbanization, industrialization, and intensified use of fertilizers, pesticides and chemical matters in agriculture, and industries processing production after harvesting are left unregulated.

The Problems of Water Resources and Watershed Management in Vietnam

At present, the Ministry of Natural Resources and Environment has the task of managing water resources, but there are overlaps in management and responsibilities. For example, in water resources, water demands for industrial activities is under the supervision of the Ministry of Industry, water demands for domestic use under the Ministry of Construction, and water demands for agriculture under the Ministry of Agriculture and Rural Development. This makes it very difficult for an integrated approach to be carried out for river basin management. This point will be further elaborated below.

There is also a lack of cooperation between companies and institutions in using water, even between the different sectors (water, forestry, energy). The problems of strategy, policy in exploitation, integrated utilization, and protection of water resources for whole the country should be approached in a more coherent and integrated manner. In the research and management of natural resources of the basins, official statistics, information, and monitoring data are not widely available, even for the river basins inside the country such as those of the Ba River or Dong Nai River. Almost all Vietnamese people in the rural areas of the river basins think that natural resources come from nature; this is one of the difficulties for river basin management by policy and laws.

SITUATION OF WATER RESOURCES AND WATERSHED MANAGEMENT IN VIETNAM

1. Organization of the Water Resources Management

Several regulations however exist. This includes the following:

The Law on Water Resources of Vietnam was approved and issued on 20 May 1998 and Decree 179/1999/ND-CP of 10 July

FIGURE 12.5
Water Resources Management in Vietnam

Organizational chart of water-related institutions

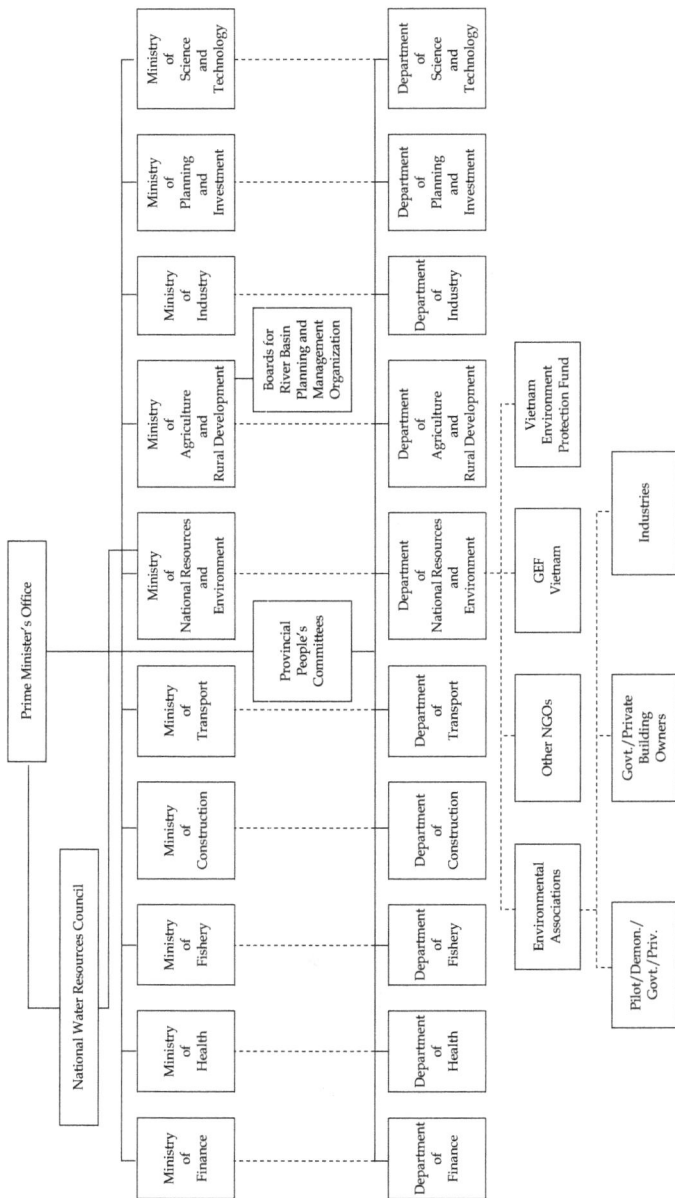

Source: The World Bank, DANIDA, MONRE, *Vietnam Environment Monitor* 2003.

1999 on implementing this law. This law includes ten chapters with 75 articles, and the implementation of this law has been commendable.

Decision Number 67/2000/QD-TTg of Prime Minister dated 15 June 2000, on establishment of National Water Resources Council, and Decision Number 99/2001/QD-TTg of Prime Minister on issuing regulations on organization and operation of National Water Resources Council.

Decision Number 37, 38, 39/2001/QD/BNN-TCCB of Ministry of Agriculture and Rural Development (MARD) dated 9 April 2001, on the establishment of boards for river basin planning and management of Mekong (Delta), Dong Nai, ThaiBinh, and Red River.

At present, the planning tasks on water resources and river basins in Vietnam rests with the Institute of Water Resources Planning (under the Ministry for Agriculture and Rural Development, MARD), while the tasks of water resources management rests with the Department of Water Resources Management (under the Ministry of Natural Resources and Environment, MONRE). The Department of Water Resources (under MARD) is concerned only with the management of irrigation systems for agriculture.

Since the passing of the Law on Water Resources of Vietnam, the activities of management are now defined as follows:

(i) To set up, report for approval and oversee the implementation of the river basin planning, ensure the unique management between river basin and administration territory.

(ii) To carry out the coordination between related institutions from different ministries, sectors and provinces in basic investigation, statistics, and assess the water resources of the basin; also to set up, report for approval and oversee the implementation of planning the river tributaries.

(iii) To propose solutions in conflicts of water resources within the river basin.

2. Water Resources and Watershed Management Practices in Vietnam

a) Overlaps in water management:

There are many "owners" in the water management of a river basin, leading to overlaps in management, for example: Water supplies for energy generation and industrial uses and are under the Ministry of Industry (MOI); water supplies for domestic use is under the Ministry of Construction (MOC); water supplies for agriculture is under the Ministry of Agriculture and Rural Development (MARD); water quantity, quality and water environment of the basins are under the Ministry of Natural Resources and Environment (MONRE). This makes it very difficult for an integrated management of river basins, because each owner has its own plan, agenda, and investments for water resources under its purview.

There has also been a lack of cooperation between the companies, and institutions in the field of water supply, drainage and environmental protection (rainfall water, wastewater from domestic and industry).

b) Water resource planning and river basin planning management are the most important first steps in water resources and watershed management in Vietnam. It can be said that water resource planning must involve the following:

- Estimating the potential of water resources of the basin and the water demand from a social-economic development perspective in order to protect water resources and prevent damage;
- Defining the orientation and task of the water resource development programme of the basin;
- Proposing the measures for exploiting and using water resources in a sustainable and effective way; and
- Proposing suitable steps to implement the proposed solutions and issues.

Depending on the scope of planning area, water resources planning is divided into the following categories: water resources planning in the river basin; water resources planning in an economic zone, or in the region (some province); nation-wide water resources planning or linked river basins water resources planning.

In order to implement watershed management, the following should be undertaken:

- Building the database and information system on water demand and water resources for the whole of the basin, and update and disseminate the information to all regions and related organizations.
- Organizing the participation of the community in the planning process frequently and systematically.
- Building a two-way comprehensive relationship with the National Water Resources Council in order to create a practical and effective consultation system; and for the transboundary river basins, there is a need to build international links and relationships with countries sharing the same basin.

3. Measures for Water Resources and Watershed Management

a) In general, the following measures should be applied:

- To raise the knowledge of people in safe water uses, environmental protection; reforestation and forest protection, strictly execute laws, especially the Water Resources Law and Environmental Protection Law and other related regulations.
- To complete and improve the quality of river basin planning; enhance the management capacity and operational efficiency of the National Water Resources Council and River Basin Management Boards.

- To improve the efficiency of water uses and reduce water demand and consumption by applying new technologies, and treatment of waste water for re-use.
- To construct multi-purpose reservoirs and exploit multiple terraced rivers to improve water supply, drought control, salt-water intrusion prevention and hydropower generation.
- Apply new technologies in groundwater investigation and exploitation, and combination between surface and groundwaters.
- Cooperate effectively and closely with the neighbouring countries in using and sharing water resources of trans-boundry river systems.

b) Flood control and the solution for drought problem and others:

Regarding flood control, the strategy should be as follows:

(1) For the Red and Thai Binh River (North Vietnam), flood control must combine six measures:

- Watershed forest planting and protection;
- Flood regulation by large reservoirs in the upstream of Da and Lo rivers;
- Dyke system in lower river basins to protect the important areas from the floods;
- Improve the flood drainage capacity of the rivers, especially for reaches of the downstream and estuary;
- Flood diversion through Day River to the sea;
- Use of flood detention areas along Red River from Phu Tho to Ha Tay provinces.

(2) For the central coastal plains, the flood control measures mainly are:

- To avoid and modify developments in areas vulnerable to natural disasters by planning for regional socio-economic development.

- Adapt to the conditions of major seasonal floods, control initial and late floods by constructing reservoirs in rivers upstream.
- Control bank erosion and river-mouth sedimentation for flood drainage, and development of waterways.
- Construct the drainage and flood control works in the coastal urban areas.
- Enlarge the span of bridges and culverts of the North-South Railway and National Road Number 1.
- Implement four lines of action on flood control and rescue by maximizing local supplies, manpower, logistics, and direction.

(3) For Mekong River Delta, the following measures should be applied:

- Ensure that residential areas are safe from floods.
- Construct houses in high elevation areas, and build embankments to protect low-lying areas.
- Regulate river beds and mouths to ensure safety for residential areas and drain floods through the river mouth including the Vam Co Tay River.
- Enlarge canals for flood drainage and water storage for users during the dry season; enlarge roads along canals to establish transport and settlement areas in combined routes.
- Extend appropriately the span of bridges and culverts to ensure rapid flood drainage.

In Vietnam, droughts are also a big problem affecting the socio-economic development of the country. In order to avoid and mitigate their impacts, several measures should be applied:

- Plan water resource development, management and protection (water quantity and quality) suitable to the conditions of the basins or regions.

- Use measures and new technologies to protect water resources.
- Construct reservoirs to regulate water flows in order to supply water and control saltwater intrusion during the dry season.
- Change crop patterns, especially in the Mekong Delta and Central Highlands in order to reduce water demand during the dry season.

Regarding water quality and pollution, firstly the water quality monitoring network should be established for the whole country, and wastewater must be treated before discharge into rivers and lakes. Integrated coastal zone management is an especially important issue for water resource management.

In conclusion, implementation of water resources and watershed management in Vietnam is a complex problem, but with the concept of sustainable development as a guiding principle and a step-by-step approach towards this will improve the practice.

Notes

1. See *World Water Balance and Water Resources of the Earth* (Paris: UNESCO, 1978).
2. See Water Utilization Program, MRC, *Overview of Hydrology of the Mekong Basin*, 2005.
3. *State of Water Resources Management in ASEAN* (Jakarta: ASEAN Secretariat, October 2005), p. 61.
4. See Le Dinh Thanh, *Extreme Rainfall and Flood in Vietnam*, Workshop on Hydrological Extremes and Climate in Tropical Areas and their Control, Bressia University, Italia, 2003.
5. Ibid.
6. *State of Water Resources Management in ASEAN*, op. cit., p. 59.
7. See Le Huy Ba and Nguyen Xuan Hien, *Assessment of Economic, Social and Environmental Impacts of the Floods of the Year 2000 in Mekong Delta* Regional Training Workshop, Ho Chi Minh City, 2002.
8. See World Bank, Asian Development Bank, FAO, UNDP and Others, *Vietnam – General Review on Water Sector*, Hanoi 1996.

9. See The World Bank, DANIDA, MONRE, *Vietnam Environment Monitor 2003.*

References

IN VIETNAMESE

Dao Xuan Hoc, et al. *Drought and the Measures for Mitigating Its Effects.* Hanoi: Agricultural Publisher, 2002.
_____. *Research the Measures for Mitigating the Drought Disaster of the Coastal Central Provinces.* State research project, 2000–02.
Le Dinh Thanh. *Potentiality of Heavy Floods on Huong River Basin.* International Symposium on Achievements of IHP-V in Hydrological Research, 2001.
_____. *Estimation of Maximum Probable Flood for Hoa Binh Reservoir.* Proceedings of 2nd Scientific Conference of the Vietnam University, Hanoi, 2000.
Le Huy Ba and Nguyen Xuan Hien. *Assessment of Economic, Social and Environmental Impacts of the Floods of the Year 2000 in Mekong Delta.* Regional Training Workshop, Ho Chi Minh City, 2002.
National Assembly of the Socialist Republic of Vietnam. *Water Resources Law*, 1998.
_____. *Environmental Protection Law*, 1993.
Ngo Dinh Tuan, Le Dinh Thanh, et al. *Water Balance for Eco-social Development in Central Coastal Provinces of Vietnam.* Hanoi, 1994.
Nguyen Dinh Tien, Le Dinh Thanh, et al. *Water Balance for Eco-social Development in Central High Land of Vietnam.* Hanoi, 1995.
Ngo Dinh Tuan, Le Dinh Thanh. *Assessment of Typhoons, Rainfall Storms, Floods and Plant Cover Effecting on Floods and Water Disasters in River Basins of Central Vietnam.* Hanoi, 1997.
Standing Office of the Central Committee for Flood and Storm Control VN. *Reviewing Floods at the Basins of Da, Lo, Red and Ca River, and the Losses due to Flood and Typhoon.* Hanoi, 1996.

IN ENGLISH

Dao Trong Tu. *Integrated Water Management in Vietnam and International Integration.* Hanoi: National Workshop, October 2001.

Kenneth N. Brooks, et al. *Hydrology and the Management of Watersheds.* USA: Iowa State University Press, 1991.

Le Dinh Thanh. *Integrated River Basin Management in Vietnam.* Regional Refresher Seminar on Integrated Management of River Basin and Coastal Zones. Hanoi, Vietnam, December 2002.

Mick van der Wegen. *Water Security Challenges in Provision and Protection.* Regional Refresher Seminar on Integrated Management of River Basin and Coastal Zones. Hanoi, Vietnam, December 2002.

National Water Resources Council. *Vietnam Water Resources Atlas,* 2004.

Ngo Dinh Tuan, Le Dinh Thanh. *Some Aspects of River Basin Management in Vietnam.* International Workshop in River Basin Management. Netherlands: The Hague, 1999.

Le Duc Trung. *Implications of Sustainable Development and Management in Integrated Planning of Quan Lo-Phung Hiep Project.* International Symposium on Achievements of IHP-V in Hydrological Research. Hanoi, Vietnam, 2001.

Le Dinh Thanh. *Extreme Rainfall and Flood in Vietnam.* Workshop on Hydrological Extremes and Climate in Tropical Areas and their Control. Italia: Bressia University, 2003.

Le Dinh Thanh, Pham Hung. *Water Quality of Typical Estuaries in Coastal Areas of Central Vietnam.* International Workshop on Water Resources. Vietnam: Doson, 2005.

Nguyen Hong Toan. *Some Aspects in International River Basin Management of Vietnam in View of Water Security Vision.* National Workshop, Hanoi, October 2001.

Nguyen Huu Phuc. *Flood Management and Mitigation in Vietnam.* International Symposium on Achievements of IHP-V in Hydrological Research. Hanoi, Vietnam, 2001.

State of Water Resources Management in ASEAN. Jakarta: ASEAN Secretariat, October 2005.

The World Bank, DANIDA, MONRE. *Vietnam Environment Monitor 2003.*

To Trung Nghia. *River Basin Planning Management in the Present Condition.* National Workshop, Hanoi, October 2001.

United Nations. *Strategy and Action Plan for Mitigating Water Disasters in Vietnam.* New York and Geneva, 1994.

Ven Te Chow, David R. Maidment, and Larry W. Mays. *Applied Hydrology.* Boston, Massachusetts: McGraw-Hill international editions, 1998.

Vietnam Association for Conservation of Natural and Environment. *Vietnam Environment and Life*. Hanoi: National Political Publisher, 2004.

Water Utilization Program, MRC. *Overview of Hydrology of the Mekong Basin*, 2005.

World Bank, Asian Development Bank, FAO, UNDP and Others. *Vietnam – General Review on Water Sector*. Hanoi, 1996.

World Water Balance and Water Resources of the Earth. Paris: UNESCO, 1978.

INDEX

A

Actiflo system in Malaysia, 171
ADB. *See* Asian Development
     Bank (ADB)
agriculture
     growth rate in Indonesia, 116
     surface water pollution in, 301
     in Thailand, 266–67
     water demand in, 105
     water usage in, 13, 259
air pollution, 178
Amur River, 28, 46
     water pollution in, 47–48
Aral Sea Basin, 65–68, 71–73
ASEAN, water quality in, 258
Asian Development Bank (ADB),
     22–23, 38, 50, 174, 187, 194,
     203n1
Asian financial crisis,
     privatization, 21, 77, 230, 232
Atienza, Lito, 189
Ayala Corporation, 225, 227, 228

B

Badawi, Abdullah, 95
Bakrie, Aburizal, 94

Bali, irrigation water in, 106
Bang Giang River, 290
Bangkok, urban areas in, 265
Bang Pakong Dialogue, 278,
     279–80
Bang Pakong River Basin, 275–78
Bang Pakong River Basin
     Committee (BP-RBC), 278,
     281–82
Ba River, 290, 305
Basin Development Programme
     (BDP), 296
basin's fishery resources, 275
Bedok project, 246
bidding
     participants, 224–27
     procedure, 21, 212, 215, 221,
     225
     requirements, 224–25
BOD, 186, 194, 196
Bonn International Freshwater
     Conference, 79
BOO contracts. *See* build-operate-
     own (BOO) contracts
BOOT. *See* build-operate-own-
     transfer (BOOT)

BOT. *See* build-operate-transfer
    (BOT)
BP-RBC. *See* Bang Pakong River
    Basin Committee (BP-RBC)
Brahamaputra River, 49
Brunei Darussalam
    surface water in, 4
    water resources in, 2
build-operate-own (BOO)
    contracts, 20, 89, 139, 216
build-operate-own-transfer
    (BOOT), 214
    contracts, 216
build-operate-transfer (BOT)
    contracts, 20, 89, 139, 216
    project, 150
bumiputra, Malaysia, 138, 142

C
Cai Nha Trang River, 303, 304
Cai Phan Rang River, 303, 304
Cambodia
    freshwater usage in, 4
    Mekong River Basin flows
        across, 287
    tributaries of Mekong River
        flow to, 290
capacity-building
    programmes in Malaysia, 131,
        132
    in Thailand, 271, 280
capital expenditures (CAPEX),
        137, 172n3
    wrong planning on, 157–58
capitalism
    pure, 77
    unbridled, 18, 77

Ca river basin, 289
Cau river basin, water quality in,
    302
Central Asia, 43–46
    damming rivers in, 36
    environmental crisis, 43
    geography of, 28
    Lake Balkhash in, 28
central coastal plains, flood
    control measures in, 310–11
Central Java, floods and
    landslides in, 104
Central Vietnam
    estuary regions of, 303
    floods in, 297
    river basins of, 289
Chay River, Thac Ba on, 295
China
    climate change in, 32, 34
    coal-fired plant in, 51
    cultural force in, 27
    damming rivers in, 36
    dams construction in, 4, 10, 41,
        42, 44
    electricity in, 29, 41, 51
    freshwater rivers in, 27, 35
    hydropower plants in, 37, 49
    irrigation systems in, 33, 48
    Mekong River Basin flows
        across, 287
    melting glaciers in, 31–34
    population in, 35
    power station in, 51
    soil erosion in, 34
    toxic spills in, 46
    water conflict in, 9–11

water crisis in, 35–36
water sharing systems in, 4
cholera, 185, 219
civilization, 56, 119
civil society
   groups, 231
   and Pasig, 196–200
climate change
   in China, 32, 34
   in Southeast Asia, 256, 257
   in Vietnam, 293
coal-fired plant in China, 51
coastal Central Vietnam, estuaries
   of, 303
coastal line, Vietnam's, 289
coastal plains, flood control
   measures in central, 310–11
coastal waters, coliform bacteria
   in, 183
community empowerment,
   dealing with environmental
   pollution, 201
community mobilization, 197
competitive bidding procedure,
   21, 221, 225
Concession Agreement and
   privatization programme,
   149, 166, 167
concessionaire
   Manila Water Company,
      227–28
   Maynilad Water Services
      Incorporated, 228–30
concessions method, PSP, 216
Construction cum Concession
   Agreement (CCOA), 149

consumer price index (CPI), 223
coordinated management of
   resources, 121
corporate agreement in Metro
   Manila, 216
cronyism, 88, 95
Czarist Russia, irrigated
   agriculture in, 66

D

DAF System. *See* Dissolve Air
   Flotation (DAF) System
Dai Estuary, 303
dams
   construction in China, 4, 10, 41,
      42, 44
   diversion, 276
   in Indonesia, 103, 114
   in Malaysia, 137, 167
   Mekong River, 37
Da Nang
   estuary parts of, 303
   solid waste from, 304
Da Nhim hydropower plant, 303
Da River
   Hoa Binh on, 295
   Huong Quang on, 295
decentralization, 77
   and environmental policy,
      15–16
   in Indonesia, 95
   in Philippines, 179–82
Deep Tunnel Sewerage System
   (DTSS), 251–52
degradation, environmental, 22,
   129, 176
democratization, 78

DENR. *See* Department of
    Environment and Natural
    Resources (DENR)
Department of Environment
    (DOE), 124, 130, 168
Department of Environment and
    Natural Resources (DENR),
    176, 180, 181, 189, 207n50
    estimated pollution sources,
    185
Department of Irrigation and
    Drainage, 168
Department of Mineral and
    Geosciences, 168
Department of Public Works and
    Highways (DPWH), 189
Department of Water Resources
    (DWR), 16, 264, 266, 274,
    277–78
Department of Water Resources
    Management, 307
Department of Water Supply
    (DWS), 129
deregulation, 87, 282
desalination
    membrane-based, 244
    water in Singapore, 17, 23
dispute settlement mechanism,
    223–24
Dissolve Air Flotation (DAF)
    System, 171
Dissolved Oxygen (DO), 183, 186,
    194
distribution supply system
    contracts project, 150
diversion dam in Thailand, 276
divestiture method, PSP, 216

Dong Nai River, 290, 305
    Tri An on, 295
Dong Nai–Saigon River Basin,
    302–3
drought
    in Thailand, 257
    in Vietnam, 311
dry season, 288, 296
    freshwater shortage during,
    303
DTSS. *See* Deep Tunnel Sewerage
    System (DTSS)
Dublin principles, 1, 58–61
Duerkop, Colin, 8
DWR. *See* Department of Water
    Resources (DWR)

E
eastern seaboard of Indochinese
    peninsula, 288
East Java, floods and landslides
    in, 104
ECAFE. *See* Economic
    Commission for Asia and the
    Far East (ECAFE)
eco-innovations, 176
Economic and Social Commission
    for Asia and the Pacific
    (ESCAP), 69
Economic Commission for Asia
    and the Far East (ECAFE),
    69
economic resource, water as, 109,
    110
ecosystem integrity, 183
ecosystem services, water
    resources for, 258

Eighth Malaysia Plan (8MP)
(2001–2005), 139, 144, 145–46
key strategies of, 129
electricity
in China, 29, 41, 51
in Thailand, 268
El Nino, 257
phenomenon, 230
and river basin damage, 101
enabling environment, 127, 132
Enron-Arthur Andersen, 79
fiasco, 82
saga, 82
environmental awareness in
Southeast Asia, 23
environmental degradation, 22,
129, 176
environmental disasters in Java,
104
Environmental Impact
Assessment Law, 40
environmental impacts of PRRP,
194–96
environmental legislation in
Philippines, 179, 182
environmental pollution. *See also*
water pollution
community empowerment
dealing with, 201
Environmental Preservation Areas
(EPAs), 190–92
Environmental Programme (EP),
201, 296
Environmental Protection Law,
309
environment policy in Philippines,
175, 180

ESCAP. *See* Economic and Social
Commission for Asia and the
Pacific (ESCAP)
esteros in Pasig River, 176, 183,
188, 196, 202
Estrada, Joseph, 96, 187
estuaries
of coastal Central Vietnam, 303
Dai, 303
Han, 303
water pollution in, 303–4
evapo-transpiration process, 122
extraordinary price adjustment
(EPA), 223

F
FDIs, 94–96
Federations of Water User
Associations (WUAFs), 115
flash floods in Thailand, 256
Flood and Typhoon Prevention
and Control Boards (FTPCB),
297
floods
control in Vietnam, 310
frequency of, 257
in Indonesia, 100, 104
in Java, 104, 118n3
in Malaysia, 13, 124
in Mekong Delta, 298–99
in Red River Delta, 297
in Thailand, 256
in Vietnam, 288
warning systems, 104
foreign currency differential
adjustment (FCDA), 230
forest and river basin, 101

Four Taps of Singapore, 16, 250
freshwater resources, 286, 290
    availability of, 1, 24n1
    demand for, 7
    largest volume of, 2
    shortage of, 303
    in Southeast Asia, 2, 5, 24n2
freshwater rivers in China, 27,
    35

G

General Comment on the Right to
    Water, 213
geographic information system
    (GIS), 269
glacial lake outburst floods
    (GLOFs), 34
globalization, 80
    harsh realities of, 83
global warming, 9, 29, 31, 32, 34
Global Water Awards 2008,
    244
Global Water Partnership (GWP),
    61, 120
global water resources, 33
GLOFs. *See* glacial lake outburst
    floods (GLOFs)
GMS. *See* Greater Mekong Sub-
    region (GMS)
Government of Indonesia (GOI),
    107
    authority and responsibility of,
    111–12
Greater Mekong Sub-region
    (GMS), 38, 50
groundwater, 258, 286, 301
    exploitable, 293

resources, 168, 260–61
    in Southeast Asia, 4
    in Thailand, 260
Gulf Coastal Plain, 261
GWP. *See* Global Water
    Partnership (GWP)

H

Han Estuary, 303
harness water, 10
Highland Towers event, 125
Himalayan region, 33, 34
Hoa Binh on Da River, 295
Ho Chih Minh City, 97
Hoi An, 303
human communities,
    infrastructure and utilities
    provision, 84–86
human development, water
    resource for, 286
Huong Quang on Da River
    system, 295
Huong River Basin, 298
hydrological cycle, 119
hydropower plant
    in China, 29, 37, 38, 49, 52
    Da Nhim, 303
    in Vietnam, 295
Hyflux, Singapore water
    company, 243

I

IACEP. *See* Inter-Agency
    Committee on Environmental
    Protection (IACEP)
IFC. *See* International Finance
    Corporation (IFC)

Ili River, 43
Indochina, hydropower projects
    in, 268
Indochinese peninsula, eastern
    seaboard of, 288
Indonesia
    agriculture growth rate in, 116
    dams in, 103, 114
    decentralization in, 95
    economy, 116
    Medium Term Development
        Plan, 116
    municipal water system in, 108
    provincial government of, 111
    river basins deterioration in,
        100–6
    sustainable water sector
        development programme
        in, 112–13
    water demand rising in, 12–13
    water resources in, 2
    water scarcity in, 100
    water sector development and
        programme in, 113–14
    water sector road map in,
        116–17
    WRL, 109–12
Indus Basin, 63–65, 71–73
Indus River basin, 11
Indus River Commission, 30
industry, water demand in, 105
Inland Vietnam, river basins in,
    291
Institute of Water Resources
    Planning, 307
integrated river basin
    management (IRBM), 121

coordinated management of,
    121
Master Plan, 168
integrated water resources
    management (IWRM), 61,
    120, 121, 131, 271–72
    definition of, 59
    principles, 110
    processes of, 272
    water governance and
        implications, 272–73
Inter-Agency Committee on
    Environmental Protection
    (IACEP), 178
International Chamber of
    Commerce (ICC), 224, 231
International Finance Corporation
    (IFC), 21, 220, 221
International Law Commission, 64
international river basin, 290
International Water Management
    Institute (IWMI), 278, 280–82
inter-state agreements, 66
investment, in wastewater
    treatment, 268–70
IRBM. *See* integrated river basin
    management (IRBM)
irrigated agriculture in Czarist
    Russia, 66
irrigated paddy field
    in Indonesia, 114
    in Java, 105
irrigation
    in China, 33, 48
    condition of, 106
    in Indonesia, 105–6
    infrastructure, 114

in Java, 103
in Malaysia, 124
water demand for, 294
water in Bali, 106
water used for, 108
Irtysh-Ob River in Russia, 45
Irtysh River, 48
in Russia, 45
IWMI. *See* International Water
Management Institute
(IWMI)
IWRM. *See* integrated water
resources management
(IWRM)

J
Jakarta
water availability in, 102–3
water supply in, 102
Java
environmental disasters in, 104
irrigation water in, 106
rainfall in, 101
water potency in, 103
Johannesburg Plan of
Implementation (2002), water
supply, 1
Johor
privatization in, 20
water revenues in, 144

K
Kazakhstan, environmental
activists in, 45
Khorat Plateau, rainfall in, 261
Kien Giang province, shortage of
water in, 298

Klang Valley water crisis (1998),
144, 158
Konsortium ABASS, 148
Ky Cung River in Lang Son, 290

L
Lake Balkhash, 43, 44
water problem in, 48
Lancang, 37
Lancang Jiang river, 10
land, management of, 120, 133
landslides, 125, 256, 257
in Java, 104, 118n3
land use planning, 133
Lang Son, Ky Cung River in, 290
La Nina, 257
Lao People's Democratic Republic
(Lao PDR), 256, 258–59
Laos
Mekong River Basin flows
across, 287
tributaries of Mekong River
flow to, 290
Law on Water Resources of
Vietnam, 305, 307
leases method, PSP, 215
Lee Kuan Yew, 246
LGC. *See* Local Government Code
(LGC)
LGUs. *See* Local Government
Units (LGUs)
LMB. *See* Lower Mekong Basin
(LMB)
Local Government Code (LGC),
180, 205n20
Local Government Units (LGUs),
15, 180, 181, 264

Lower Central Plain, 261
Lower Mekong Basin (LMB), 68
Lower Peirce Reservoir, 245

M

Malaysia, 119
  Actiflo system in, 171
  bumiputra in, 138, 142
  capacity-building programmes
    in, 131, 132
  current initiatives, 128–32
  dams in, 137, 167
  development projects in, 131
  diminishing biodiversity in, 123,
    124, 127
  emerging issues in, 123–25
  financial crisis in, 151
  flood occurrences in, 123
  forest management in, 168
  groundwater resources in, 122
  land based developments, 128
  management issues, 125–28
  Ministry of Agriculture, 168
  national development policy in,
    138
  national policies and plans, 130
  National Privatization Policy in,
    20, 142
  peat swamp areas, 125
  pollution of water in, 14
  privatization in water supply.
    See privatization in water
    supply, Malaysia
  privatization of water, 20–21
  privatized projects in, 139–42
  project financing in, 152–53
  water demand in, 12, 124

water-related agencies, 127
water resource management in,
  132
water resources in, 2, 122–23
water revenue, 145
Malaysia Environmental Quality
  Report 2003, 169
Malaysia Incorporated Policy, 138
Malaysian Constitution, natural
  resources management, 15
Malaysian rivers
  deterioration by pollution, 146
  quality of, 146
Malaysia Water Forum, 128
management contracts method,
  PSP, 215
Manila
  water privatization in, 213
  water system, 21–22
Manila Bay, 183, 186, 220
Manilad project, 96
Manila Water Company, 227–28
  promising case of, 233–35
MARD. *See* Ministry of
  Agriculture and Rural
  Development (MARD)
Mar del Plata Action Plan (1979),
  1
Marina Basin, Singapore, 17
Marina reservoir, 250–51
Ma River, 288, 289
massive clean-up operation in
  Singapore, 247
Maynilad Water Services, 21–22,
  25n14, 213
Maynilad Water Services
  Incorporated, 228–30, 231–33

MDGs. *See* Millennium
    Development Goals (MDGs)
Medium Term Development Plan
    (MTDP), 116, 206n49
Mekong Agreement, 11, 69, 70, 73,
    296
Mekong Basin, 22, 51, 68–73
    fisheries in, 38
    water problem in, 48
Mekong River, 29, 33, 36, 287, 295
    and China's dam-building
        activities, 10
    dams, 37
    riparian countries of, 4
    tributaries of, 290
Mekong River Commission
    (MRC), 11, 22, 23, 30, 37, 38,
    41, 42, 69, 296
Mekong River Delta, 290, 293, 296
    flood control measures, 311
    flood in, 297, 298–300
melting
    glaciers in China, 31–34
    point of Mount Everest, 32
membrane-based desalination, 244
Membrane Bioreactor (MBR), 250
membrane technology, 249, 250
Metro Manila, 221
    case of, 218–20
    chronic water pollution in, 176
    corporate agreement in, 216
    environmental issues in, 179
    pre-privatization water
        provision in, 217–20
    privatization in. *See*
        privatization in Metro
        Manila

river pollution in, 185
solid waste in, 183
urbanization of, 186
Metro Manila Development
    Authority (MMDA), 189
Metropolitan Manila. *See* Metro
    Manila
Metropolitan Waterworks and
    Sewerage System (MWSS), 21,
    22, 212, 218, 219
    pre-privatized, 219
    privatization of, 212
    Regulatory Office (RO), 222
Metropolitan Waterworks
    Authority (MWA), 265
Meulle del Rio linear park, 190,
    191
mgd. *See* million gallons per day
    (mgd)
Millennium Development Goals
    (MDGs), 1, 213, 263
million gallons per day (mgd),
    249, 250
Ministry of Agriculture and Rural
    Development (MARD), 305,
    307, 308
Ministry of Construction (MOC),
    305, 308
Ministry of Industry (MOI), 305,
    308
Ministry of Natural Resources and
    Environment (MONRE), 168,
    307, 308
Ministry of Public Works (MPW),
    129
MOC. *See* Ministry of
    Construction (MOC)

Monterrey Consensus, 80–82
Morgan, Jennifer, 34
Mount Everest, melting point of, 32
MRC. *See* Mekong River Commission (MRC)
muddy banks, 248
municipal water system
  in Indonesia, 108
  in Jakarta, 102
MWA. *See* Metropolitan Waterworks Authority (MWA)
MWSS. *See* Metropolitan Waterworks and Sewerage System (MWSS)
Myanmar
  hydropower development plan in, 41
  Mekong River Basin flows across, 287
  MRC meetings, 37
  water resources in, 2

N
Nam Rom, 290
national development policy, in Malaysia, 138
National Economic Action Council (NEAC), 95
National Environmental Protection Council (NEPC), 178
national leadership, in Russia, 47
National Medium Term Development Plan, 114

National Pollution Control Commission (NPCC), 177, 178, 186
National Privatization Policy, in Malaysia, 20, 142
national river basin, 290
National Water and Air Pollution Control Commission (NWAPCC), 177
National Water Crisis Act, 220
national water management, challenges of, 12–18
National Water Master Plan, 148
national water policy (NWP), 129, 130, 147
National Water Resources Committee (NWRC), 273, 274
National Water Resources Council (NWRC), 16, 129, 130, 148, 168, 307, 309
National Water Resources Study, 122
  in Malaysia, 137
nationwide distribution, of water, 267
natural disasters, in Vietnam, 296–300
natural environment, 121
Navatos-Tullajan-Tenejeros River system, 183
NEAC. *See* National Economic Action Council (NEAC)
Negri Sembilan, water crisis in, 12
neo-liberalism, 76, 77
NEWater, 244
  plants, 93, 250
  in Singapore, 7, 17, 23, 249–50

NGOs. *See* non-governmental organizations (NGOs)
Nhan Dan newspaper, 298–99
Nha Trang, 304
Nhue-Day River Basin, water quality problems in, 301–2
Ninh Hai district, 298
Ninh Phuoc district, 298
Ninh Thuan province, 297
Ninth Malaysian Plan (2006–10), 140, 145, 146
nitrobenzene, 47
non-consumptive water sectors, 294, 295
non-governmental organizations (NGOs), 128, 189, 190, 198
non-municipal water system, in Jakarta, 102
non-revenue water (NRW), 219, 223
  increasing rate of, 145–46
  problem of, 157
North Central Vietnam, Ma River in, 288
northern sea, salinity of, 65
NRW. *See* non-revenue water (NRW)
Nu River, hydropower project on, 39, 40
NWP. *See* national water policy (NWP)
NWRC. *See* National Water Resources Committee (NWRC); National Water Resources Council (NWRC)

O
Office of National Water Resources Committee (ONWRC), 273
old Peirce Reservoir, 245
ONWRC. *See* Office of National Water Resources Committee (ONWRC)
Operations and Management (O&M) fund, 106
OPP3. *See* Third Outline Perspective Plan
Oregon State University, 30
ozone layer, 31

P
paddy field irrigation
  in Indonesia, 114
  in Java, 105
Pahang, water revenues in, 144
PAM JAYA, in Jakarta, 102
Pangestu, Marie, 94
participatory irrigation management (PIM), 115–16
Pasig River, 182–85, 207n52
  chronic pollution of, 200
  civil society, 196–200
  environmental impacts, 194–96
  rehabilitation of, 196–200
  relocation and resistance, 193–94
  reviving, 186–88, 200–3
  solid waste in, 183
  ten-metre easements, 190–92

Pasig River Rehabilitation
Commission (PRRC), 188–90,
194
Pasig River Rehabilitation Project
(PRRP), 175, 200
environmental impacts of,
194–96
relocation and resistance,
193–94
ten-metre easements in, 190–92
peat swamp areas, in Malaysia,
125
Penang
privatization, 20
water revenues in, 144
3P engagement approach, 252–53
Perusahaan Daerah Air Minum
(PDAM), 108
Phan Rang–Thap Cham, 298, 304
Phathum Thani Water Supply
Project, 266
Philippines
community involvement in,
179
environmental legislation, 179,
182
environment policy in, 175, 180
foremost urban centre, 218
government conflict in, 179–82
groundwater sources in, 4
incomplete decentralization in,
179–82
institutional capacity, 15
LGUs, 15
limitations of state authority,
176–79

local-central government
conflict, 179–82
Marcos Martial Law, 190
Medium Term Development
Plan (MTDP), 206n49
rainfall in, 217
river pollution in, 4
water demand rising in, 13
water pollution in, 14, 176
water privatization in, 21–22,
212
water supply in, 217
Phuoc Son commune, 298
Phu Yen province, 297
PIM. *See* participatory irrigation
management (PIM)
Ping River Basin, Chiang Mai of,
270
piped water system, private sector
in, 265–66
polluter-pays-principle (PPP),
269–70
pollution, 181
air, 178
estuaries, 303–4
in Indonesia, 101
Malaysian rivers deterioration
by, 146
river banks, 248
source of, 185–86
in Southeast Asian countries,
13–14
of surface water, 301–4
water. *See* water pollution
population
in China, 10, 35

estimation of, 259
and Indonesia's water supply,
        108
rural, 259
post-Cold War, 80
potable water, 250
    to NEWater, 253
    provision of, 84
    reliable supply of, 245–46
    and sanitation, 86
poverty, in Indonesia, 116
power station, in China, 51
PPP. *See* polluter-pays-principle
        (PPP); public-private
        partnership (PPP)
pre-privatization water provision,
        in Metro Manila, 217–20
Presidential Decree 984, 177
Presidential Decree 1151, 177
Presidential Decree 1152, 177
Presidential Taskforce on the
        Rehabilitation of the Pasig
        River (PTRPR), 187
private concessionaire, 216
private-public partnerships, 92–93
private sector, 221, 261
    in piped water system, 265–66
    role in Malaysian economy, 137,
        138
    role in water supply industry,
        144
    in urban WSS, 214
    in water sector, 18–20
private sector participation (PSP)
    BOT/BOOT/BOO contracts,
        216
    concessions, 216

divestiture, 216
    leases, 216
    management contracts, 215
    service contracts, 215
privatization, 136
    key issues in, 86–88
    Philippines, 21–22
    of water sector, 18–21
Privatization Cum Concession
        Agreement (PCCA), 149
privatization debate, global trends
        impacting on, 76–78
privatization in Metro Manila, 19,
        213, 221
    dispute settlement mechanism,
        223–24
    minimal opposition to, 224
    MWSS-Regulatory Office, 222
    process of, 230
    pros and cons of, 213–17
    rate-setting procedures, 223
    service obligations, 222–23
    of urban water services, 217
privatization in water supply,
        Malaysia
    achievement, 139–42
    benefits of, 171
    ensuring water for future,
        147–48
    historical development, 138–39
    investment, 144–45
    issues and challenges, 167–71
    need for, 145–48
    treated water distribution by
        SYABAS, 153–64
    of water distribution, 164–67

of water services, 142–44
of water treatment, 148–50
Privatization Master Plan (PMP),
    in Malaysia, 138
privatized projects
    financing by PNSB, 150–53
    in Malaysia, 139–42
privitization of water services,
    Southeast Asia
    failures and emerging trends,
        86–88
    infrastructure and utilities
        provision, 84–86
    privatization debate, global
        trends impacting on,
        76–78
    public-private partnership. *See*
        public-private partnership
        (PPP), Southeast Asia
    social goods and services
        privatizing, 89–90
    water and social reform sectors,
        78–84
PR management, of PPP, 91–92
Provincial Waterworks Authority
    (PWA), 265, 266
PRRC. *See* Pasig River
    Rehabilitation Commission
    (PRRC)
PRRP. *See* Pasig River
    Rehabilitation Project (PRRP)
3P (people, public and private)
    sectors, 18
PSP. *See* private sector
    participation (PSP)
PUB. *See* Public Utilities Board
    (PUB)

public-private partnership (PPP),
    Southeast Asia, 87, 93–97
    concept of, 89–90
    different rationales and
        challenges, 93–97
    economic advantages of, 91
    hazards of, 90–91
    to high sovereign risks, 91
    importance of, 81
    as privatization, 18–19
    PR management of, 91–92
    social goods and services,
        privatizing, 89–90
public sector, 264
Public Utilities Board (PUB), 17,
    18, 243, 245, 248, 249
    3P partners, 253
    strategy in stormwater, 252
    tagline, 244, 253
Puncak Niaga Holdings Berhad
    (PNHB)
    external borrowings, 152–53
    flotation of, 151–52
Puncak Niaga (M) Sdn Bhd
    (PNSB)
    challenges faced by, 172
    privatized projects financing by,
        150–53
    technological commitments,
        170–71
    water treatment by, 148–50
pure capitalism, 77
PWA. *See* Provincial Waterworks
    Authority (PWA)

Q
Qinghai-Tibet Plateau, 27, 31, 32

Quang Ngai, 304

R

rainfall
  in Java, 101
  in Malaysia, 122
  in Philippines, 217
  in Vietnam, 13, 289, 296
rainy season, 288, 296
Ramos, Fidel, 220
rapid economic development, 259,
    262
Rasa water treatment plants
    (WTPs), development of,
    157–58
Rate of Return on Base (RORB),
    223
raw water
  demand in urban areas, 105
  deterioration of quality, 20,
    146–47
  pollution, 169
  quality, 168
  supply, 114, 122
RBCs. *See* River Basin Committees
    (RBCs)
recreational activities
  indulge in, 251
  reservoirs for, 253
Red River, 48, 288, 289, 293, 295
  flood control measures, 310
Red River Delta, flood on, 297
Registry of River Basins (RRB),
    131
regulatory environment, for water
    supply services, 167–68

Regulatory Office (RO), 221
  creation of, 236
  MWSS, 222
reservoirs, for recreational
    activities, 253
rice production in Indonesia
  self-sufficiency in, 105
  slowdown in, 108
river banks, pollution in, 248
river basin, 120, 123, 126, 129, 133
  agreements as facilitators,
    11–12, 24
  Chinese actions in, 11
  deterioration in Indonesia,
    100–6
  development principles, 113,
    114
  establishment of organization,
    274
  human activities in, 121
  management, 271–72
  planning, 308
  in Vietnam, 288–94
River Basin Committees (RBCs),
    271, 274, 277–78
River basin management units
    (RBMUs), 131
river beds, 248
river pollution
  in Metro Manila, 185
  in Philippines, 4
RO. *See* Regulatory Office (RO)
"roof of the world", 32
Royal Irrigation Department, 267
rural areas, 263–65
Russia, 46–48

environmental activists in, 45
geography, 28
Irtysh-Ob River in, 45
Irtysh River in, 44
transboundary rivers, 28
water-dependent neighbours
    in, 27
Russian revolution, 66

S

Sabah, water revenues in, 144
Salween River
    in China, 48
    in Myanmar, 39
sanitation services, 213, 214, 234
SeBang Hien, 290
Second Water Forum of The
    Hague, 79
Second World Water Forum, 136
sedimentation, 106
Sekong, 290
Selangor
    pollution in, 146
    raw water pollution, 169
    water supply privatization in,
        140, 142, 144
Sembcorp Industries, 243
SEPA. *See* State Environmental
    Protection Agency (SEPA)
service contracts methods, PSP,
    215
Se San River, 290
    Yaly on, 295
Seventh Malaysia Plan, 144
sewerage, 219, 234
    department, 247

privatization project, 240
Shanghai Cooperation
    Organization (SCO), 50
shared water resources, among
    nation-states, 9
Singapore, 287
    application of technology, 243
    cleaning up of river, 246–48
    desalinated water in, 17, 23
    Four Taps, 16, 250
    freshwater usage in, 4
    massive clean-up operation in,
        247
    NEWater, 249–50
    PPP in, 97
    PUB corporate tagline, 244
    reservoir in, 251, 252
    sustainable water supply in, 244
    United Nations World Water
        Development Report, 244
    water constraints in, 16–18
    water infrastructure in, 7
    water resources in, 2
    water supply management in,
        248–52
Singapore International Water
    Week, 17, 244
Singapore's first seawater
    desalination project, 93
social goods and service
    importance of, 78
    privatization, 89–90
    social redistribution for, 88
social reform sectors, 78–84
socio-economic development, 311
    sustainable, 78, 80, 81

Soc Trang, 300
soil erosion
  in China, 34
  in South Asia, 34
solid waste, from Da Nang city,
  304
Songhua River, 28, 46
  toxic spill, 48
Son La Upper Hoa Binh dam, on
  Da River, 295
South Asia
  agriculture in, 28
  glaciers in, 33
  industry in, 28
  soil erosion in, 34
Southeast Asia, 36–43
  agriculture in, 28
  average water availability per
    capita in, 286
  climate change in, 256, 257
  demands and available of water
    in, 5, 6
  downstream countries in, 29
  environmental activists in, 42
  environmental awareness in, 23
  environmental crisis in, 174,
    175
  freshwater resources in, 2, 5,
    24n2
  glaciers in, 33
  groundwater in, 4
  industry in, 28
  Mekong basin in, 37
  Mekong River in, 33
  privitization of water services.
    See privitization of water
    services, Southeast Asia

public-private partnership.
    See public-private
    partnership (PPP),
    Southeast Asia
  soil erosion in, 34
  stock of water resources, 256
  urban planning in, 175
  water-dependent neighbours
    in, 27
  water in, 5–8
  water pollution in, 174
  water statistics in, 4
Southeast Asian region
  water conflict in, 9–12
  water scarcity in, 12
Soviet Union, water management
  in, 67
space, water resources variation
  with, 296–300
spillover effects, 10
Sre Pok, 290
state authority limitations, in
  Philippines, 176–79
State Environmental Protection
  Agency (SEPA), 47
State of Water Resources
  Management Report, 2, 24n3
stormwater management, PUB's
  strategy in, 252
Sungai Selangor Phase 2 (SSP2),
  149, 150
surface water
  in Brunei Darussalam, 4
  pollution of, 301–4
  resources, 168, 292, 295
  utilization, licence issues for,
    111

sustainability, forms of, 176
sustainable development,
    Johannesburg summit on, 83
sustainable irrigation, 108
sustainable socio-economic
    development, 78, 80, 81
sustainable sources, of water, 2, 3
sustainable water management
    strategy, 243, 244
sustainable water resources
    management, 58, 295–301
    essential elements of, 61–63, 71,
    72
sustainable water sector
    development programme,
    112–13
sustainable water supply, in
    Singapore, 244
Syarikat Bekalan Air Selangor Sdn
    Bhd (SYABAS), 148
    challenges faced by, 172
    client charter, 166
    concept of penalty, 165
    financial, 164–65
    indebtness, 153–56
    operating deficit, 158–60
    poor billing, 160–62
    poor planning in capacity
        development, 162–64
    privatization of water
        distribution by, 153
    problem of high NRW, 157
    to reducing NRW, 170
    regulation by government,
        166–67
    wrong planning on CAPEX
        works, 157–58

Syarikat Pengeluar Air Selangor
    Sdn Bhd (SPLASH), 148, 157
Syr Darya river, 65

T
technological commitments, in
    water supply services, 170–71
Telekom Malaysia, 139
Tenaga Nasional Berhad, 139
Thac Ba, on Chay River, 295
Thach Nham irrigation system,
    downstream of, 304
Thai Binh River, 290
    flood control measures, 310
Thailand
    Bang Pakong dialogue, 278,
        279–80
    Bang Pakong river basin, 275–76
    capacity-building in, 271, 280
    diversion dam in, 276
    drought in, 257
    establishment of river basin
        organization, 274
    factors affecting water uses in,
        258
    flash floods in, 256
    governments of, 41
    groundwater system in, 260
    hydrological balance studies on,
        260
    hydropower development plan
        in, 41
    institutional capacity, 15
    introduction, 255–58
    IWRM, 271–73
    Mekong River Basin flows
        across, 287

MWAs and PWA, 265–66
NWRC and ONWRC, 273
population of, 260
river basin management, 271–72
river basins in, 260
surface water resources, 260
water and agriculture, 266–67
water and electricity, 268
water demand rising in, 13, 262
water governance in, 272–73
water management in, 262
water provision, 262
water quality and investment
    in wastewater treatment,
    268–70
water resources, 258–59
water resources management,
    262, 276–78
watershed management and
    conservation, 270–71
water supply to rural areas,
    263–65
water supply to urban areas,
    265
Third Outline Perspective Plan
    (OPP3), 128, 129
Third World Water Forum,
    themes for, 60
Three Gorges Dam, on Yangtze
    River, 37, 40, 49
Thua Thien Hue province, 298
Thu Bon-Vu Gia, estuary regions
    of, 303, 304
Tibetan Plateau, 27, 31, 32, 33–34,
    36
Tibet, Yarlung Zangbo in, 49

time, water resources variation
    with, 296–300
toxic spill
    in China, 46
    in Songhua River, 48
trade, in China, 51
Tra Khuc River, 303
transboundary maze, 29–30
transboundary river, 28
transboundary river basin, 290
Tri An, on Dong Nai River, 295
tropical land, 258
Tu Duc project, 97

U
UK, water privatization in, 87
Ultraviolet B (UVB) radiation,
    31
unbridled capitalism, 77
UN Committee on Economic,
    Social and Cultural Rights,
    213
UN Environment Programme
    (UNEP), 44
UNEP. *See* UN Environment
    Programme (UNEP)
UNESCO, 40
United Nationals World Water
    Development Report, 2, 7,
    25n11
United Nations agencies, risk of
    wars, 30
United Nations Development
    Programme (UNDP), 69
United Nations Environment
    Programme (UNEP), 203n2

United Nations World Water
 Development Report, 244
Upper Central Plain, 260–61
URAs. *See* urban renewal areas
 (URAs)
urban areas, 265
 surface and groundwater use
  in, 102
 water supplies in, 265
urban development, 176
urbanization, 38, 119
urban management, of water, 24
urban population, statistical
 survey of, 259
Urban Redevelopment Authority,
 247
urban renewal areas (URAs), 188,
 199
urban water services, privatization
 of, 217
urban water supply and sanitation
 systems, 214

V
Vam Co Tay River, 311
Variable Salinity Plant (VSP), 250
Vietnam, 287
 climate change in, 293
 coastal line, 289
 floods control in, 310
 institutional problem, 15
 Mekong River Basin flows
  across, 287
 natural disasters in, 296–300
 pollution of water in, 14
 rainfall of, 289, 296

 river basins in, 288–90
 water consumption by, 300
 water demand rising in, 13
 water quality in, 293, 301–3
 water resources in, 290–94
 water resources management
  in, 305–12
 water utilization in, 294–95

W
Wangsa Maju water treatment
 plants, 149
 DAF for, 171
Washington Consensus, 81
wastewater
 discharge, 301
 treatment, 268–70
water
 for consumption, 263
 demand, 261–62
 inefficient use of, 261
 legal jurisdiction, 15
 legislations, 168
 loss, 146, 219, 231
 management of, 120, 133
 nationwide distribution of, 265
 need for, 257
 private sector participation in,
  214, 215–16
 provision, 261–62
 stealing, 169
 trends in, 6
water absorption capacity, in
 riverside, 104
water allocation, for agriculture,
 267

water availability, 102, 255
  in Jakarta and West Java, 102–3
  and sanitation, 2, 3
water catchment areas, 250–51,
  252
water constraints, in Singapore,
  16–18
water consumption, 294–95
  conflicts from rapid increase in,
  300–1
  in Southeast Asia, 5, 10, 12–13
water crisis, 2, 16, 21
  in China, 35–36
  Klang Valley, 144, 158
water demand, 12–13, 162, 163
  in agriculture, 105
  domestic and industrial, 124
  for irrigation, 294
  management, 252–53
  resources, 296
  rising, 12–13
  water provision and, 261–62
water distribution, privatization of
  client charter, 166
  concept of penalty, 165
  financial, 164–65
  regulation by government,
  166–67
Water Efficient Buildings
  Programme, 18, 253
Water Efficient Homes
  Programme, 18, 253
water governance, in Thailand,
  272–73
water infrastructure, 116, 117
  damaging, 106

Water in Thailand, 255–57
  and agriculture, 266–67
  Bang Pakong dialogue, 278,
  279–80
  Bang Pakong River Basin,
  275–78
  and electricity, 268
  ground water resources, 260–61
  provision and demand, 261–62
  resources, 258–59
  resources management, 262
  rural areas, 263
  surface water resources, 260
  urban areas, 265
water issues
  institutional capacity and, 14–16
  on political agenda, 168
  research programme on, 7
water management
  challenges of national, 12–18
  issues in Southeast Asia, 2, 5
  sustainable, 71, 72
  in Thailand, 262
  in watersheds, 288
water management system
  formulation of, 62
  in Soviet Union, 67
water pollution, 268, 288
  in Amur River, 47–48
  benzene compounds in Amur
  River, 46–48
  control practices in Thailand,
  269
  crisis, 46
  in estuaries, 303–4
  in Malaysia, 14, 146

in Metro Manila, 176
raw, 169
in Southeast Asia, 2, 3, 13–14,
   174
water privatization
   in Philippines, 212
   in UK, 87
water privatization in Metro
   Manila, 213
   dispute settlement mechanism,
      223–24
   MWSS-Regulatory Office (RO),
      222
   pros and cons of, 213–17
   rate-setting procedures, 223
water quality, 257, 269, 312
   in ASEAN, 258
   in Cau river basin, 302
   in Jakarta, 108
   in Vietnam, 293, 301–3
   in wastewater treatment, 268–70
water reform sectors, international
   exigencies in, 78–84
water resources, 255, 257
   availability of, 260
   in Brunei Darussalam, 2
   budget development, 259
   development of, 167–68
   for ecosystem services, 258
   in Indonesia, 2
   in Myanmar, 2
   planning, 308–9
   policy lessons for managing,
      22–24
   population growth and, 256
   projects, 148

protection of, 258
Southeast Asia's stock of, 256
surface, 260
water resources act, 272
water resources in Vietnam,
   288–94
   facing environmental problems,
      303–4
   problems of, 305
   sustainable management of,
      295–301
   variation of, 296–300
Water Resources Law (WRL),
   109–12, 309
water resources management, 15,
   276–78
   challenges in, 263–72
   integrated, 58–61
   IWRM, 280–82
   measures for, 309–12
   organization of, 305–7
   practices, 308–9
   sustainable. *See* sustainable
      water resources
      management
   in Thailand, 262
water scarcity, 5, 7
   growing, 12
   in Jakarta, 102
water sector
   development in Indonesia,
      113–14
   infrastructure, 117
water sector reform, Indonesia,
   101
   need for, 107–8

origins of, 107
principles of, 108–9
water sharing systems, 4, 5
watershed management, and
    conservation, 270–71
watershed management in
    Vietnam, 305
    measures for, 309–12
    practices, 308–9
water shortage, on future, 2
water statistics, in Southeast Asia,
    4
water supply, 215, 218, 263
    MWR and PWR, 282
    in Philippines, 217
    private operators in, 137
    privatization in Selangor, 140,
        142, 144
    quality control of, 265
    to rural areas, 263–65
water supply and sanitation
    systems (WSS), 213, 214,
    215
water supply, Malaysia
    coverage level, 165
    planning, 164
    privatization of. See
        privatization in water
        supply, Malaysia
water supply management
    desalination, 249
    DTSS, 251–52
    Marina reservoir, 250–51
    NEWater, 249–50
    new technologies, 250

in Singapore, 16, 248–52
    stormwater management, 252
water treatment, 250, 251
    operators, 154
    privatization of, 148–50
    process, 146
water treatment plants (WTPs),
    20, 148, 149
    development of, 157–58
    operators, 153–55
water utilization, in Vietnam,
    294–95
Water Utilization Programme
    (WUP), 296
Wen Jiabao, 40, 50
West Java, water availability in,
    103
World Bank, 35, 63, 81, 185, 214
World Conservation Union
    (IUCN), 52n1
World Economic Forum Global
    Competitiveness Index, 94
World Environment Day, 44
World Summit on Sustainable
    Development (WSSD), 120
World Water Forum, Third, 60
World Wide Fund for Nature
    (WWF), 34
WRL. See Water Resources Law
    (WRL)
WSS. See water supply and
    sanitation systems (WSS)
WSSD. See World Summit on
    Sustainable Development
    (WSSD)

WTPs. *See* water treatment plants (WTPs)

WWF. *See* World Wide Fund for Nature (WWF)

X

Xiaowan, hydroelectric power dam on, 37

Xinhua News Agency, 32, 52n7

Xinjiang Uighur Autonomous Region, 43

Y

Yaly, on Se San River, 295

Yangtze River, 35

  Three Gorges Dam on, 37, 40, 49

Yarlung Zangbo, in Tibet, 49